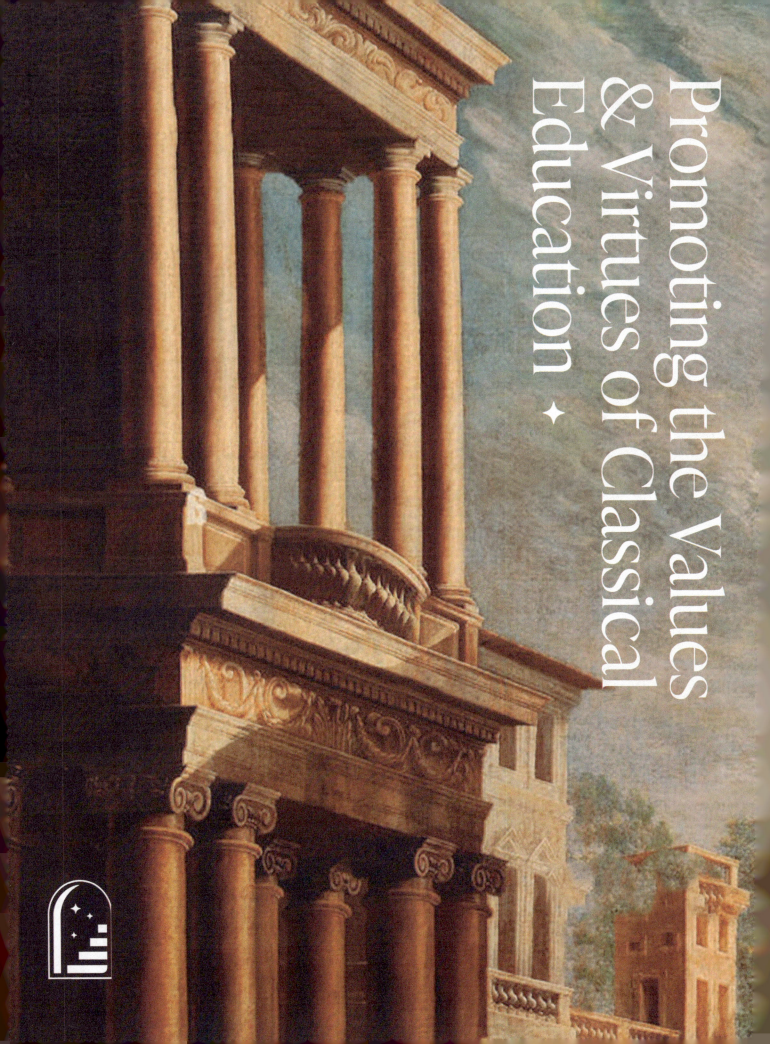

Promoting the Values & Virtues of Classical Education

# Terms & Propositions

*Logic & Writing*, Volume I

Thales Press          Raleigh, North Carolina

*This book is the property of:*

⸻

**Humane Letters II: Logic and Writing.**

Copyright 2024 by Thales Press.

First Edition. All rights reserved, including the right to reproduce this book or portions thereof in any form whatsoever without permission from the publisher, except as permitted by U.S. copyright law. To request permission, contact the publisher at thalespress@thalesacademy.org. This book was written by Winston Brady, Director of Curriculum & Thales Press.

**Humane Letters II: Logic and Writing** was published in Raleigh, North Carolina for use in Thales Academy, a network of low-cost, high-quality private schools in North Carolina, South Carolina, Tennessee, and Virginia.

For more information and supplementary resources that include pacing guides, assessments, project ideas, and other elements, email us at thalespress@thalesacademy.org

All photos, unless otherwise noted, are available in the public domain.

**Special thanks** to Elizabeth Jetton, Kelly Ellis, Holly Clark, Zach Wiggin, Josh Herring, Travis Copeland, Matt Ogle, Isaac Jennings, and Alex Nolette for providing further edits and improvements to this work.

**Cover photo** is *The School of Athens* by Raphael (1509-1511).

# Table of Contents

| | |
|---|---|
| **INTRODUCTION** | 06 |
| | |
| **SECTION I: TERMS & METAPHYSICS** | 10 |
| Chapter 1: The Importance of Logic | 12 |
| Chapter 2: The Three Acts of the Mind | 30 |
| Chapter 3: The Kinds of Terms | 58 |
| Chapter 4: Terms According to Aristotle | 100 |
| | |
| **SECTION II: PROPOSITIONS & EPISTEMOLOGY** | 142 |
| Chapter 5: The Medieval Consensus | 144 |
| Chapter 6: Epistemology & Truth | 172 |
| Chapter 7: Categorical Propositions | 190 |
| Chapter 8: Relationships of Equivalence | 206 |
| Chapter 9: The Square of Opposition | 246 |
| | |
| **APPENDIX** | 272 |
| **WORKS CITED** | 278 |
| **PHOTOGRAPHY CREDITS** | 282 |
| **GLOSSARY** | 286 |

# Introduction to Logic & Writing

**THIS LOGIC TEXTBOOK** seeks to integrate the concepts of logic with the reading and analysis of meaningful primary source texts. These texts are drawn from across the Western canon and include Plato, Aristotle, René Descartes, John Locke, Thomas Hobbes, James Madison, Alexander Hamilton, David Ricardo, Friedrich Hayek, and many more examples. We chose these texts because their authors employed the art of argumentation exceptionally well in their works. Each of these authors changed the course of world history—some for the better, but others for the worse. We need to employ the tools of logical reasoning to determine which authors and which ideas meaningfully contribute to our understanding of the good life, and which authors used some kind of sophistry to curtail and constrain real human freedom. In this way, we hope to impart meaningful content knowledge from the seminal authors in the Western tradition and provide the aspiring logician—i.e., the students reading this book—with good, concept-rich texts to read and evaluate.

To streamline the integration of these texts, we divided this textbook into two volumes, each volume into two sections, and each section associated with one act of the mind. The acts of the mind are ways of thinking about thinking, all of which we will cover in greater detail over the next few chapters. This introduction is meant to provide a brief explanation for each section and the kinds of texts paired with each act of the mind. This particular textbook—*Volume I: Terms & Propositions*—includes *Sections I* and *II*.

*Section I: Terms & Metaphysics* focuses on the first act of the mind, an act known as simple apprehension. Simple apprehension operates on *terms*, the simplest and most fundamental unit of meaning. Within this section, we have included texts from the branch of philosophy known as *metaphysics*. Accordingly, *Section I* incorporates readings from Plato, Euclid, and Aristotle. *Section II: Propositions & Epistemology*, meanwhile, focuses on the second act of the mind, known as the act of judgment, and focuses on a special kind of sentence called a *proposition*. In this section, we include readings from the branch of philosophy known as *epistemology* from René Descartes, John Locke, and David Hume.

*Volume II: Deductive & Inductive Reasoning* focuses on the *Third Act of the Mind* and the act of making inferences. *Section III: Syllogisms & Political Theory* focuses on inferences by way of deductive reasoning

*Logic is the art of right thinking and the habits needed to distinguish between truth and falsehood, and such skills could not be more valuable or more needed in the world today.*

and syllogisms—and incorporates readings from the field of academic study known as *political theory*. *Section III* incorporates readings from Thomas Hobbes, John Locke, James Madison, and Alexander Hamilton. *Section IV* also focuses on the *Third Act of the Mind*—inference-making—but focuses on the nature of inductive reasoning or the act of forming conclusions from examples or observations. *Section IV* incorporates readings from the academic field of economics and includes readings from David Hume, Frédéric Bastiat, David Ricardo, and Friedrich Hayek.

## Lessons & Activities

A series of exercises follow each lesson in logic, meant to help students master the topic under review. Following each primary source text are a series of exercises meant to encourage analytical reading follow after each reading. These activities help aspiring logicians break down difficult but worthwhile texts and analyze them according to the Three Acts of the Mind, a concept covered in Chapter 2. These exercises help students break down the important terms in the text, followed by a worksheet with propositions drawn from the text. These exercises should draw the logician's attention to some key word or phrase that the author uses to build his or her argument up to his or her conclusion. The last activity in each chapter is called an *argument map* and is meant to help students make sense of the author's argument as a whole. What is the author saying, and is it true? An argument map is a visual and verbal way to record all the terms, propositions, assumptions, and other relevant information needed to analyze an argument and determine whether or not its conclusion is *true* or *false*.

That closing question will be a prompt for an expository essay comprised of one introduction, one body paragraph, and one conclusion. After all, logic is the art of right thinking, and few exercises compel the student to *think* better than writing on a meaningful topic. Each chapter ends with a writing prompt that teachers may assign for formal essays as time allows in the semester. All citations should be done in MLA format.

## Note-Taking

Write down the vocabulary words for each chapter. These include grammar concepts, terms and ideas from the writing lesson, and difficult vocabulary from the primary source included in each section. The terms, concepts, tips, and strategies are covered in each writing lesson. As a result, students may want to consider writing down as part of their notes the text beneath the section heading and subheading titles, the content for which students should summarize in their notes, as well as the terms and ideas covered in each logic lesson and in the primary source texts. Generally, any information that is **bolded, underlined**, or highlighted in a textbook is important enough to write down in a notebook.

Lastly, to support the values of classical education, ***Logic & Writing*** *uses* cathedrals as a kind of guiding metaphor to bring together all of the skills and concepts needed to understand logic. A cathedral is a church that was constructed during the medieval period, and they constitute some of the most beautiful and enduring architectural marvels in the world. We have included photos of various Gothic cathedrals at the beginning of each chapter because a Gothic cathedral is not unlike an argument in that it is composed of building blocks, requires great skill in its construction, and ultimately can lead people to a deeper understanding of the truth. Such is the goal of classical education: to cultivate students of excellence through the contemplation of truth, beauty, and goodness.

The following pages contain a detailed table of contents, volume by volume and the kinds of lessons, activities, and readings you can find in ***Logic & Writing***.

**Volume I:** *Terms & Propositions*

| Section | Act of the Mind | Philosophical & Academic Field | Primary Source Texts |
|---|---|---|---|
| **Section I** *First Act of the Mind* | **Simple Apprehension** | Metaphysics | Plato's "The Allegory of the Cave" <br> Euclid's *Elements* <br> Plato's *Euthyphro* <br> Aristotle's *Metaphysics* |
| **Section II** *Second Act of the Mind* | **Judgment** | Epistemology | Thomas Aquinas' *Summa Theologiae* <br> René Descartes' *Discourse on Method* <br> John Locke's *Essay Concerning Human Understanding* <br> David Hume's *Enquiry Concerning Human Understanding* |

**Volume II:** *Deductive & Inductive Reasoning*

| Section | Act of the Mind | Philosophical & Academic Field | Primary Source Texts |
|---|---|---|---|
| **Section III** *Third Act of the Mind* | **Inference / Deductive Reasoning** | Political Theory | Thomas Hobbes' *Leviathan* <br> John Locke's *Second Treatise on Government* <br> Montesquieu's *Spirit of the Laws* <br> The Federalist Papers |
| **Section IV** *Third Act of the Mind* | **Inference / Inductive Reasoning** | Economics | David Ricardo's *Principles of Political Economy* <br> Frédéric Bastiat's "Parable of the Broken Window" <br> Friedrich Hayek's *Road to Serfdom* |

## Volume I, Section I: *Terms & Propositions*

| Chapter | Chapter Title | Topics | Primary Source Texts |
|---|---|---|---|
| Chapter 1 | **The Importance of Logic** | The trivium; the liberal arts | Plato's "The Allegory of the Cave" |
| Chapter 2 | **The Three Acts of the Mind** | Terms, propositions, and arguments | Euclid's *Elements* |
| Chapter 3 | **The Kinds of Terms** | Introduction to metaphysics; universals versus particulars; various kinds of terms | Plato's *Euthyphro* |
| Chapter 4 | **Terms According to Aristotle** | Aristotle's causes, predicables, categories | Aristotle's *Metaphysics* |

## Volume I, Section II: *Propositions & Epistemology*

| Chapter | Chapter Title | Topics | Primary Source Texts |
|---|---|---|---|
| Chapter 5 | **The Medieval Consensus** | Survey of medieval thought and philosophy | Augustine's *Confessions*; Aquinas' *Summa* |
| Chapter 6 | **Introduction to Epistemology** | Survey of epistemology, rationalism, and empiricism | René Descartes' *Discourse on Method* |
| Chapter 7 | **Categorical Propositions** | A, E, I, and O Statements | This chapter does not include a primary source text |
| Chapter 8 | **Relationships of Equivalence** | Obversion, conversion, and contraposition | John Locke's *Essay Concerning Human Understanding* |
| Chapter 9 | **The Square of Opposition** | Contradiction, contrariety, subcontrariety, etc. | David Hume's *Enquiry Concerning Human Understanding* |

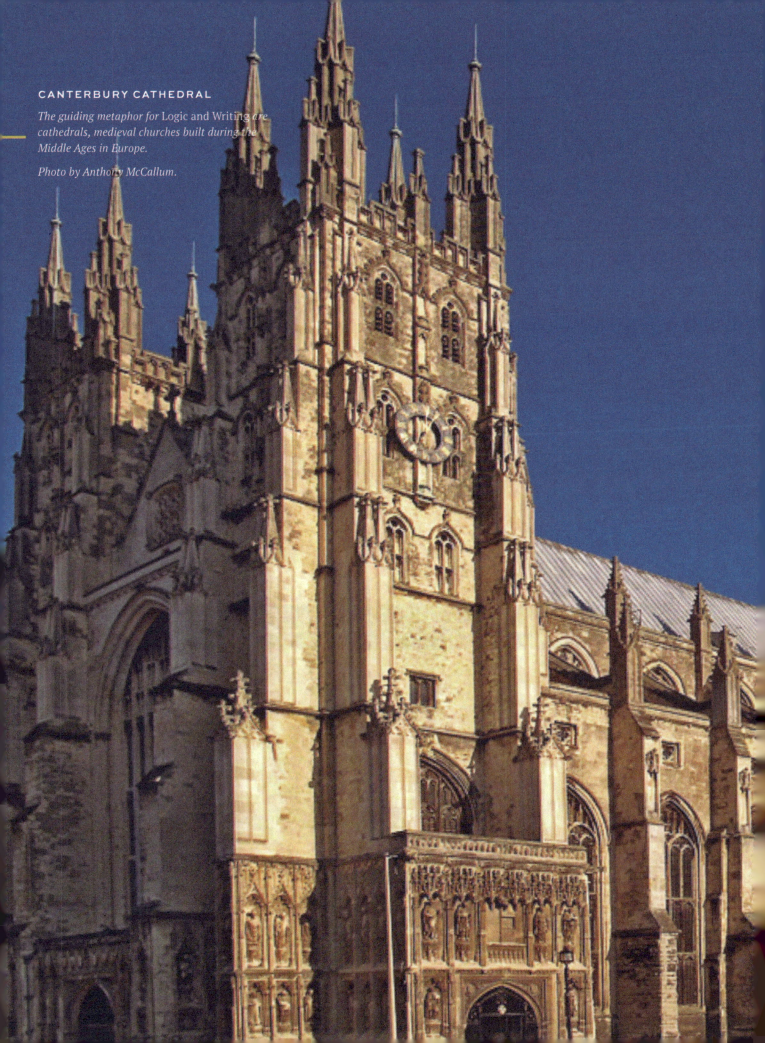

**CANTERBURY CATHEDRAL**

*The guiding metaphor for Logic and Writing are cathedrals, medieval churches built during the Middle Ages in Europe.*

*Photo by Anthony McCallum.*

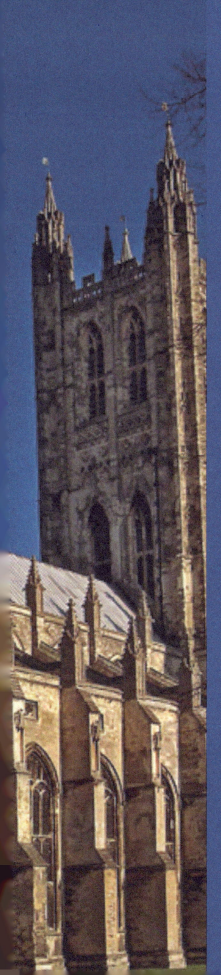

# Section I
# Terms & Metaphysics

**CHAPTERS**

01 The Importance of Logic

02 The Three Acts of the Mind

03 The Kinds of Terms

04 Terms According to Aristotle

**CANTERBURY CATHEDRAL / INTERIOR**

*As we will explain in this chapter, a cathedral's architecture was meant to transport visitors upwards to the heavens; in the same way, an argument helps us reach new, unknown conclusions beyond what we can know through experience.*

*Photo by Zoltan Tasi.*

CHAPTER

# The Importance of Logic

ROADMAP

✦ Learn about logic and its role in cultivating the habits of thought.

✦ Learn how the liberal arts contribute to human flourishing.

✦ Read "The Allegory of the Cave" from Plato's *Republic*.

THALES OUTCOME

Nº 4

**A Critical Thinker** analyzes a variety of truth statements and/or observations through a dialectic examination of facts and assumptions.

Logic is the art of right thinking, the ability to sift through large amounts of information and identify truth from falsehood, necessary from superfluous, good from evil. Dorothy Sayers expresses a similar sentiment in "The Lost Tools of Learning": "The disrepute into which Formal Logic has fallen is entirely unjustified; and its neglect is the root cause of nearly all those disquieting symptoms which we may note in the modern intellectual constitution."

CHAPTER 1   The Importance of Logic   ✦   13

# The Importance of Logic

IMAGINE THE BUILDING of a great cathedral, for its construction is not unlike the building of an argument. A cathedral may take well over a hundred years to build so that the workers who laid its foundations passed away before artisans finished adorning the cathedral's spires and vaults. Cathedrals were made from rough, unhewn stones, massive blocks of limestone and marble dug out of quarries and dragged overland to towns or cities in Europe. Some of these cities may have already been great capitals bustling with kings and princes, merchants and knights, or they may have been towns of some minor importance, whose residents hoped that a grand cathedral might encourage the world not to pass them over. But as the cathedrals took shape and slowly grew taller and grander, a profound transformation took place in the stonework of these soaring edifices.

Artisans, stonecutters, and sculptors all went to work to turn the rough crags into something that resembled light. Suppose we look at the stonework of Europe's great cathedrals at Chartres, Notre Dame, and Cologne. In that case, their soaring spires imitate the beams of light that penetrate through dark thunderclouds hanging overhead. A series of spires ascending to the heavens has the effect of a beautiful and illuminated cloudscape, the kind which we might see from the window of an airplane and which the builders may have only seen in the most delightful daydream. Light symbolizes truth, and the airy, ethereal beams of stone are meant to point the viewer of such a cathedral toward the beauty and glory of truth.

The cathedral's interior aimed to replicate such an impression upon its visitors. First, the interior of a cathedral is breathtakingly tall. Chartres Cathedral in France boasts a vaulted ceiling almost 400 feet high, and Germany's Cologne Cathedral is nearly 600 feet. The reason that their architects intentionally built these man-made mountains so tall was not only to ensure the cathedral would dominate the city skyline (Cologne Cathedral was the tallest building in the world for a brief, ten-year period), but they hoped that anyone walking inside the cathedral would feel small in comparison. They hoped that visitors would be taken up in the grand, ethereal space created by the vaulted ceiling towering overhead, that their eyes would be drawn upwards by the lines of the barrel vaults, an arch projected in space that intersected other arches supporting the cathedral's ceiling. In short, the architects hoped that any visitor might be transported to another world the moment they stepped inside the cathedral.

*Logic is like a cathedral in that a logical argument is composed of different components, namely, terms and propositions, and logic leads us to understand what is true and what is false, just like a the lines of a cathedral leads the eyes of anyone who steps inside a cathedral upwards to the heavens.*

## Vocabulary

*Write down this vocabulary in your notebook. These terms will help you better learn and understand the material in this chapter.*

### Cathedral
A church constructed during the medieval period made of marble or limestone. They were hundreds of feet in height and were constructed to resemble beams of light.

### Logic
The art of right thinking and the rules for organizing a wide array of thoughts, facts, and propositions into a coherent and organized system.

### Argument
In logic, an argument is composed of two or more propositions called "premises" that, if those premises contain clear terms and true propositions, lead to a true conclusion.

### Trivium
The place "where three roads meet", this concept was an ancient and medieval way of organizing education, whose "three roads" included the study of grammar, logic, and rhetoric.

**CHARTRES CATHEDRAL / VAULTED CEILING & INTERIOR**
*Photo by K. Mitch Hodge*

**Logic** and the building of an argument do the very same for our thoughts. Thought is much like stone in that thoughts can be rough and formless. A single, fleeting thought requires the careful application of skilled, reasoned argumentation for that thought to take shape and gain clarity, a process we will learn this year in logic. A careful expression of that thought is an argument, and an argument, like a building, is composed of fundamental building blocks. If we remove the blocks, the entire edifice collapses upon itself. Cathedrals have their foundations, barrel vaults, and flying buttresses to help support these massive structures, whereas arguments are built upon clear terms, true propositions, and valid argumentation. Should an argument be lacking in any one of these areas, the whole argument might come crashing down.

But an **argument** resembles a cathedral in another grand and unexpected way. An argument, like a cathedral, can transport individuals into another world, for logic gives us tools that would help us reach new conclusions we could not reach by experience alone. An argument takes two or more propositions, each of which is composed of clear terms and conveys some meaningful, true idea, and builds to a conclusion not evident in either one of those two propositions. Our ability to create arguments and make such inferences about the world is one of the grandest and most beautiful gifts we human beings have.

The ability to make such inferences allows us to know more about our world and what happens in it than any other creature in the universe. This ability, which learned men refer to as man's reason, helps us go above and beyond the normal realm of human experience. Like the lines of a vaulted ceiling, logic allows us to be carried away by the grandeur and beauty of truth. This

CHAPTER 1  The Importance of Logic  ♦  15

power to know is why it is essential to study logic because logic is not merely one more subject to become acquainted with in high school. Indeed, logic is composed of all the tools needed to organize all our thought.

In the ancient and medieval world, students went through the coursework of the **trivium**. The word trivium is itself composed of two different Latin words: *tres, trium* meaning "three", and *via* meaning "road". The trivium began with **grammar**, principally Latin grammar, which included the basic, fundamental building blocks of any subject matter. Those basic building blocks may consist of facts and dates in history class, laws and theories in science class, and other kinds of simple but essential information that we simply have to know as the mark of a well-educated person.

The second road was logic, the art of right thinking. Logic offers a series of rules, strategies, and habits that equip students to organize their thoughts into a coherent system. It is not enough for us to know many facts; we have to understand how they fit together, and logic equips us to refine our thought and bring them together into an argument. To handle those challenges, students have to be capable of solving problems and communicating the solutions to those problems in a meaningful way. As a result, coursework in the trivium is of vital importance in preparing students for the challenges of the modern world. If we cannot explain our solutions, we can hardly expect anyone to entertain, let alone act upon, our suggestions. To paraphrase C. S. Lewis, if we cannot translate our thoughts into words, then those thoughts are not clear. Logic is the means to transform such raw thought into clear and intelligible speech.

The final road in the trivium was **rhetoric**, the art of public speaking. For ancient logicians and rhetoricians (such as Aristotle and Quintilian, among others), rhetoric was the counterpart to logic. The skills one needed to create an argument formed an indispensable component of writing and delivering speeches. Ancient teachers of rhetoric argued that it was not enough for an orator to be eloquent and capable of delivering great speeches. An eloquent speaker should not only know how to build an effective argument but should also commit themselves to the pursuit of wisdom and the cultivation of virtue that was typical of philosophers.

This counterpart of rhetoric is important because ultimately we desire to know what is true, and logic helps us to sift through the vast array of facts, opinions, and arguments whose conclusions about the world may or may not be true. If rhetoric is the art of public speaking, and if we want to be honest, truthful, and genuine in the words we say, then logic becomes all the more important for us

# Vocabulary

### Grammar
The subject of grammar focuses on the rules of language and communication to read and understand texts and write in clear, intelligible prose; at times, grammar, as a road of the trivium, may also refer to the basic, fundamental building blocks of a subject.

### Rhetoric
The art of public speaking and the skills and strategies needed to compose and deliver a stirring speech.

### The Liberal Arts
The liberal arts are the subject areas that free the mind from ignorance; they are composed of the trivium and the quadrivium and thus include grammar, logic, and rhetoric (known as the trivium) and music, arithmetic, geometry, and astronomy (known as the quadrivium).

### Quadrivium
Literally, the place where "four roads meet"; metaphorically, those "four roads" are the arts of music, arithmetic, geometry, and astronomy.

to study. Logic helps us know the truth, and if we are to speak well in public, we ought to speak from our commitment to, and our delight in, what is true.

As the art of right thinking, logic is one of the seven liberal arts. The **liberal arts** include **grammar**, **logic**, and **rhetoric** (the **trivium**), and arithmetic, geometry, music, and astronomy (the **quadrivium**). Students in the medieval world would complete the coursework of the trivium first at around the age of thirteen or fourteen before going on to the more advanced coursework of the quadrivium. But what makes the liberal arts liberal? The word *liberal* derives from two interrelated words in the Latin language: *libertas* and *liber*. The word *liber*, from which we derive our English word library, simply means "book," whereas *libertas* means "liberty" or "freedom." In the minds of the ancient Romans, an education marked individuals as being free—an education is exceedingly expensive, after all—and also prepared those individuals to enjoy that freedom. The liberal arts are so named because they are the subjects that are free from the necessities of daily life, the subjects that people study because they (the people) are free, and the subjects that prepare an individual to use that freedom well. Most simply, the liberal arts free an individual from ignorance.

Today, we may take the ability to read and understand texts (i.e., grammar) for granted, since almost everyone we know can read, but from the ancient world to the modern world, the ability to read distinguished slaves from freemen. The noted American orator Frederick Douglass (circa 1817-1895) said as much in his autobiography. He recognized that his masters tried to keep him from learning how to read because that would make Douglass, then a slave, easier to control and manipulate. Slowly but surely, Douglass taught himself how to read and write before ultimately escaping from slavery and gaining his freedom. Then, as now, a good education helps impart confidence to students to take on challenges that seem impossible.

**PHILOSOPHIA ET SEPTEM ARTES LIBERALES**
*Herrad of Landsberg, Hortus deliciarum* (12th century)

**FREDERICK DOUGLASS / 1817-1895**

Moreover, the liberal arts are subjects typically studied for their own sake, freed from the physical, rigorous constraints of daily living. Subjects like grammar and rhetoric are qualitatively different from the technical knowledge required to practice a craft like agriculture, weaving, or architecture. The art of astronomy or the study of the heavens may impart joy and improve one's ability to grasp complex mathematical concepts, but astronomy will never help us grow the food or weave the clothing that we need to survive in a harsh, often uncaring world. Still, we study the liberal arts (and every other subject, really) because they help us think, solve problems, and cultivate the kind of confidence and character needed to take on the challenges of the modern world. The liberal arts may not directly correlate to the activities that we perform in our jobs, but they do teach us to think, and that correlates with everything else.

One learned the liberal arts because these subjects helped prepare an individual to handle the challenges and responsibilities of freedom. In a country like the United States, we have an overabundance of choices: some choices, ideas, and activities are good and lead to better opportunities. Other choices, ideas, and activities are bad and do not lead anywhere at all—at least, not anywhere worth going. On top of that, many people in various fields of politics, culture, entertainment, YouTube, or wherever else the voice may come from, all cry out that their way is the best way and encourage their adherents to follow them in their pursuits. In such a climate, the liberal arts, that is, the study of the trivium and the quadrivium, are more important now than ever. The trivium teaches the skills of reading and writing (grammar), building and evaluating arguments (logic), and public speaking and communication (rhetoric). More importantly, the liberal arts help teach us what it means to be human and impart the intellectual and academic skills needed to pursue the nature of the good life.

In this way, logic is not a subject matter to learn about. Instead, logic is a tool to help us evaluate everything else we learn. The builders of those grand, medieval cathedrals carved huge blocks of stone to resemble light, and logic is not unlike light in that it helps to see and understand the world around us. By learning logic, we can become more critical and confident thinkers, thinkers capable of evaluating arguments and having a greater appreciation for what is true, good, and beautiful.

We hold these truths as the goals of classical education in general and the mission of Thales in particular: to educate students to their highest potential and to help students achieve everything of which they are capable. If the trivium refers to the *place where the three roads meet*, that place can be found in a student who can write, reason, and speak well. Moreover, they have developed such excellent character that they can not only choose what is good but persuade others to pursue what is good, what is true, and what is beautiful, too. Shortly, we will examine this principle in further detail through one of the most influential texts in the Western canon: Plato's "Allegory of the Cave," from Book VII of Plato's *Republic*, a massive work on the idea of justice and its relationship to the nature of the good life.

> *The **trivium** is the "place where the **three** roads" of grammar, logic, and rhetoric meet.*
>
> *The **quadrivium** is the "place where the **four** roads" of arithmetic, geometry, astronomy, and music meet.*
>
> *Together, the **quadrivium** and the **trivium** comprise the original seven **liberal arts**, those arts that **free** an individual from ignorance.*

## Reading Comprehension Questions

1. How is a cathedral a metaphor for logic?

2. What is logic, and how does logic help cultivate good thinking?

3. What are the liberal arts?

4. How are the liberal arts "liberal"?

# Logic, Philosophy, and the Truth

ALFRED NORTH WHITEHEAD, a British mathematician and logician, once said that much of Western philosophy is a series of footnotes to Plato. By this description, Whitehead meant that Plato's work was so influential and enduring that every philosopher preceding him has been in a dialogue with the famed Greek philosopher. We know little about Plato outside of the details that Plato provides in his dialogues. He was born in the 4th century to a wealthy, well-connected family, and he later started a school called the Academy to teach others about Socrates, Plato's teacher and mentor.

Socrates is the principal character in the massive collection of dialogues that Plato wrote. Far more is known about Socrates as a result. Socrates lived from 470 to 399 BC, and by occupation, he was a stonecutter. Like many of his fellow Athenians, Socrates served in the Peloponnesian War between Athens and Sparta (431-404 BC), an event that may have forced Socrates to question many of the fundamental assumptions that he held about the world. The story of how Socrates went from a stonecutter to a philosopher is the stuff

| SOCRATES: 470-399 BC

of philosophical legend: one of Socrates' friends went to the Oracle at Delphi and asked the oracle if anyone was "wiser" than Socrates. The oracle answered "no," and Socrates was dumbfounded because he believed that he possessed so little knowledge about the world. He endeavored to try and prove the oracle "wrong" by going about and asking questions of the Athenians he

*Philosophers like Socrates and Plato wanted to connect knowledge and content with virtue and character because they hoped that the knowledge they gained about truth, beauty, and goodness would help them to improve their character and do good to their souls.*

## Vocabulary

### Philosophy
Literally, the "love of wisdom", philosophy is the academic subject that examines significant, overarching questions of the human condition concerning ethics, values, epistemology, and ontology.

### Plato
An Athenian philosopher whose writings serve as the basis for much of Western philosophy; he wrote dialogues that explored the fundamental nature of reality and morality.

### Socrates
A Greek philosopher and "gadfly of Athens" whose incessant questioning and probing into the nature of the good life led to his execution in 399 BC.

### Forms
Plato's term for ideas such as truth, beauty, and goodness that, for Socrates and Plato, exist in an independent spiritual realm known as the "World of Forms". The term is derived from the Greek word for "seeing", so the term is ironic since the Forms can only be seen with the *mind*.

### Allegory
An allegory is an extended metaphor where different people, places, and things have a deeper meaning that is often moral, philosophical, or theological.

‖ **JACQUES LOUIS-DAVID'S *THE DEATH OF SOCRATES* (1787)**

met about wisdom, virtue, and the nature of the good life. Famously, Socrates bothered so many people in Athens that his enemies accused Socrates of "corrupting" the youth of Athens. For this crime, the Athenian court sentenced Socrates to death by drinking hemlock.

Plato depicts Socrates as one utterly consumed by the contemplation of truth, beauty, and goodness. Central to Socrates' philosophy is the idea of forms, which are effectively ideas. These ideas exist independently of true statements, good people, or beautiful things that we see in the real world, and these things are only true, good, and beautiful in as much as they imitate the forms. The forms are essentially ideas, pure, unchanging, perfect, and timeless ideas, and many of Plato's dialogues focus on one of these significant ideas. One dialogue might concentrate on an idea such as justice, piety, or beauty as Socrates asked a series of sustained, almost exasperating questions to whomever happened to be willing to talk with him. By asking so many questions, Socrates hoped he could understand that idea better and then shape his behavior in light of his new understanding. We have provided a sample text from Plato's dialogues, "The Allegory of the Cave" from Plato's *Republic*, Book VII.

*The Republic* is one of Plato's most significant and important dialogues, one that focuses on the nature of justice and investigates how an understanding of justice might lead an individual (like Socrates or the reader) to live a life marked by justice. In this particular selection, Socrates offers an illustration, an allegory, to distinguish between the world of forms and the world we see around us. In "The Allegory of the Cave," all of humanity is chained in a cave and watching shadows on the cave wall, and because the shadows are all that the people see, they mistake them for reality.

# Allegory of the Cave / By Plato

## The Republic, Book VII

*Socrates is speaking to Glaucon, Plato's brother.*

**Socrates:** And now, let me show in a figure how far our nature is enlightened or unenlightened: Behold, we find human beings living in an underground den, which has a mouth open towards the light and reaching all along the den; here they have been from their childhood, and have their legs and necks chained so that they cannot move, and can only see before them, being prevented by the chains from turning round their heads. Above and behind them a fire is blazing at a distance, and between the fire and the prisoners there is a raised way; and you will see, if you look, a low wall built along the way, like the screen which marionette players have in front of them, over which they show the puppets.

**Glaucon:** I see.

**Socrates:** And do you see men passing along the wall carrying all sorts of vessels, and statues and figures of animals made of wood and stone and various materials, which appear over the wall? Some of them are talking, others silent.

**Glaucon:** You have shown me a strange image, and they are strange prisoners.

**Socrates:** Like ourselves, and they see only their own shadows, or the shadows of one another, which the fire throws on the opposite wall of the cave?

**Glaucon:** True, how could they see anything but the shadows if they were never allowed to move their heads?

**Socrates:** And of the objects which are being carried in like manner they would only see the shadows?

**Glaucon:** Yes.

**Socrates:** And if they were able to converse with one another, would they not suppose that they were naming what was actually before them?

**Glaucon:** Very true.

**Socrates:** And suppose further that the prison had an echo which came from the other side, would they not be sure to fancy when one of the passers-by spoke that the voice which they heard came from the passing shadow?

**Glaucon:** No question.

**Socrates:** To them, the truth would be literally nothing but the shadows of the images.

**Glaucon:** That is certain.

**Socrates:** And now look again, and see what will naturally follow if the prisoners are released and told of their error. At first, when any of them is liberated and compelled suddenly to stand up and turn his neck round and walk and look towards the light, he will suffer sharp pains; the glare will distress him, and he will be unable to see the realities of which in his former state he had seen the shadows. Then, he can conceive someone saying to him, that what he saw before was an illusion, but that now, when he is approaching nearer to being and his eye is turned towards more real existence, he has a clearer vision—what will be his reply? And you may further imagine that his instructor is pointing to the objects as they pass and requiring him to name them—will he not be perplexed? Will he not fancy that

## Vocabulary & Annotations

**...see men passing**
Notice how some men are *not* chained in the cave and, in fact, control what everyone else is seeing.

**...shadows of the images**
The people in the cave see shadows on the wall in the same way that what we see and experience in the world around is not as real as the world of Forms..

**...rugged ascent**
The philosopher "ascends" to the world of the Forms via reflection on, and conversation about, the nature of wisdom, virtue, and the Forms.

**...realities**
The word *realities* refers to the Forms themselves and seeing the Forms for what they really are.

**...put him to death**
Such was the fate that happened to Socrates.

---

the shadows which he formerly saw are truer than the objects which are now shown to him?

**Glaucon**: Far truer.

**Socrates**: And if he is compelled to look straight at the light, will he not have a pain in his eyes which will make him turn away to take refuge in the objects of vision which he can see, and which he will conceive to be in reality clearer than the things which are now being shown to him?

**Glaucon**: True.

**Socrates**: And suppose once more, that he is reluctantly dragged up a steep and **rugged ascent**, and held fast until he is forced into the presence of the sun himself, is he not likely to be pained and irritated? When he approaches the light his eyes will be dazzled, and he will not be able to see anything at all of what are now called **realities**.

**Glaucon**: Not all in a moment.

**Socrates**: He will have to grow accustomed to the sight of the upper world. And first, he will see the shadows best, next the reflections of men and other objects in the water, and then the objects themselves; then he will gaze upon the light of the moon and the stars and the heavens; and he will see the sky and the stars by night better than the sun or the light of the sun by day?

**Glaucon**: Certainly.

**Socrates**: Last of all he will be able to see the sun, and not mere reflections of him in the water, but he will see him in his own proper place, and not in another; and he will contemplate him as he is.

**Glaucon**: Certainly.

**Socrates**: He will then proceed to argue that this is he who gives the season and the years, and is the guardian of all that is in the visible world, and in a certain way the cause of all things which he and his fellows have been accustomed to behold?

**Glaucon**: Clearly, he said, he would first see the sun and then reason about him.

**Socrates**: And when he remembered his old quarters, and the wisdom of the den and his fellow-prisoners, do you not suppose that he would be happy about the change and thus pity them?

Glaucon: Certainly, he would.

Socrates: And if they were in the habit of conferring honors among themselves on those who were quickest to observe the passing shadows and to remark which of them went before, and which followed after, and which were together; and who were therefore best able to draw conclusions as to the future, do you think that he would care for such honors and glories, or envy the possessors of them? Would he not say with Homer, *Better to be the poor servant of a poor master, and to endure anything, rather than think as they do and live after their manner?*

Glaucon: Yes, he said, I think that he would rather suffer anything than entertain these false notions and live in this miserable manner.

Socrates: Imagine once more, such an individual coming suddenly out of the sun and found himself again in his old situation; would he not be certain to have his eyes full of darkness?

Glaucon: To be sure.

Socrates: And if there were a contest, and he had to compete in measuring the shadows with the prisoners who had never moved out of the den, while his sight was still weak, and before his eyes had become steady (and the time which would be needed to acquire this new habit of sight might be very considerable), would he not be ridiculous? Men would say of him that up he went and down he came without his eyes; and that it was better not even to think of ascending; and if anyone tried to loose another and lead him up to the light, let them only catch the offender, and they would put him to death.

Glaucon: No question.

Socrates: This entire allegory, I said, you may now append, dear Glaucon, to the previous argument; the prison-house is the world of sight, the light of the fire is the sun, and you will not misapprehend me if you interpret the journey upwards to be the ascent of the soul into the intellectual world according to my poor belief, which, at your desire, I have expressed—whether rightly or wrongly God knows. But, whether true or false, my opinion is that in the world of knowledge the idea of good appears last of all, and is seen only with an effort; and, when seen, is also inferred to be the universal author of all things beautiful and right, parent of light and of the lord of light in this visible world, and the immediate source of reason and truth in the intellectual; and that this is the power upon which he who would act rationally either in public or private life must have his eye fixed.

Glaucon: I agree as far as I understand you.

Socrates: Moreover, you must not wonder that those who attain to this beatific vision are unwilling to descend to human affairs; for their souls are ever hastening into the upper world where they desire to dwell; which desire of theirs is very natural, if our allegory may be trusted.

Glaucon: Yes, very natural.

Socrates: And is there anything surprising in one who passes from divine contemplations to the evil state of man, misbehaving himself in a ridiculous manner; if, while his eyes are blinking and before he has become accustomed to the surrounding darkness, he is compelled to fight in courts of law, or in other places, about the images or the shadows of images of justice, and is endeavoring to meet the conceptions of those who have never yet seen absolute justice?

Glaucon: Anything but surprising.

Socrates: Anyone who has common sense will remember that the bewilderments of the eyes are of two kinds, and arise from two causes, either from coming out of the light or from going into the light, which is true of the mind's eye, quite as much as of the bodily eye; and he who remembers this when he sees anyone whose vision is perplexed and weak, will not be too ready to laugh; he will first ask whether that soul of man has come out of the brighter life, and is unable to see because unaccustomed to the dark, or having turned from darkness to the day is dazzled by the excess of light. And he will count the one happy in his condition and state of being, and he will pity the other; or, if he has a mind to laugh at the soul which comes from below into the light, there will be more reason in this than in the laugh which greets him who returns from above out of the light into the den.

## Reading Comprehension Questions

1. According to Plato, the cave is an allegory for … what?

2. What are the shadows on the wall? Are they real? What do the shadows signify?

3. What does the world outside the cave look like? What might it symbolize?

4. Is the state of man, apart from pursuing philosophy, really nothing more than a prisoner chained in a cave?

ACTIVITY

# Socratic Seminar Prep Sheet

A Socratic Seminar is a guided yet free-flowing discussion about ideas that matter. They are lively conversations between teachers and students around the investigation of a great text, an inspiring work of art, or some other meaningful idea or concept worth discussing. To prepare for our Socratic seminar, let's examine some key pieces of information about this text by filling in the blank spaces of this Socratic Seminar Prep Sheet. This worksheet can also be found in the Appendix.

| | |
|---|---|
| **Author** | |
| **Title** | |
| **Literary Genre** | |
| **Date of Composition** | |
| **Key Ideas** *The ideas we should understand well enough to analyze this particular text and evaluate the ideas within it.* | |
| **Key Vocabulary** *Words that are either so difficult, so crucial, or so abstract that they merit special consideration.* | |
| **The "Big Idea"** *This point may be the central claim (or claims) that the author is trying to advance in his or her work, or it may be an idea that speaks to transcendent values such as truth, beauty, justice, and virtue. Or the text may interact with deeply-rooted issues in the human condition so that no matter how long ago the text was written, it can speak to and inspire us today.* *In short, what is the "Big Idea", the most important idea or ideas, circulating through this text?* | |

WRITING

# Writing Prompt

Remember, writing is thinking. To help us to write and think more clearly, we will spend considerable time this year writing essays based on the texts we read in class. These essays are descriptive in nature and answer one question that arises from the material we are reading in class. In such an essay, the writer wants to explain the meaningful ideas contained in this text by reading and rereading the text under analysis to better explain that author's argument and the consequences of his or her ideas.

**Question**: *How does "The Allegory of the Cave" reinforce the ideas of logic and reasoned argumentation, as covered in this chapter? Explain your reasoning.*

WRITING

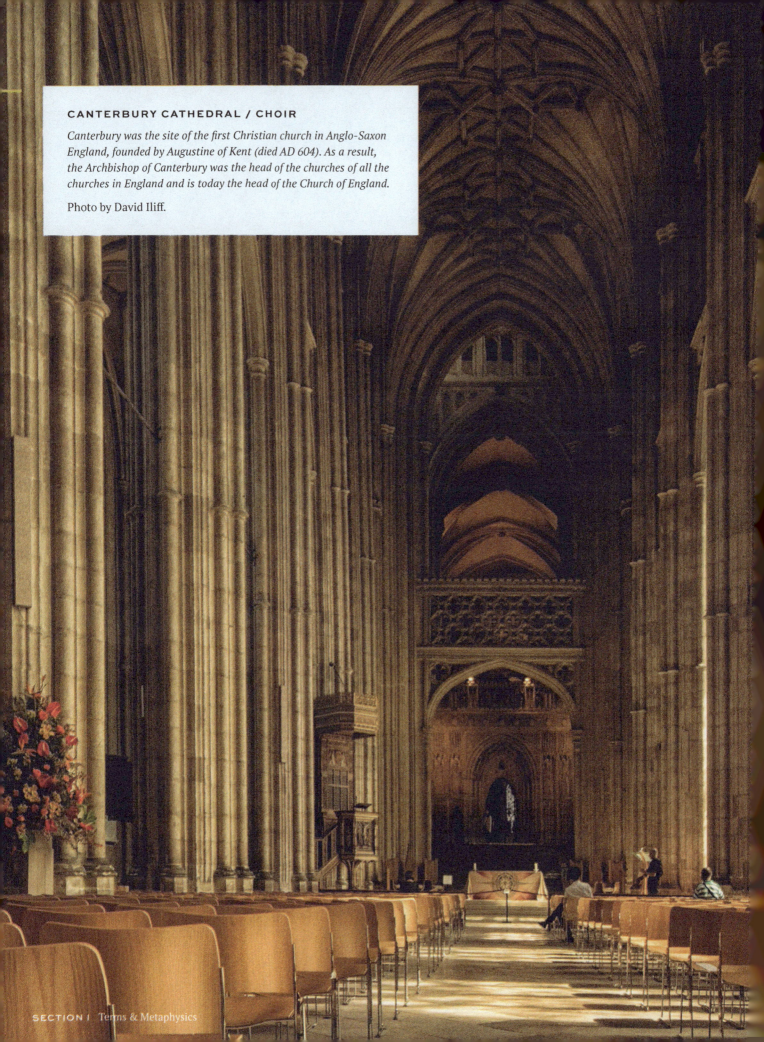

**CANTERBURY CATHEDRAL / CHOIR**

*Canterbury was the site of the first Christian church in Anglo-Saxon England, founded by Augustine of Kent (died AD 604). As a result, the Archbishop of Canterbury was the head of the churches of all the churches in England and is today the head of the Church of England.*

Photo by David Iliff.

## CHAPTER 2

# The Three Acts of the Mind

### ROADMAP

- Learn about simple apprehension, judgments, and arguments.
- Learn how to evaluate arguments according to their terms, their propositions, and the way in which those arguments are constructed.
- Read a selection from Euclid's *Elements*.

**THALES OUTCOME N°. 3**

*A person with* **Self-Reliance** *evaluates his/her interdependence, independence, and dependence to local, national, and global communities in relation to oneself.*

Logic is not merely a subject but the means of learning all subjects. Moreover, if you can't think for yourself—that is, if you can't evaluate arguments or form arguments of your own, you'll be reliant on other people to do that kind of thinking for you. As students of logic, we want to identify fallacies (errors in reasoning) in the arguments that we use or are used against us.

# The Three Acts of the Mind

LOGIC IS PREDICATED on the conviction that truth is real and can be known. We human beings are endowed with a faculty called **reason**, our ability to work out problems and make inferences about subject matter that goes above and beyond human experience. An animal may be able to escape from a maze through trial and error, but they are incapable of thinking above and beyond in a way we would call "reasoning". That is, the kind of thinking that allows us to work out complex problems or contemplate things that are true, good, and beautiful. The mind and its ability to reason is typically divided into three distinct acts, the three principal ways that the mind takes in information from the world and uses that information to reach new conclusions.

Simply enough, the **three acts of the mind** are ways of thinking about thinking. They include the acts of simple apprehension, judgment, and inference. These three acts subsequently correspond to the three fundamental building blocks of an argument—namely, terms, propositions, and arguments. Our minds can "apprehend" and understand terms; our minds can evaluate the accuracy of a proposition; and our minds can use clear terms and true propositions in such a way as to reason from premises to a conclusion in an argument. Terms correspond to the act known as apprehension, propositions to the act of judgment, and arguments to inference and reasoning. For the conclusion of an argument to be true, that argument must employ clear terms, and true propositions, and those propositions must be arranged and formulated in such a way that the argument is valid. The word "valid" means that the argument follows the rules governing the construction of syllogisms (more on that in Section III). To evaluate an argument, a logician must carefully consider the terms of the argument, the propositions of that argument, and its structure if he or she wants to have certainty that the conclusion of that argument is true.

## The First Act of the Mind: Simple Apprehension

The first act of the mind is called **simple apprehension**. To *apprehend* something is to understand it, to hold it in the mind, and to know what that term is in itself in the same manner a detective might apprehend a criminal at the end of a puzzling mystery novel. Often, this process happens automatically and implicitly within our minds, such as when we see a furry, four-legged animal and immediately recognize it as a dog. The act of *apprehension* operates on **terms**, the basic, most fundamental unit of meaning. Ideally, in an argument, the terms must be clearly understood by both the maker

*The three acts of the mind are ways of thinking about thinking and include the acts of simple apprehension, judgment, and inferences. Apprehension focuses on terms, the simplest units of meaning; judgment on propositions, wherein one term is connected to another; and inferences on arguments, wherein we use information that we already know to reach new conclusions.*

## Vocabulary

*Write down this vocabulary into your notebook. These terms will help you better learn and understand the material in this chapter.*

### Reason
The unique ability to solve problems, make inferences, and think about subjects that go above and beyond human experience.

### Three Acts of the Mind
The three ways that human beings can think about thinking, which are the acts of simple apprehension, judgment, and inference.

### Simple Apprehension
This act is the first act of the mind and focuses on the clear understanding of terms.

### Terms
The simplest, most fundamental unit of meaning. A term is a concept that is "held" or "apprehended" in the mind when we think of a particular idea or concept.

### Judgment
The second act of the mind, a process that evaluates whether or not a proposition is true or false.

### Proposition
A sentence that joins together a term with another term in order to communicate some idea about the world, an idea that could either be true or false.

▌ **FRANCIS BACON / 1561-1626**

of that argument and the recipient of it. Otherwise, the writer or the logician risks losing his or her reader either by confusing them or in talking past them. Throughout history, the writers of complicated, philosophical treatises have taken the time to define their terms first so that the forceful, well-reasoned content of their prose cannot help but move the reader to their conclusion.

The use of clear terms in communication is so important, yet we often neglect to clarify the meaning of the words that we use. The tendency is so common that the sixteenth-century English writer Francis Bacon described it as one of the "Four Idols," those errors in reasoning to which all people are susceptible. Bacon described the "Idol of the Marketplace" as an error that arises whenever we do not use clearly defined terms when we speak, write, or argue. This certainty is as hard to reach as haggling with a street vendor in a crowded, frenzied marketplace where prices change as frequently as the meaning of the terms we use. In Francis Bacon's famous work, the *Novum Organum*, he describes the "Idol of the Marketplace", or the real, very human tendency to use unclear terms, in the following way:

> *There are also idols formed by the reciprocal intercourse and society of man with man, which we call idols of the market, from the commerce and association of men with each other; for men converse by means of language, but words are formed at the will of the generality, and there arises from a bad and unapt formation of words a wonderful obstruction to the mind.*

CHAPTER 2  The Three Acts of the Mind  ◆  33

To overcome such problems, we should strive to use clear terms in formal writing and argumentation. That way, the people reading or listening to our arguments can understand what we are trying to argue for.

## The Second Act of the Mind: Judgment

The second act of the mind is **judgment**, and this particular act focuses on **propositions**. A proposition is a statement that contains both a subject—a person, place, or thing that *is* something or *does* something—and a predicate—the part of the sentence that says something about the subject, its actions, or its state of being. Essentially, a proposition is a sentence that affirms (or denies) something is true about the subject, and thus we can say that a proposition can be either true or false. That is, a proposition makes a statement that either does (or does not) correspond to reality, a correspondence that we can verify by observation or by argumentation.

Take, for example, a proposition like *the weather outside is sunny*. Such a proposition may or may not be true, and we can *judge* whether or not it is true simply by looking outside. Other propositions require more than simple observation to verify their truth content, propositions such as *man has free will, the universe is not governed by random chance*, or Aristotle's famous proposition that *man is a rational animal*. These propositions require argumentation, evidence, and careful reflection upon the significance of the subject matter being discussed to *judge* whether or not such propositions are true or false. Yet, they are still statements that affirm that something is true about the world. While logic focuses on the building and evaluation of arguments, propositions may be more important than arguments. That is because only propositions can be *true* or *false*, and logic aims at truth (Kreeft 3).

The final and third act of the mind resides in making an **inference** or reasoning, and this act of the mind operates upon arguments. The act of making an inference is the process of taking what is already known and using that information to reach a new, previously unknown conclusion. Typically, an argument will have a word that signals an argument is being made, words like "therefore", "because", "subsequently", "so", or other similar conclusion-indicator words. The key idea is that in making an inference, we take information we know and use it to reach a conclusion that was not previously apparent. Logic distinguishes between two kinds of reasoning: deductive reasoning and inductive reasoning. Let's examine deductive reasoning first.

## Vocabulary

**Inference**
The third act of the mind, a process that takes information we already know and uses that information to reach a new conclusion.

**Deductive Reasoning**
Reasoning that goes "from premises to particulars" that utilizes clear terms, true propositions, and valid reasoning in the construction of formal arguments.

**Syllogism**
A formal, well-structured argument composed of two premises leading to a conclusion; the written expression of the mental act of inference.

**Valid**
An argument that follows the rules governing the formal construction of syllogisms.

**Sound**
An argument that employs valid reasoning and contains true propositions.

**Organon**
The title of Aristotle's work on logic and reasoning; the word comes from the Greek word for "tool" or "instrument" in the same way that logic is very much a tool for constructing and evaluating arguments.

## Deductive Reasoning

The term **deductive reasoning** comes from two Latin words: the preposition *de* meaning "down from" or "about" and the verb *duco, ducere*, meaning "to lead". In this sense, *deductive reasoning* "leads down from" broad premises to particular instances of that broad, general, premise. Typically, deductive reasoning focuses more on structure and form instead of content.

Often, deductive reasoning appears in the form of a syllogism. A **syllogism** is a highly structured argument consisting of three terms and three propositions. If the terms are clear, the propositions true, and the argument **valid**—that is, the argument follows the *rules* that govern syllogisms—then the conclusion of that argument *must* be true. Here, we have italicized the word *must* to signify the idea of *necessity*—that because the argument contains clear terms, true propositions, and valid reasoning, then by necessity the conclusion of that argument is true. If human beings delight in what is true, then we should find joy in deductive reasoning since it can give us the certainty that our conclusion is true. An argument that is valid in form and contains true propositions is said to be **sound**.

One famous example of a syllogism is as follows:

Premise 1: *All men are mortal*

Premise 2: *Socrates is a man.*

Conclusion: *Socrates is a mortal.*

A broad, universal proposition like *all men are mortal* goes *down* to a specific, particular subject, *Socrates*. *Socrates*, being a *man*, must also be *mortal*. From these premises, we can infer that because *all men are mortal*, and *Socrates is a man*, *Socrates* must also be a *mortal*.

To put it another way, one can think of deductive reasoning as moving in one direction: down. Deductive reasoning goes down from universal principles to real,

# DEDUCTIVE REASONING
### FROM PRINCIPLES

### TO PARTICULARS

**DEDUCTIVE / FROM PREMISES TO PARTICULARS**

*This form of reasoning is often associated with Aristotle's* Organon.

individual applications of that principle. Moreover, deductive reasoning takes information we already know and uses it to reach a conclusion not previously apparent. In the *Posterior Analytics*, a treatise included in the **Organon** (Aristotle's logic textbook), Aristotle writes the following about deductive reasoning: "Both produce their teaching through what we are already aware of, the former [deduction] getting their premises as from men who grasp them, the latter [induction] proving the universal through the particular's being" (Barnes 114).

In the *Topics*, another text included in the *Organon*, Aristotle defined deduction as "an argument in which, certain things being laid down [in a broad premise], something other than these necessarily comes about through them" (Barnes 167). That is, we begin with premises comprised of information we already know and use that information to reach a conclusion that we did not know before.

To illustrate this unique facet of deductive reasoning, we have included a reading from Euclid's *Elements*, a geometry textbook written in the 3rd century BC. In this section, Euclid takes information we do know about circles and triangles and uses that understanding to reach a conclusion not immediately apparent in a proposition known as Thales' theorem.

## Inductive Reasoning

Inductive reasoning works, meanwhile, by taking general observations of "stuff" happening out in the world (sometimes called "phenomena") to reach a conclusion that is generally broader and more universal in nature.

The word *inductive* comes from the Latin preposition *in* and the Latin verb *duco, ducere,* meaning "to lead", so that inductive reasoning leads into or up to a broad, universal principle. A logician using inductive reasoning would take multiple observations about one particular thing happening in the world and, from those observations, make a reasoned, well-informed, well-researched conclusion about the cause, the effects, the relationship, etc. about the pieces of the observed "stuff".

Inductive reasoning is based more on content than form, since the more observations or evidence that an inductive argument has, the more likely the conclusion is to be true. If, for example, we were curious about the effect of sunlight on plants, we might place one plant outside in the sun and another in a dark closet and then observe how much either plant grows. We could reason inductively from our observations of said plants to the general principle that plants grow best in sunlight.

As one may surmise, inductive reasoning constitutes the bedrock of modern, empirical science. We use inductive reasoning in the science classroom whenever we form a hypothesis and devise an experiment to test that hypothesis, an experiment by which we make observations about one particular thing happening in the classroom and then analyze our data once we're finished. Inductive reasoning is a powerful tool for discovering and testing new sources of information, a tool so powerful that Francis Bacon, the same English author referenced earlier, wrote an entire book on induction's potential called the *Novum Organum*, Latin for the *New Instrument*. Published in 1620, Bacon contrasted the *new* instrument of inductive reasoning with that of deductive reasoning, the kind of reasoning that Aristotle expounded upon in the *Organon*. Bacon writes in the *Novum Organum*:

> *But the true method of experience on the contrary first lights* **the candle**, *and then by means of the candle shows the way; commencing as it does with experience duly ordered and digested, not bungling or erratic, and from it* **educing axioms**, *and from* **established axioms again new experiments** *... Let men therefore cease to wonder that the course of science is not yet wholly run ... [and that] a method rightly ordered leads by an unbroken route through the woods of experience to the open ground of axioms.*

Recall that Aristotle's treatise on logic was named the Organon from the Greek word for *tool* or *instrument*. Logic in general and deductive reasoning in particular are tools to evaluate arguments and determine whether or not those arguments point to a true conclusion. In contrast, Bacon's Novum Organum, extols the immense possibilities offered by inductive reasoning—the *new instrument*—and empirical, experimental science. That is, beginning with intellectual curiosity (the "candle"), we form a hypothesis, devise an experiment, and make observations about some particular phenomenon out in the world.

## Vocabulary

### Inductive Reasoning
A form of reasoning that goes from observations to broad, universal principles; these arguments depend more on content and evidence than on form or structure.

### Novum Organum
Francis Bacon's work on the potential of inductive reasoning, the "new instrument" in contrast to the deductive reasoning of Aristotle. The title is Latin for "New Instrument".

### Phenomenon
Things that we can observe to exist in the real world and whose characteristics we can record and measure, and make inquiries about their nature and their causes.

*To Principles*

*From Particulars*

## INDUCTIVE REASONING

> **INDUCTION / FROM PARTICULARS TO PREMISES**
> *This form of reasoning is often associated with Francis Bacon's* Novum Organum.

The word *phenomenon* refers to things we can observe and experience in the world and use as the basis of our inquiries in classes like biology and physics.

By way of induction, we can reach or "educe" new axioms that lead to greater and greater knowledge about our world. The potential of science and induction is encapsulated in the famous title page of the *Novum Organum,* featuring a ship sailing past the Pillars of Hercules, the metaphorical boundaries of the ancient and medieval world. Now, through science, mankind could finally go beyond the boundaries previously placed upon him. However, in reality, inductive reasoning has strict limits. Unlike deductive reasoning, we can never have certainty that the conclusion of an inductive argument is correct.

We can never have this certainty because we could always discover new evidence or make new observations that prove our conclusion false. We may also wrongly assume that one event caused another when, in reality, they only happened in close proximity, a phenomenon called *correlation*. Or, we analyze past events and assume that the future will be like the past, even though the past provides no guarantee of future events. Generally, the past is a good indicator of future events, and the observations of past events provide helpful data in an inductive argument. But, we still cannot be certain that the conclusion of such an argument is *true*—only that its conclusion is *strong* or *weak*. Indeed, any conclusion we reach through inductive reasoning can only be *strong* or *weak*—strong if it has many observations supporting it and weak if it only has a few.

We may also come across more data that disproves the broad, universal premise that we thought our conclusion led to.

As a famous example, individuals living in Western Europe once believed that all swans were white. They believed that this assertion was so because the only swans they had ever seen waddling around Western Europe were white. But then Dutch and British seafarers discovered the continent of Australia and found black swans living there, thereby shattering the universal claim that "all swans are white". In short, we can never be certain that the conclusion of an inductive argument is true because we can always discover new information which refutes it.

## Conclusion & Summary

In conclusion, the three acts of the mind are three ways in which we can think about thinking. The first act of the mind is apprehension, which focuses on terms. The second act of the mind is judgment, which focuses on propositions and in evaluating whether a proposition is true or false. The third act of the mind is inference, a process that includes two kinds of reasoning: deductive reasoning and inductive reasoning. *Deductive* reasoning is reasoning *from broad premises* and is most often found in the form of a syllogism. A syllogism is a highly structured form of argumentation comprised of two premises leading to a conclusion. In contrast, an inductive argument is usually cast in ordinary, everyday language, going from observations and evidence to conclusions and principles. Often, we think of deductive reasoning going in a downward direction *from broad premises to particulars*, and inductive reasoning *going up from particulars to broad conclusions*.

The primary difference between *deductive* and *inductive* reasoning lies in the certainty that we can gain from a deductive or inductive argument. In this sense, certainty means that the conclusion of the argument must be

**FRONTISPIECE OF FRANCIS BACON'S *NOVUM ORGANUM* / 1620**

true, but only deductive arguments can give us any kind of certainty. If a deductive argument has clear terms, true propositions, and valid reasoning—that is, the argument follows the rules governing syllogisms—then the conclusion of that argument must necessarily be true. Inductive arguments are built upon observations and evidence and, as such, can never be *certain* but only *strong* or *weak*.

On the other hand, the strength of an inductive argument is determined by the amount or the quality of the evidence found in the argument. In this sense, an inductive is probable but not certain. An inductive argument may include whether or not the sun will rise tomorrow: based on the untold numbers of days in which the sun rose, we can have confidence the sun will rise tomorrow, even though such an event is highly probable.

ACTIVITY

# Guided Notes / The Three Acts of the Mind

**Instructions**: Given the amount of specialized terminology and nuanced definitions in this chapter, you may use this page to take notes concerning the Three Acts of the Mind.

| Act of the Mind | Space for Notes |
| --- | --- |
| Simple Apprehension | |
| Judgment | |
| Inference | |

CHAPTER 2 The Three Acts of the Mind ♦ 39

## Reading Comprehension Questions

What is apprehension? On what does the mental act of apprehension focus?

What is judgment? On what does the mental act of making judgments focus?

What is inference? On what does the mental act of making inferences focus?

What is deductive reasoning? What is inductive reasoning?

ACTIVITY

# Three Acts of the Mind

**Instructions:** Read over each of the following word(s) and identify whether it is a term, a proposition, or an inference. Each of these terms, propositions, and inferences are out of order but are all used in advance of one particular argument.

| Example | Term, Proposition, or Inference |
|---|---|
| 1. Happiness | |
| 2. I see an apple. | |
| 3. Happiness is a kind of life lived in accordance with virtue and the contemplation of meaningful ideas. | |
| 4. Animals do not have the ability to make meaningful choices. | |
| 5. If happiness requires good character (virtue) and a good education (the contemplation of meaningful ideas), then we ought to educate ourselves to our fullest potential. | |
| 6. Republics | |

ACTIVITY

# Three Acts of the Mind

**Instructions:** Continue the exercise from the previous page. An answer key is available at the bottom of this page.

| Example | Term, Proposition, or Inference |
|---|---|
| 7. A republic is a form of government that divides power between several branches. | |
| 8. Apples | |
| 9. Free will is defined as the ability to make meaningful choices. | |
| 10. I see an apple, so I eat it. | |
| 11. Since humans do have the ability to make meaningful choices, they are not merely animals. | |
| 12. Because republics divide power between several branches, they, by design, require much debate and compromise between the individuals serving in those branches. | |

*Answer key:* 1. Term 2. Proposition 3. Proposition 4. Proposition 5. Argument 6. Term 7. Proposition 8. Term 9. Proposition #1, 3, & 5 10. Argument #2, 8, & 10 11. Argument #4, 9, & 11 12. Argument #6, 7, & 12

# Three Acts of the Mind / via Euclid

**TO HELP US IN OUR STUDY** of the three acts of the mind, we will read a text from the Greek mathematician **Euclid** (mid-4th BC). Euclid was from **Alexandria**, a large, cosmopolitan city that served as the capital of Ptolemaic Egypt. Euclid is known as the *Father of Geometry* because he wrote what is perhaps the most influential mathematics textbook in history: the *Elements*, a work that focused on geometry and the nature of shapes.

Before individuals like Euclid, mathematics was used almost entirely for practical applications. Engineers used math and geometry for building pyramids, as in Egypt, and bureaucrats used an early form of algebra to predict crop yields, as in Sumer and many other regions practicing intensive agriculture. With Greek mathematicians came the attempt to bring mathematics into the realm of universal and transcendent ideas. Euclid himself stands near the front of this shift, along with individuals like Pythagoras and our spiritual founder, Thales of Miletus, who attempted to ground mathematics in the world of ideas. That is, mathematics in general and geometry in particular could point to ideas that were true, independent of human experience.

Moreover, Euclid's *Elements* utilizes logic in a simple but profound way. Euclid begins with simple definitions of key terms, employs those terms in propositions, and then builds upon those propositions to reach a previously unknown conclusion. Indeed, Euclid's method is so thorough that, according to legend, Abraham Lincoln taught himself the rules of logic and argumentation by reading not a logic textbook but Euclid's *Elements*. Euclid's method follows the same rigorous chain of reasoning that all aspiring logicians should cultivate. In both math and geometry, the student has to build

‖ EUCLID / MID-4TH C.

proofs upon theorems and axioms that, if true, require that the resulting proof would be true as well. As the geometer's proof would stand or fall upon such axioms, so an argument stands or falls on the clarity of its terms and the truth content of its propositions.

Perhaps the most important idea in this text is *Proposition 31*:

> *In a circle the angle in the semicircle is right, that in a greater segment less than a right angle, and that in a less segment greater than a right angle; further the angle of the greater segment is greater than a right angle, and the angle of the less segment is less than a right angle.*

**EUCLID'S ELEMENTS / ADELARD OF BARTH'S**
*A page from an illuminated manuscript* (14<sup>th</sup> century)

This proposition is known as **Thales' Theorem**. A **theorem** is a statement that is not self-evident, but it has been proven to be true on the basis of other axioms or other theorems. Ancient writers and mathematicians attributed this theorem to either Thales of Miletus or Thales' student, Pythagoras. We have culled the terms and propositions to help students evaluate and understand this particular theorem as if it were the conclusion Euclid is building to in this section of the *Elements*, Book III. Euclid builds upon definitions previously given in the *Elements*, like that of triangles and right angles, and provides definitions for other key terms in Book III.

In this way, we hope to showcase the workings of the Three Acts of the Mind regarding the building and evaluation of arguments. In the *Topics*, a text included in Aristotle's *Organon*, Aristotle defined deduction as "an argument in which, certain things being laid down [in a broad premise], something other than these necessarily comes about through them" (Barnes 167). Euclid's Elements demonstrates this definition of deductive reasoning. Here in the Elements, we begin with our knowledge concerning the properties of circles and triangles and builds upon that knowledge to reach a new conclusion—namely, Thales' Theorem, that "the angle in a semicircle is a right angle"—a conclusion not readily apparent from our initial starting place of circles and triangles. For the conclusion of an argument to be true, that argument must employ clear terms, true propositions, and valid reasoning. In this way get our first experience with the power of logical reasoning through the writings of one of history's greatest thinkers: Euclid.

# Vocabulary

### Euclid
A mathematician from Alexandria, Egypt and author of the *Elements*, perhaps the most influential math textbook in history.

### Alexandria, Egypt
A cosmopolitan port city that was founded by Alexander the Great and located in the Nile delta; the city was one of the largest in the ancient world and, despite being in Egypt, was a center for Greek culture.

### Geometry
One of the four *roads* of the quadrivium, geometry is the study of space relative to the size and distance of shapes.

### Theorem
A theorem is a statement that is not self-evident (that is, it is not obviously true) but has been proven to be true on the basis of other axioms or other theorems.

### Corollary
A proposition that derived from a proposition that has already been proved.

# Elements / Euclid

## Book III: Theory of the Circle

### 01 Definition 1

Equal circles are those whose radii are equal.

### 02 Definition 2

A chord of a circle is the line joining two points in its circumference.

### 03 Definition 3

A right line is said to touch a circle when it meets the circle, and, being produced both ways, does not cut it; the line is called a tangent to the circle, and the point where it touches it the *point of contact*.

**FIGURE 1 / DEFINITION 3**
*"...the line is called a tangent to the circle..."*

### 04 Definition 4

Circles are said to touch one another when they meet, but do not intersect.

There are two species of contact: (1) When each circle is external to the other; (2) When one is inside the other.

**FIGURE 2 / DEFINITION 4**
*Circles are said to touch one another when they meet, but do not intersect*

### 05 Definition 5

A segment of a circle is a figure bounded by a chord and one of the arcs into which it divides the circumference

### 06 Definition 6

Chords are said to be equally distant from the center when the perpendiculars drawn to them from the center are equal.

### 01 Proposition 01

*Problem* / To find the center of a given circle (*ADB*).

*Solution* Take any two points *A*, *B* in the circumference. Join *AB*. Bisect it in *C*. Erect *CD* at right angles to *AB*. Produce *DC* to meet the circle again in *E*. Bisect *DE* in *F*. Then *F* is the center.

*Demonstration* / If possible, let any other point *G* be the center. Join *GA, GC, GB*. Then in the triangles *ACG, BCG* we have *AC* equal to *CB* (const.), *CG* common, and the base *GA* equal to *GB*, because they are drawn from *G*, which is, by hypothesis, the center, to the circumference. Hence [I. viii.] the angle *ACG* is equal to the adjacent angle *BCG*, and therefore each is a right angle; but the angle *ACD* is right (const.); therefore *ACD* is equal to *ACG*—a part equal to the whole—which is absurd. Hence no point can be the center which is not in the line *DE*. Therefore *F*, the middle point of *DE*, must be the center.

The foregoing proof may be abridged as follows: Because *ED* bisects *AB* at right angles, every point equally distant from, the points *A*, *B* must lie in *ED*; but the center is equally distant from *A* and *B*; hence the center must be in *ED*; and since it must be equally distant from *E* and *D*, it must be the middle point of *DE*.

## 09 Proposition 09

*A point (P) within a circle (ABC), from which more than two equal lines (PA, PB, PC, &c.) can be drawn to the circumference, is the center.*

*Dem.* / If *P* be not the center, let *O* be the center. Join *OP*, and produce it to meet the circle in *D* and *E*; then *DE* is the diameter, and *P* is a point in it which is not the center: therefore only two equal lines can be drawn from *P* to the circumference; but three equal lines are drawn (hyp.), which is absurd. *Hence P must be the center.*

## 10 Proposition 10

*If two circles have more than two points common, they must coincide.*

*Dem.* / Let *X* be one of the circles; and if possible let another circle *Y* have three points, *A*, *B*, *C*, in common with *X*, without coinciding with it. Find *P*, the center of *X*. Join *PA*, *PB*, *PC*. Then since *P* is the center of *X*, the three lines *PA*, *PB*, *PC* are equal to one another.

Again, since *Y* is a circle and *P* a point, from which three equal lines *PA*, *PB*, *PC* can be drawn to its circumference, *P* must be the center of *Y*. Hence *X* and *Y* are concentric, which is impossible.

*Corollary* / Two circles not coinciding cannot have more than two points common.

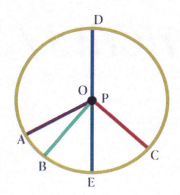

**FIGURE 3 / PROPOSITION 9**
*"...If P be not the centre, let O be the centre..."*

Compare I., Axiom x., that two right lines not coinciding cannot have more than one point common.

## 14 Proposition 14

*In equal circles (1) equal chords (AB, CD) are equally distant from the center. (2) Chords which are equally distant from the center are equal.*

*Dem. 1* / Let *O* be the center. Draw the perpendiculars *OE*, *OF*. Join *AO*, *CO*. Then because *AB* is a chord in a circle, and *OE* is drawn from the center cutting it at right angles, it bisects it [iii.]; therefore *AE* is the half of *AB*. In like manner, *CF* is the half of *CD*; but *AB* is equal to *CD* (hyp.). Therefore *AE* is equal to *CF* [I., Axiom vii.]. And because *E* is a right angle, $AO^2$ is equal to $AE^2 + EO^2$. In like manner, $CO^2$ is equal to $CF^2 + FO^2$; but $AO^2$ is equal to $CO^2$. Therefore $AE^2 + EO^2$ is equal to $CF^2 + FO^2$; and $AE^2$ has been proved equal to $CF^2$. Hence $EO^2$ is equal to $FO^2$; therefore *EO* is equal to *FO*. Hence *AB*, *CD* are (Def. vi.) *equally distant from the center.*

## 15 Proposition 15

*The diameter (AB) is the greatest chord in a circle; and of the others, the chord (CD) which is nearer to the center is greater than (EF) one more remote, and the greater is nearer to the center than the less.*

*Dem. 1* / Join *OC*, *OD*, *OE*, and draw the perpendiculars *OG*, *OH*; then because *O* is the center, *OA* is equal to *OC* [I., Def. xxxii.], and *OB* is equal to *OD*. Hence *AB* is equal to the sum of *OC* and *OD*; but the sum of *OC*, *OD* is greater than *CD* [I. xx.]. *Therefore AB is greater than CD.*

**Dem. 2** / Because the chord *CD* is nearer to the center than *EF*, *OG* is less than *OH*; and since the triangles *OGC*, *OHE* are right-angled, we have $OC^2 = OG^2 + GC^2$, and $OE^2 = OH^2 + HE^2$; therefore $OG^2 + GC^2 = OH^2 + HE^2$; but $OG^2$ is less than $OH^2$; therefore $GC^2$ is greater than $HE^2$, and *GC* is greater than *HE*, but *CD* and *EF* are the doubles of *GC* and *HE*. Hence *CD* is greater than *EF*.

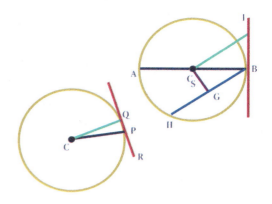

**FIGURE 6 / PROPOSITION 16**
*"...Take any point I, and join it to the center C..."*

**Dem. 2** / To prove that *BH*, which is not perpendicular to *AB*, cuts the circle. Draw *CG* perpendicular to *HB*. Now $BC^2$ is equal to $CG^2 + GB^2$. Therefore $BC^2$ is greater than $CG^2$, and *BC* is greater than *CG*. Hence [note on I., Def. xxxii.] the point *G* must be within the circle, and consequently the line *BG* produced must meet the circle again, *and must therefore cut it.*

This Proposition may be proved as follows:

*At every point on a circle the tangent is perpendicular to the radius.*

Let *P* and *Q* be two consecutive points on the circumference. Join *CP*, *CQ*, *PQ*; produce *PQ* both ways. Now since *P* and *Q* are consecutive points, *PQ* is a tangent (Def. iii.). Again, the sum of the three angles of the triangle *CPQ* is equal to two right angles; but the angle *C* is infinitely small, and the others are equal. Hence each of them is a right angle. *Therefore the tangent is perpendicular to the diameter.*

*Or thus:* A tangent is a limiting position of a secant, namely, when the secant moves out until the two points of intersection with the circle become consecutive; but the line through the center which bisects the part of the secant within the circle [iii.] is perpendicular to it. Hence, in the limit the tangent is perpendicular to the line from the center to the point of contact.

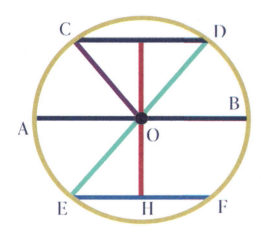

**FIGURE 5 / PROPOSITION 15**
*"... The diameter (AB) is the greatest chord in a circle..."*

## 16 Proposition 16

*The perpendicular (BI) to the diameter (AB) of a circle at its extremity (B) touches the circle at that point. 2. Any other line (BH) through the same point cuts the circle.*

**Dem. 1** / Take any point *I*, and join it to the center *C*. Then because the angle *CBI* is a right angle, $CI^2$ is equal to $CB^2 + BI^2$ [I. xlvii.]; therefore $CI^2$ is greater than $CB^2$. Hence *CI* is greater than *CB*, and the point *I* [note on I., Def. xxxii.] is without the circle. In like manner, every other point in *BI*, except *B*, is without the circle. Hence, since *BI* meets the circle at *B*, but does not cut it, it must touch it.

*Or again:* The angle *CPR* is always equal to *CQS*; hence, when *P* and *Q* come together each is a right angle, *and the tangent is perpendicular to the radius.*

## Proposition 31

*In a circle, (1). The angle in a semicircle is a right angle. (2). The angle in a segment greater than a semicircle is an acute angle. (3). The angle in a segment less than a semicircle is an obtuse angle.*

*Dem. 1* / Let *AB* be the diameter, *C* any point in the semicircle. Join *AC*, *CB*. The angle *ACB* is a right angle.

For let *O* be the center. Join *OC*, and produce *AC* to *F*. Then because *AO* is equal to *OC*, the angle *ACO* is equal to the angle *OAC*. In like manner, the angle *OCB* is equal to *CBO*. Hence the angle *ACB* is equal to the sum of the two angles *BAC*, *CBA*; but [I. xxxii.] the angle *FCB* is equal to the sum of the two interior angles *BAC*, *CBA* of the angle *ABC*. Hence the angle *ACB* is equal to its adjacent angle *FCB*, and therefore it is a right angle [I. Def. xiii.].

*Dem. 2* / Let the arc *ACE* be greater than a semicircle. Join *CE*. Then the angle *ACE* is evidently less than *ACB*; but *ACB* is right; *therefore ACE is acute.*

*Dem. 3* / Let the arc *ACD* be less than a semicircle; then evidently, from (1), *the angle ACD is obtuse.*

*Corollary 1* / If a parallelogram be inscribed in a circle, its diagonals intersect at the center of the circle.

*Corollary 2* / Find the center of a circle by means of a carpenter's square.

*Corollary 2* / From a point outside a circle draw two tangents to the circle.

***Teachers and parents***: You may want to consider posing **Proposition #31 / Thales' Theorem** *first and with little prior instruction. Then, ask students to prove this theorem for themselves. In this way, students have to take what they know about circles and triangles and combine that information in such a way to reach a conclusion that was not apparent at the very beginning: a right triangle inscribed inside a circle, with one side being the diameter, will always be a right triangle.*

**Primary Source Questions**

1. Draw a circle and inscribe a triangle inside the circle, with one side of the triangle being the diameter. What is the size of the angle opposite the diameter?

2. Repeat the steps in the previous question, except draw the angle opposite the diameter in an extreme location on the circle, whether to the very left or the very right of the circle. Is that angle, the angle opposite the diameter, still a right angle?

3. How does Euclid's reasoning take the idea of circles and the idea of triangles and combine them together to reach a new conclusion?

ACTIVITY

# The First Act of the Mind / Terms

Each row contains a term, the author's use of that term, or a definition of that term suitable for students. If the row contains a quotation, write down a clear, intelligible definition of that term in the box provided. If the term is already defined for you, please find the quotation from the text that supports the appropriate definition.

| Term | Quotations from the Text | Quotations Rephrased as Definitions |
|---|---|---|
| Triangle | *A triangle is a shape composed of three line segments whose interior angles add up to 180 degrees.* [This is assumed.] | |
| Circle | | A shape whose points lie on a plane, all of which are equally distant from the center. [This is assumed.] |
| Definition 1 | *Equal circles are those whose radii are equal.* | |

SECTION I Terms & Metaphysics

ACTIVITY

# The First Act of the Mind / Terms

Each row contains a term, the author's use of that term, or a definition of that term suitable for students. If the row contains a quotation, write down a clear, intelligible definition of that term in the box provided. If the term is already defined for you, please find the quotation from the text that supports the appropriate definition.

| Term | Quotations from the Text | Quotations Rephrased as Definitions |
|---|---|---|
| Definition 4 | *Circles are said to touch one another when they meet, but do not intersect.*<br><br>*There are two species of contact: (1) When each circle is external to the other; (2) When one is inside the other.* | |
| Right Angle | | A right angle measures exactly 90 degrees; a right triangle has one right angle and two forty-five degree angles. [This is assumed.] |

CHAPTER 2 The Three Acts of the Mind

ACTIVITY

# The Second Act of the Mind / Propositions

Each row contains an excerpt from the significant text included in this chapter. These selections include significant points and ideas the author uses to build his argument and reach a meaningful conclusion, one that was not apparent at the beginning of their work. In the space provided, write a summary of the quotation and try to express it in the form of a proposition. You may express it as one or more propositions, but try to paraphrase the author's ideas in your own words—that way, you can come to a much deeper understanding of the argument the author is advancing.

| Quotations from Text | Quotations rephrased as one (or more) Proposition(s) |
|---|---|
| **Proposition 9**<br><br>*A point (P) within a circle (ABC), from which more than two equal lines (PA, PB, PC, &c.) can be drawn to the circumference, is the center.* | |
| **Proposition 14**<br><br>*In equal circles equal chords (AB, CD) are equally distant from the center. (2) Chords which are equally distant from the center are equal.* | |

ACTIVITY

# The Second Act of the Mind / Propositions

Each row contains an excerpt from the significant text included in this chapter. These selections include significant points and ideas that the author uses to build his argument and reach a meaningful conclusion, one that was not apparent at the beginning of their work. In the space provided, write a summary of the quotation and try to express it in the form of a proposition. You may express it as one or more propositions, but try to paraphrase the author's ideas in your own words—that way, you can come to a much deeper understanding of the argument the author is advancing.

| Quotations from Text | Quotations rephrased as one (or more) Proposition(s) |
| --- | --- |
| **Proposition 16**<br><br>*The perpendicular (BI) to the diameter (AB) of a circle at its extremity (B) touches the circle at that point. Any other line (BH) through the same point cuts the circle.* | |
| **Proposition 31**<br><br>*In a circle, (1). The angle in a semicircle is a right angle. (2). The angle in a segment greater than a semicircle is an acute angle. (3). The angle in a segment less than a semicircle is an obtuse angle.* | |

ACTIVITY

# The Third Act of the Mind / Inferences

In the space below, create an "argument map", a visual way of representing the premises, assumptions, and ultimately the conclusion that a writer is making in his or her work. You can also use this blank space provided to draw a "conversation map", a visual way of recording the discussion your class had over this text.

ACTIVITY

# The Third Act of the Mind / Inferences

In the space below, we have created our own "argument map" to prove Thales' Theorem and to demonstrate what an argument map may look like.

## Starting Point / *How can we prove Thales' Theorem?*

### 31 Proposition 31

*In a circle the angle in the semicircle is right, that in a greater segment less than a right angle, and that in a less segment greater than a right angle; further the angle of the greater segment is greater than a right angle, and the angle of the less segment is less than a right angle.*

**Premise 1:** Lines from the center of a circle to the circumference of that circle will be equal to each other.

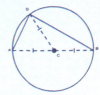

C = Center of Circle
AC = Radius; AB = Diameter
Line AC = Line BC = Line CD

*Refer to Proposition 9, Proposition 14, Proposition 16.*

**Premise 2:** Any triangle formed inside a circle with one side the diameter and with one point on the circumference will be an isosceles triangle.

*Triangle ADC and BCD are isosceles triangles*

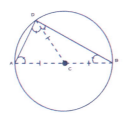

*Angles ADC and CAB are equal to each other.*
*Angles CDB and CBD are equal to each other.*
*Angles ACD and DCB lie on line AB and sum to 180°.*

*The interior angles of a triangle must sum to 180°; thus, angles ADC and CDB must sum to 90°.*

## The Conclusion / Thales' Theorem

If we circumscribe a triangle inside a circle, with one side being the diameter, that triangle will always be a right triangle, regardless of where that point is located on the circumference.

Ex. 1 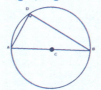   Ex. 2    Ex. 3

Notice that we began with information that we knew—the properties of circles and triangles—and came to a conclusion (Thales' Theorem) that was, in Aristotle's words, a proposition "other than these [properties so that the conclusion] necessarily comes about through them". Euclid's *Elements* demonstrates deductive reasoning in that we take information we do know to come to a conclusion that was not readily apparent.

WRITING

# Writing Prompt

Remember, writing is thinking. To help us to write and think more clearly, we will spend considerable time this year writing essays based on the texts we read in class. These essays are descriptive in nature and answer one question that arises from the material we are reading in class. In such an essay, the writer wants to explain the meaningful ideas contained in this text by reading and rereading the text under analysis to better explain that author's argument and the consequences of his or her ideas.

**Question**: *How does Euclid's* Elements *demonstrate the three acts of the mind, as well as the nature of deductive reasoning? In your essay, be sure to reference quotations and ideas from both Euclid and Aristotle.*

## Writing

CANTERBURY CATHEDRAL / CHOIR

*Augustine of Kent became the first Archbishop of Canterbury and built the first cathedral inside the city of Canterbury. The site underwent several renovations during Anglo-Saxon England, but it was the Normans who rebuilt Canterbury into the soaring Gothic cathedral it is today.*

Photo by K. Mitch Hodge.

CHAPTER 3

# The Kinds of Terms

**ROADMAP**

- Learn about metaphysics and its relationship to logic
- Study terms and how terms constitute the most basic, fundamental unit of meaning
- Complete exercises related to the Tree of Porphyry, the different kinds of terms, and the Comprehension & Extension of terms
- Read a selection from Plato's *Euthyphro*

**THALES OUTCOME Nº 3**

*A Truth-Seeker* critiques a variety of truth statements and/or observations through research and scientific methodology.

Logic is the art of right thinking, and the logician aspires to know, and have some degree of certainty of the truth. As a study in and of itself, metaphysics aims to better understand the fundamental nature of reality itself, to know the causes of things and why they occur, and to have confidence that they occur the way that they do.

# Terms & Metaphysics

**WE DIVIDED OUR LOGIC** textbook into four parts and paired each section and its act of the mind with an appropriate branch of philosophy. That way, we could integrate primary source readings that would allow us to explore that particular concept in logic from the vantage point of the writers, philosophers, and thinkers who used logic particularly well in their writing. For example, the first section of our textbook focuses on terms and the first act of the mind, which we have paired with metaphysics. Metaphysics is the branch of philosophy that focuses on the fundamental nature of reality, being, and existence. Metaphysics is a complex, obscure subject, but perhaps this metaphor may help us better understand it: a swimming pool.

Imagine a swimming pool and a swimming team preparing for practice. The coach has set the lanes out so that each swimmer can compete and practice in his or her lane. The lanes stretch the entire length of the pool, and they keep each swimmer moving in the right direction. Every swimmer steps up, pushes off the wall with their feet, and dives into the pool heading for the other wall. No matter how many laps the swimmers swim or what stroke they use to get to the other end, they all must push off the wall or starting block to begin swimming. Metaphysics is much like that wall. Each subject area or discipline is much like that pool. History, English literature, mathematics, science, and many other subjects swim in their respective lanes, all heading for the other end of the pool. However, they all push off the same wall. Metaphysics is that wall that everyone uses to understand the world around them. But from where does the term metaphysics come?

As with many ideas in the Western tradition, metaphysics originates with Aristotle. The Greek philosopher Aristotle wrote treatises on subjects ranging from literary criticism to political theory, with the title of each treatise derived from its subject; *Poetics* is a work on literary criticism, *Politics* on political theory, and so on. However, the treatise containing the material of *Metaphysics* was notoriously hard to describe, let alone define, and an editor of Aristotle's works simply called the treatise *Metaphysics*, drawn from two Greek words. First, the Greek preposition meta means merely "with" or "after," and the Greek word physics means "nature." Thus, the term *metaphysics* simply means "after nature" or "after physics", with *Physics* being the title of a treatise on motion and causality that comes just before *Metaphysics* in an ancient edition of Aristotle's works. Put another way, the title *Metaphysics* was given to the book that came just after Aristotle's *Physics*, so this work on the fundamental nature and essence of being was simply called *Metaphysics*. Aristotle himself defined

*Metaphysics is the branch of philosophy that focuses on the fundamental nature of causes, as well as certain issues concerning the nature of being and reality; as a result, metaphysics is the most appropriate field of philosophy to pair with terms, the most fundamental unit of meaning.*

## Vocabulary

*Write down this vocabulary in your notebook. These terms will help you better learn and understand the material in this chapter.*

### Philosophy
From the Latin *philosophia* meaning the "love of wisdom".

### Metaphysics
The branch of philosophy that focuses on the fundamental nature of causes, as well as certain issues concerning the nature of being and reality. The word comes from the title of a book that literally came after Aristotle's *Physics*—hence, *Metaphysics*.

### Aristotle
A Greek philosopher whose writings on *Politics, Poetics, Physics, Metaphysics,* and *Rhetoric* form the basis for the Western canon. He lived from 384 to 322 BC.

### Universals
One idea or concept that can be predicated, or said about, many other ideas or concepts. For example, the idea of the color *blue* may be predicated of many different things such as the sky, the ocean, eye color, etc.

### Particulars
The individual thing that exists in the observable world.

**ARISTOTLE / 384 - 322 BC**
*Greek philosopher and author of Metaphysics, Poetics, and Rhetoric*

metaphysics as the *first philosophy* and the *wisdom to deal with 'first causes' and the principles of things*. Since metaphysics focuses on what a thing is, metaphysics stands at the heart of philosophy and logic.

Metaphysics deals with the existence of things and what they are as we know them. Metaphysics, subsequently, helps answer the question: what is? As we will see in Section II, once we know what things 'are', we can begin to consider whether or not they are true, how we as human beings come to know them, and why we can be sure of their truth or falsehood. Our coming to understand the nature of terms is like pushing off the wall in the swimming pool. Each lane will study history, literature, or biology, but they must first consider what exists. What makes something what it is? Metaphysics will help us to answer that question and better understand the essence or substance of a thing. Now that we understand what metaphysics is, let us turn to the subject on which metaphysics focuses—existence and what makes a thing what it is.

This section will examine the relationship between words, terms, and concepts, and then address the problem of **universals**—how one thing (such as a color) can apply to, or be predicated of, many different **particular** things. The problem of universals, the understanding that one thing may apply to many different things, is one of the most difficult problems in all of Western philosophy. What, after all, makes something beautiful? How might a painting, a tree, or a sunset all be beautiful, even if each of those things is radically different from the other? Later in this chapter, we will look at three of the most commonly held positions on the *problem of universals* from the philosophers Plato (late-5th century BC), Aristotle (mid-4th century), and the medieval scholastic William of Ockham (AD 1285-1347).

CHAPTER 3 The Kinds of Terms ♦ 61

## Reading Comprehension Questions

1. From where did the term *metaphysics* come?

2. Why is metaphysics important?

## Reading Comprehension Questions

3. What is the problem of universals?

4. In your opinion, how might a painting, a tree, or a sunset all be beautiful, and yet all be different things?

# The Nature of Terms

A TERM MAY BE SIMPLY, but not fully, described as a word. If we think of a word with real, concrete meaning to it—something like an orange or a penguin—that word brings to mind the image of that particular thing. The image we have in our minds is that of an orange or a penguin we have seen somewhere in the world. The word orange or penguin may differ from language to language, such as *naranja* and *pingüino* in Spanish, but the image conjured in our minds remains the same. That image is immaterial in that it exists in the mind and not in the real world in the way an actual orange or a real penguin exists. The word may exist physically on a page (like the word *orange* or *naranja* printed right here) or travel physically through the air as human speech, but it is the image conveyed to the mind upon which the logician focuses (Kreeft 37). That image is of vast importance to us as we study logic.

First, that image could very well be real in a way that is even more real than a real orange one can eat. That image is an idea, almost like a picture inside our heads, and an idea does not break down or decay with time, as does an actual orange. That is because an idea can endure, transcending spatial and temporal boundaries above and beyond what we human beings are capable of appreciating. The fact that we communicate one word—and words more important than orange and penguin, perhaps, words like freedom, dignity, and happiness—and convey it into the mind of another human being is an astounding ability that we human beings often take for granted. We can train an animal to fetch some object for us, but animals are seemingly incapable of understanding things in such a way that we human beings can (Arryn, *Aristotle's Ethics*).

A **term**, subsequently, is the most fundamental unit of meaning. A term brings to mind an image of the thing that it refers to, and such an image is often referred to as a **concept**. The first act of the mind is called **apprehension,** because this act holds or apprehends a concept in the mind in the way we think about things. In differentiating between concepts, terms, and words, we must emphasize first that a concept exists in the mind and is immaterial. In contrast, a term expresses what that concept is in itself. The term is the most important, fundamental component of meaning, and it often represents a category of things (Hodges, Larsen, Johnson 9; Kreeft, 40-41). Words can change across languages so that different words can refer to the same concept, and a word is also the physical representation of that term as that word is written on a page or heard audibly in conversation (Kreeft 40-41).

*The problem of universals and how the one relates to the many is resolved in three ways: extreme realism, in that ideas like truth and beauty really exist; modified realism, in that the universal idea exists in the particulars; and nominalism, in that the idea is just a name we use to refer to a category of things that exist.*

## Vocabulary

**Term**
A term is the most basic, most fundamental unit of meaning; terms are *held* or *apprehended* in the mind when we think of a particular idea or concept.

**Concept**
The image in our mind of a thing, which transcends space and time.

**Apprehension**
The first act of the mind that focuses on the clear understanding of terms. Also known as *simple apprehension*.

**Form**
Forms are ideas such as truth, beauty, and goodness that, for Socrates and Plato, exist in an independent spiritual realm known as the *World of Forms*.

**Necessity**
A necessary truth is one that cannot exist otherwise.

**Contingent**
A proposition or state of affairs that could have existed otherwise.

The concept brought up by a term has several essential characteristics. One, concepts are immaterial because concepts only exist in our minds. In this immaterial nature, they have a near-synonym with the word *idea*, although the English word *idea* is much broader than simply the idea of an orange or a penguin. Then, concepts are abstract in that they can apply to many different things without necessarily existing as an entirely separate thing (Kreeft 37-39). The word *abstract* is derived from the Latin preposition *ab* ("from") and the verb *traho, trahere* ("to draw from") so that an abstract idea is drawn from, or separated from, the real world (Kreeft 38). The *color* orange does not exist in the same way an *orange* orange exists, or an *orange* basketball exists, although we can think of the color orange in our minds. We can hold it in our minds because we can isolate and abstract the idea of *orange* from some orange thing.

Such concepts are universal in that they can apply to many different things even while that idea remains only one thing. The idea that a vegetable, a flower, or some other broad category of things can apply to many different things even while it remains that one thing is one of the most difficult problems in philosophy. How does the many or the universal relate to the one and the particular? We can see an individual person, yet we cannot see the universal idea of *man* (Kreeft 39). Concepts exist in the mind, and, as a result, concepts are unchanging. Since they are unchanging, they are in some sense perfect. The image that we have in our minds of a tree may even bear some passing similarity to the concept of a tree held in the mind of an individual like Socrates and Plato. These two eminent philosophers focused on the importance of terms, the concepts they produced in the mind, and how we can shape our behavior in light of truly understanding what these ideas mean. They focused not just on relatively simple concepts (like geometric shapes in Plato's *Meno*) but deep, abstract, and immaterial ones like truth, goodness, and beauty. (Kreeft 39-40).

A form, idea, or concept does not take up space in how physical, concrete objects do in the world around us. For instance, the color blue is abstract, as we can hold the color blue in our minds independent of anything in the real world that is blue—the ocean, the sky, or someone's eye color, for instance (Kreeft 42). We can also examine a just act and extract from it ideas of justice that may help us understand what justice is, just as Socrates attempts to do in Plato's *Republic*. In short, because concepts are spiritual, immaterial, and abstract, we can take such a concept and apply it to many different things in the real world, but such a concept does not exist in the same way that particulars exist (Kreeft 41-43). Concepts, moreover, illustrate the difference between necessity and contingency. The idea of **necessity** means that it cannot exist otherwise: the concept of a

**PLATO (LEFT) & ARISTOTLE (RIGHT) / RAPHAEL'S SCHOOL OF ATHENS**
*Plato points upwards to the World of Forms while Aristotle points to the earth and the world of particulars*

triangle is, by definition, a three-angled shape whose interior angles add up to 180 degrees. Anything that deviates from this definition ceases to be a triangle and instead becomes some other shape (Kreeft 37-39). By contrast, propositions or states of affairs that are **contingent** are true and do correspond to reality, but they could have occurred in some other way. A triangle cannot be anything other than a three-sided shape, whereas a student at Thales could have gone to a different school. A state of affairs that is contingent is one that could have happened in a way other than it did without presenting a contradiction.

But does a concept really exist? I can entertain the idea of a unicorn in my mind, but I know that unicorns do not exist in the real world. If I think hard enough, I can separate the horn of a unicorn from the body of a horse; I am left with two different ideas, one of a horse, one of a horn, and I can recognize that someone, long ago, thought that they could make an extraordinary fantastical creature by combining these ideas. If an idea like a unicorn does not exist, do other ideas exist, ideas that are much more meaningful, ideas like truth, beauty, and goodness?

**Plato's** most famous student, the Greek philosopher **Aristotle**, broke with Plato on the independent existence of universals. Aristotle defined a universal as that which "belongs to something both of every case and in itself and as such" (Barnes 119), but he did not believe that such a universal existed in the way that Plato described. Instead, Aristotle countered that even if a concept may exist in several different things—the color *blue* existing in blue skies, blue oceans, and blue eyes, for example—one does not need to assume that the idea of blue exists in a realm independent of a world where blue things exist (Kreeft 41-43).

## Vocabulary

**Plato**
An Athenian philosopher whose dialogues explored the fundamental nature of reality and morality.

**Aristotle**
A Greek philosopher whose writings on *Politics, Poetics, Physics, Metaphysics*, and *Rhetoric* form the basis for much of the Western canon. He lived from 384 to 322 BC.

**Porphyry**
Roman philosopher and author of commentaries on the works of Aristotle. He lived from AD 234 to 305.

**Particulars**
The individual thing that exists in the observable world.

**Extreme Realism**
Ideas really exist outside of minds and in another world as real entities; this view derives from the writings of the philosopher Plato.

**Modified Realism**
A universal exists in the world in the particulars, and in our mind as universal concepts abstracted from other real things; also called *moderate realism*.

**Nominalism**
Universals exist only as names that we use for convenience, but don't express anything true outside of the idea brought to our minds by that name; identified with the English philosopher William of Ockham.

In *De Interpretatione*, or in English, *On Interpretation*, Aristotle says that of

> *actual things some are universal, others particular (I call universal that which is by its nature predicated of several things, and particular that which is not man; man, for instance, is a universal, Callias [an ancient Greek worthy of being referenced by Aristotle] a particular"* (Barnes 27).

If the particular did not exist, then the things we would say of the particular—that is, the universal—would not exist either. The universal exists in the particular but is not independent of that particular. This view, most famously associated with Aristotle, is often referred to as *modified realism*. This view holds that universals exist, but they exist in the particulars and not independently of those particulars. The idea of blue exists in blue things but not independently of them (Kreeft 42). The Tyrian philosopher **Porphyry** expressed the dilemma in the opening pages of the *Isagoge*, a commentary he wrote on Aristotle's *Categories*:

> *I shall omit to speak about genera and species, as to whether they subsist (in the nature of things) or in mere conceptions only; whether also if subsistent, they are bodies or incorporeal, and whether they are separate from, or in, sensibles, and subsist about these, for such a treatise is most profound, and requires another more extensive investigation.*

Per such an investigation, check out the **Closer Look at the Tree of Porphyry** on pages 78 and 79.

Socrates, Plato, and Aristotle believed and argued based on human reason and logic that universal ideas exist in a meaningful way. Such a concept may exist independently of particulars (**extreme realism**, per Plato), or these ideas exist in the particulars we see and experience in the real world (**modified realism**, per Aristotle). Later Christian theologians like St. Augustine of Hippo (AD 354-430), who studied Platonism and other philosophical schools before he became a Christian, found that the idea of the forms seemed to fit with the Christian faith. Augustine wrote that the Forms of truth, beauty, and goodness originate in the mind of God, who formulated all values from the basis of his excellent character. The issue continued to be debated amongst philosophers and theologians long into the Middle Ages.

The Scholastic theologian St. Thomas Aquinas (1225-1274) endeavored to reconcile Aristotelian rationalism to the Catholic Church's teachings in his magnum opus, the *Summa Theologia*. Aquinas called Aristotle "the Philosopher" and as such, adopted much of Aristotle's thinking into his own writings and thinking, albeit subordinated to Aquinas' Christian faith. Aquinas argued that faith and reason, with reason being the problem-solving abilities of man are two different but non-contradicting avenues for understanding and delighting in truth. Through reason, we are capable of apprehending some forms of knowledge but not divine truths, the knowledge of God which impart the greatest happiness to human beings. To understand and contemplate divine truth, reason needs faith (McInerny).

However, a third view, the one most prevalent in our day and age, arose during the Middle Ages, a position known as **nominalism** (Kreeft 42-43). Nominalism derives from a Scholastic theologian and monk named William of Ockham (1287-1347). The term *nominalism* derives from the Latin word *nomen*, *nominis* for "name", in that abstract, universal, unchanging ideas like blue, liberty, goodness, justice, and other concepts do not actually exist, opposing Plato and Aristotle. Instead, these abstract ideas are merely names for concepts we find very useful and convenient (Kreeft 42; Weaver 3). In fairness, William of Ockham was trying to simplify a complex, almost intractable philosophical problem; after all, William of Ockham is most famous for an idea called *Ockham's Razor*, which states, most simply, that the simplest explanation is most likely correct or true. If we cannot see the color *blue* but only hold it in our minds, what proof do we have that such a thing exists in any meaningful way?

According to nominalists, the straightforward solution is to say that such an idea is merely a name for a concept we find convenient, even meaningful ideas like truth and beauty, justice and goodness, liberty and dignity. But if these are names that we use for the sake of convenience, then it stands to reason that neither the names nor their definitions make any real difference to human beings. By extension, if we believe that justice is just a name and so does not bear any resemblance to any transcendent value above and beyond human experience (Weaver 4), then the name of justice and its corresponding definition cannot shape human behavior for the better either.

If justice does not exist, but is instead relative and subjective, then an individual may have no reason to tell the truth unless it personally benefits them. If friendship and love do not exist apart from subjective, emotional feelings that we may have for one but not for another, we have little reason to pursue such meaningful relationships or endure the sacrifices needed to sustain them. If such ideas are just names and nothing more, then the pursuit of wisdom and the cultivation of the good life do not seem to matter much. The American scholar and philosopher Richard Weaver (1910-1963) argued that William of Ockham's nominalism constituted a massive turning point in Western history because, for the first time in the broad consensus of Western thinking, ideas were separated from reality so that they could not influence behavior (3-5). Weaver argued that upon accepting Ockham's nominalism, Western civilization fell off a cliff.

In contrast, classical education aims to help us scale the heights of clear, logical thinking and virtuous character. Taking as our exemplar the philosopher Socrates, classical education hopes to encourage students to take ideas seriously. Socrates himself fell in love with the idea of ideas because he hoped that such an understanding would transform his character for the better. Socrates stated at his trial, "I say again that the greatest good of man is daily to converse about virtue, and all that concerning which you hear me examining myself and others, and that the life which is unexamined is not worth living" (Jowett, *The Apology*). Likewise, classical education aims to reinvigorate that examined life and impart the same sort of love for things that are good, things that are true, and things that are beautiful. Such an understanding would ideally accompany the study of logic, beginning with both the apprehension and the appreciation of terms as the most fundamental unit of meaning.

ACTIVITY

# Guided Notes / The Nature of Terms

**Instructions**: Given the amount of vocabulary in this chapter, take a moment to write down a definition for each term in the table provided below as they appear in the reading. Fill in the blank provided in the middle column, and provide a short definition of the word in the third column.

| Vocabulary Word | Quotation | Definition |
|---|---|---|
| Term | ...a term, subsequently, is the most _____ unit of meaning... | |
| Concept | ...such an _____ is often referred to as a concept... | |
| Abstract | ...in that they can _____ to many _____ things... | |
| Necessary (*or* Necessity) | ... it cannot _____ otherwise... | |
| Unchanging | ... they are in some sense _____ | |
| Universal | ...they can apply to _____ things even while it remains one thing... | |
| Particular | ...Callias...a _____... | |
| Realism | ...that universal ideas exist in a _____... | |
| Nominalism | ...abstract ideas are merely _____ for concepts we find useful and convenient... | |

CHAPTER 3  The Kinds of Terms  ♦  69

# The Kinds of Terms

A TERM MAY BE THE MOST fundamental unit of meaning, but we still have much to learn about the nature of terms. While a term should bring one concept or idea to our minds, a term may impart multiple concepts or carry a series of nuanced understandings that can be applied in multiple ways. Let's begin by looking at three different kinds of terms: univocal, equivocal, and analogical terms (Kreeft 48). Then we will look at the comprehension and extension of Terms.

## The Kinds of Terms: Univocal to Metaphorical

As its Latin root suggests, **univocal terms** have only one meaning. That is, univocal terms have one relatively clear definition, and they impart one relatively consistent concept to the mind.

In contrast, **equivocal terms** have two or more meanings unrelated to each other such as the stars in the sky and the stars in Hollywood or television (very different concepts, to be sure). Think of the word *equivocate*, which is the use of a word that has multiple definitions. At times, people use equivocal terms purposefully to confuse people.

Then, there are **analogical terms**. Analogical terms have two or more meanings that are partly the same and partly different, even if their meanings are still related to each other. One can think of the word good as an analogical term, since a person, a dog, or a work of art may all be described as good but are good in radically different ways. Although we might define good as something "worthy of imitation", we would still not say that a person is good in the same way that a dog is good (Kreeft 48-49). We can also think of **metaphorical terms**, terms that have one meaning but can be (and are commonly) used as part of a metaphor. That is, these metaphorical terms can be used to compare two unlike objects.

We differentiate terms into these categories to emphasize the importance of using clear terms in our thinking, writing, and speaking. For the conclusion of an argument to be true, it must rest upon valid reasoning, true propositions, and, of course, clear terms. We cannot use a term so that its meaning is obscured; we have to be clear about what we are saying. We should strive to clarify the terms that we use in writing and speaking so that these terms are not vague, ambiguous, or in any way difficult to understand (Kreeft 47). If our terms carry with them such a nuanced understanding, then we must carefully define our terms so that people will understand what we are saying.

## Comprehension & Extension

We can think of a term in two different ways: by its comprehension and its extension. The word **comprehension** refers to a term's *inner meaning* and what that term means in itself (Kreeft 44). A term's *comprehension* is generally a qualitative and subjective understanding, one that refers to the various attributes of a term. The word comprehension, moreover, can be used somewhat synonymously with connotation (Kreeft 44). The word **connotation** refers to the feeling invoked by the use of a word alongside its dictionary definition. The comprehension of a term like "superhero" might include the characteristics of a superhero including justice-seeking, crime-fighting, and cape-wearing, among others. In short, the comprehension of a term refers to

## Vocabulary

**Univocal Terms**
A term that has only one meaning.

**Equivocal Terms**
A term that has two or more definitions.

**Analogical Terms**
A term that has multiple but related shades of meaning and thus can describe many different things; such terms include adjectives like "good", "bad", "love", etc.

**Metaphorical Terms**
One term that can be (and is commonly used) to make a comparison between two unlike objects to illustrate an important idea.

**Comprehension**
The inward, subjective understanding of a term and the various attributes of that term.

**Connotation**
The thought or feeling invoked by the use of a word alongside its dictionary definition.

**Extension**
All the real things to which a term refers (i.e., the population of a species), and is generally quantitative.

**Denotation**
The dictionary definition of a world.

the inner, subjective, and qualitative understanding of a term and the various attributes associated with that term.

**Extension**, meanwhile, refers to all the things to which a term refers or how far a term extends. The word extension is used somewhat synonymously with **denotation**, which refers to the literal, dictionary definition of a word. In general, the word *extension* refers to all the things which a term includes. If the comprehension of the term *superheroes* involves fighting crime, then the extension of the term "superheroes" might include Batman, Spider-man, Iron Man, Captain America, and others.

To better understand comprehension and extension, it can be helpful to look at the relationship between the two. When examining two related terms, comprehension and extension have an inverse relationship; as one increases, the other decreases and vice versa. Consider, for example, the terms "people" and "superheroes". "People" has a greater extension than "superheroes" because more beings fit into the category of the former than the latter. Every human being to exist fits into the category of "people", but only a select few fit into the category of "superhero". Conversely, the term "superhero" has a greater comprehension than "people" because we more specifically define the term "superhero". A superhero has all the same characteristics as that of a person (assuming we are excluding the League of Super-Pets), but it has additional characteristics that cannot be applied to all people such as "justice-seeking" and "crime-fighting". All in all, if one term has a higher extension than another term, you know that it also has a lower comprehension, and vice versa.

## Conclusion & Summary

Let's recap the most important details from this chapter. A term is the most basic, fundamental unit of meaning, whereas a word is either a visible, physical, or audible expression of such a term. Words may also differ from language to language. A term refers to a concept that exists in the mind and is thus immaterial—that is, it does not exist in time and space the way that particulars, things that exist in the real world, really exist. Concepts are immaterial and exist in the mind, so all of the following ideas also apply uniquely to concepts, and not things that exist in the world:

*Abstract, in that a concept can be drawn out from a particular thing;*

*Universal, since a concept can apply to many different things even while it remains one thing;*

*Unchanging, in that ideas do not change or decay in the same way that particulars change and decay;*

*Necessary, in that a concept must exist in a certain way or it cannot exist otherwise.*

*Terms can have one meaning (univocal), multiple unrelated meanings (equivocal), or multiple related meanings (analogical). Terms can also be used as part of a comparison between two unlike objects that illustrates an important idea.*

As an example, let us consider a triangle: the concept of a triangle is abstract in that we can separate the idea of a triangle from real triangles we might find in the real world; universal in that the idea of a triangle might apply to many different triangles; the fundamental understanding of a triangle is unchanging; and is by nature necessary since a triangle cannot be anything other than a three-sided shape whose three interior angles sum to 180 degrees.

Plato & *Extreme Realism*: Ideas, which Plato calls forms, exist in a world independent of human experience, whereas things in the real world such as a beautiful painting, good character, or true speech are themselves beautiful, good, and true in as much as they derive from, or attempt, the forms themselves. Later Christian philosophers and theologians, most notably St. Augustine of Hippo would merge this idea with that of the Christian faith, principally in how the Bible describes God as the ultimate arbiter or definer of what is good and true.

Aristotle & *Modified Realism*: A universal idea exists in the world in the particulars and in our mind

**PLATO'S ACADEMY / ROMAN MOSAIC**
*Circa 79 AD from a villa in Pompeii*

as universal concepts abstracted from other real, tangible things. These ideas, however, do not exist in a world independent of human experiences such as the World of Forms. Per Aristotle, just because two things are alike somehow (such as blue eyes and blue skies) does not mean one must assume the independent, immaterial existence of some third thing as in the idea of blueness. Later, the Christian philosopher and Scholastic theologian St. Thomas Aquinas (1225-1274) would integrate the philosophical system of Aristotle with that of the Christian faith.

William of Ockham & *Nominalism*: Beginning with William of Ockham, *nominalism* is the idea that universals do not exist in any meaningful way. Instead, a universal is just a name that we use for convenience and does not express anything true outside of the idea brought to our minds by that name.

## Reading Comprehension Questions

1. What is a term, and how does a term differ from a word?

2. What is a concept, and how is a concept or an idea so unique?

3. What does it mean that a concept is abstract, universal, unchanging, and necessary?

4. What is the comprehension and the extension of a term?

ACTIVITY

# The Kinds of Terms

**Instructions**: For the following terms, identify whether it is be a univocal, an equivocal, or an analogical term. We will work in groups, and the teacher should provide adequate time for this exercise so that students can look up each word and debate whether or not it is an univocal, equivocal, metaphorical, or analogical term. Explain your reasoning in the space provided in one or two sentences.

*Example: The term* right *is an example of a/an analogical term because it has multiple meanings, most of which are related to each other. Such examples include the* right *way of doing things, the* right *directions, etc., and even the idea of being* right *came from the fact that most people in a given population are right handed.*

1. The term *bank* is an example of a/an _____ term because _____
_____
_____

2. The term *star* is an example of a/an _____ term because _____
_____
_____

3. The term *lead* is an example of a/an _____ term because _____
_____
_____

4. The term *fruit* is an example of a/an _____ term because _____
_____
_____

5. The term *good* is an example of a/an _____ term because _____
_____
_____

6. The term *bad* is an example of a/an _____ term because _____
_____
_____

ACTIVITY

# The Kinds of Terms

**Instructions**: Continue the exercise from the previous page, labeling each term as a *univocal, equivocal, analogical,* or *metaphorical* term.

7. The term *just* is an example of a/an _____ term because _____
_____
_____

8. The term *happy* is an example of a/an _____ term because _____
_____
_____

9. The term *gas* is an example of a/an _____ term because _____
_____
_____

10. The term *idol* is an example of a/an _____ term because _____
_____
_____

11. The term *virtuous* is an example of a/an _____ term because _____
_____
_____

12. The term *healthy* is an example of a/an _____ term because _____
_____
_____

13. The term *chaff* is an example of a/an _____ term because _____
_____
_____

ACTIVITY

# Comprehension & Extension

**Instructions**: Recall that the *comprehension* of a term is the inward, subjective understanding of a term whereas *extension* refers to all the possible instances that term may include. In the table below, identify the *comprehension* and the *extension* of each term provided in the left column.

| Term | Comprehension | Extension |
|---|---|---|
| Flowers | | |
| Sharks | | |
| Forest Creatures | | |

ACTIVITY

# Comprehension & Extension

**Instructions**: Recall that the *comprehension* of a term is the inward, subjective understanding of a term, whereas *extension* refers to all the possible instances that term may include. In the table below, identify the *comprehension* and the *extension* of each term provided in the left column.

| Term | Comprehension | Extension |
| --- | --- | --- |
| Primates | | |
| Passions | | |
| Virtues | | |

CHAPTER 3 The Kinds of Terms

ACTIVITY

# Closer Look at the Tree of Porphyry

Recall the philosopher Porphyry, who hailed from the city of Tyre and lived from AD 234 to 305. His accomplishments include a number of commentaries on earlier, more famous works of philosophy. A commentary is a work explaining the more difficult points of other works, and Porphyry wrote commentaries on works like *The Enneads* of Plotinus and Euclid's *Elements*. Porphyry ranks high among logicians for the *Isagoge*, an introduction that Porphyry wrote for Aristotle's *Categories*. The work became the standard logic textbook throughout the Middle Ages up to the time of William of Ockham. Moreover, the *Isagoge* contains one of Porphyry's most original contributions to logic and philosophy, a concept called the *Tree of Porphyry*. The *Tree of Porphyry* is essentially a diagram based on Aristotle's *predicables*. The term *predicable* comes from the term *predicate*, the part of the sentence that affirms or denies something about a subject. In a treatise called the *Categories*, Aristotle expands on the nature of predicables and explains how *predicables* help us to make sense of the substance or the essence of a thing. We will cover *predicables* more in the next chapter.

The idea behind the *Tree of Porphyry* is to highlight the *scale of being* based on the *genus* and *species* of a secondary substance. The *Tree of Porphyry* grows and extends as these secondary substances grow more and more distinct (see below).

**PORPHYRY / AD 234 - 305**

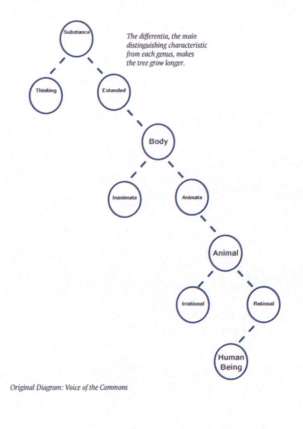

*The differentia, the main distinguishing characteristic from each genus, makes the tree grow longer.*

Original Diagram: Voice of the Commons

**TREE OF PORPHYRY**

ACTIVITY
# The Tree of Porphyry

**Instructions**: Below, one extending from *Substance* down to the mythical creature known as the *chimera*. Fill in the missing spots in the Tree of Porphyry between *Substance* and this monster from Greek mythology.

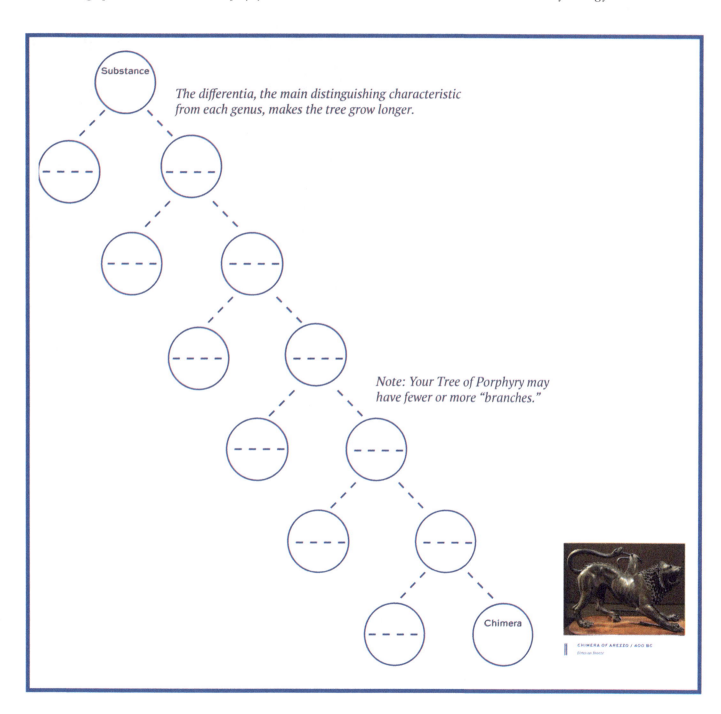

*The differentia, the main distinguishing characteristic from each genus, makes the tree grow longer.*

*Note: Your Tree of Porphyry may have fewer or more "branches."*

CHIMERA OF AREZZO / 400 BC
*Etruscan Bronze*

# Terms & Euthyphro's Dilemma

**PLATO'S DIALOGUES OFTEN** focus on the precise meaning of one or two terms. The protagonist of Plato's dialogues was always the Greek philosopher Socrates, a former stonecutter and soldier upon whom the Oracle of Delphi had given the title of "wisest man in Greece." Socrates suspected that the oracle might be wrong, and he went about Athens trying to find someone more intelligent than he was. He would ask questions of everyday Athenians about the nature of the "good life" and the meaning of abstract terms like piety, justice, and beauty. What were these concepts, and what did they really mean? If someone like Socrates could understand what piety is in and of itself, would it help him be more pious and virtuous? Socrates hoped that by understanding what justice is, he could live more justly and honorably. In short, Socrates was convinced of the metaphysical connection between ideas and actions, and if he knew what was good, he could also *be* good.

Socrates' quest focused on the understanding of what he called the *forms*. As we discussed earlier, the word *forms* come (ironically) from the Greek word *eidon* for "something having been seen"; the word *form* is ironic because a form cannot be seen with the eye but only held in the mind as an abstract, unchanging concept (Brann). Per Plato and Socrates, these forms are, in a sense, more real than the things we see around us because the forms are absolute and unchanging. Such forms exist in a world of their own, yet the things we see in this world derive from these forms. Socrates hoped to understand the forms by his persistent questioning and logical reasoning until he could express

**SOCRATES / 470 - 399 BC**
*1ˢᵗ c. AD Bust (Louvre)*

that term in words and phrases that adequately captured whatever that term meant. Once he understood that term, he hoped that his newfound understanding would influence his actions and help him live a better, more virtuous life.

This tension is particularly evident in Plato's *Euthyphro*, a dialogue that famously revolves around the idea of piety. The dialogue takes place as Socrates is walking to the Athenian courthouse for his trial on charges of impiety and of "corrupting" the youth of Athens. Along the way, Socrates encounters Euthyphro, a youth indicting his father on charges of murder. Ironically, Euthyphro could be accused of being impious himself for doing so. A servant on the estate of Euthyphro's father had murdered another servant, and in disciplining that servant, Euthyphro's father bound him and cast him into a ditch where the slave later died. Euthyphro, subsequently, accused his father of murder, an action that could be considered impious. Believing that Euthyphro must have a correct understanding of piety to be so sure about condemning his father before a court, Socrates debates with Euthyphro about the essence of piety and what makes actions *pious* or *impious*. Socrates' dialogue details the difference between what is "pious" and "good" versus what are merely examples of what is pious and good, and the difference between "essences" and "particulars". So, what exactly is piety? What does it mean that an action *is* pious rather than *an example of* a pious action? What makes any action just or good or pious?

# Euthyphro / By Plato

## Plato's *Euthyphro*

Socrates: And what is **piety**, and what is impiety?

Euthyphro: Piety is doing as I am doing; that is to say, prosecuting anyone who is guilty of murder, sacrilege, or of any similar crime—whether he be your father or mother, or whoever he may be—that makes no difference; and not to prosecute them is impiety. And please to consider, Socrates, what a notable proof I will give you of the truth of my words, a proof which I have already given to others—of the principle, I mean, that the impious, whoever he may be, ought not to go unpunished. For do not men regard Zeus as the best and most righteous of the gods? Yet, they admit that he bound his father (**Cronus**) because he wickedly devoured his sons and that he too had punished his own father (**Uranus**) for a similar reason, in a nameless manner. And yet when I proceed against my father, they are angry with me. So inconsistent are they in their way of talking when the gods are concerned, and when I am concerned.

Socrates: May not this be the reason, Euthyphro, why I am charged with impiety—that I cannot dismiss these stories about the gods? Therefore, I suppose that people think me wrong. But, as you who are well informed about them approve of them, I cannot do better than assent to your superior wisdom. What else can I say, confessing as I do, that I know nothing about them? Tell me, for the love of Zeus, whether you really believe that they are true.

Euthyphro: Yes, Socrates; and things more wonderful still, of which the world is in ignorance.

Socrates: And do you really believe that the gods fought with one another, and had dire quarrels, battles, and the like, as the poets say, and as you may see represented in the works of great artists? The temples are full of them; and notably the robe of Athena, which is carried up to the **Acropolis** at the great **Panathenaea**, is embroidered with them. Are all these tales of the gods true, Euthyphro?

Euthyphro: Yes, Socrates; and, as I was saying, I can tell you, if you would like to hear them, many other things about the gods which would quite amaze you.

Socrates: I dare say; pray tell me about them at some other time when I have leisure. But at present, I would rather hear from you a more precise answer, which you have not as yet given, my friend, to the question, What is piety? When asked, you only replied, Doing as you do, charging your father with murder.

Euthyphro: And what I said was true, Socrates.

Socrates: No doubt, Euthyphro; but you would admit that there are many other pious acts?

Euthyphro: There are.

Socrates: Remember that I did not ask you to give me two or three examples of piety, but to explain the general idea which makes **all pious things to be pious**. Do you not recollect that there was one idea which made the impious, impious, and the pious, pious?

Euthyphro: I remember.

Socrates: Tell me what is the nature of this idea, and then I shall have a standard to which I may look, and by which I may measure actions, whether yours or those of anyone else and then I shall be able to say that such and such an action is pious, such another impious.

Euthyphro: I will tell you, if you like.

Socrates: I should very much like you to do so.

Euthyphro: Piety, then, is that which is dear to the gods, and impiety is that which is not dear to them.

Socrates: Very good, Euthyphro; you have now given me the sort of answer which I wanted. But whether what you say is true or not I cannot as yet tell, although I make no doubt that you will prove the truth of your words.

Euthyphro: Of course.

Socrates: Come, then, and let us examine what we are saying. That thing or person which is dear to the gods is pious, and that thing or person which is hateful to the gods is impious, these two being the extreme opposites of one another. Was not that said?

Euthyphro: It was.

Socrates: And well said?

Euthyphro: Yes, Socrates, I thought so; it was certainly said.

Socrates: And further, Euthyphro, the **gods were admitted to have enmities** and hatreds and differences?

Euthyphro: Yes, that was also said.

Socrates: And what sort of difference creates enmity and anger? Suppose for example that you and I, my good friend, differ about a number; do differences of this sort make us enemies and set us at variance with one another? Do we not go at once to arithmetic, and put an end to them **by a sum**?

Euthyphro: True.

Socrates: Or suppose that we differ about magnitudes, do we not quickly end the differences by measuring?

Euthyphro: Very true.

Socrates: And we end a controversy about heavy and light by resorting to a weighing machine?

Euthyphro: To be sure.

Socrates: But what differences are there which cannot be thus decided, and which therefore make us angry and set us at enmity with one another? I dare say the answer does not occur to you at the moment, and therefore I will suggest that these enmities arise when the matters of difference are the just and unjust, good and evil, honorable and dishonorable. Are not these the points about which men differ, and about which when we are unable satisfactorily to decide our differences, you and I and all of us quarrel, when we do quarrel?

Euthyphro: Yes, Socrates, the nature of the differences about which we quarrel is such as you describe.

Socrates: And the quarrels of the gods, noble Euthy-

## Vocabulary & Annotations

### Piety
As an abstract value, *piety* refers to one's respectful and reverential dealings with one's superiors, including one's parents and the gods.

### Cronos & Uranus
Cronos & Uranus were deities that existed before the Olympians; Cronos rebelled against Uranus and took his kingdom, and Zeus rebelled against Cronos and took his kingdom.

### Acropolis
The Acropolis was the main citadel at Athens, located on top of a massive, rocky outcropping in the center of the city.

### Panathenaea
A festival held in ancient Athens celebrated every four years that included religious ceremonies and athletic events, alongside other events.

### ...all pious things to be pious
Socrates wants to know what piety is in itself, not mere examples of pious things.

### ...gods were admitted to have enmities
As any student of Greek mythology will recognize, the gods of ancient Greece rarely, if ever, agreed on anything.

### ...by a sum
Some questions may be resolved by some sort of empirical observation, such as measuring or weighing an object.

---

phro, when they occur, are of a like nature?

**Euthyphro**: Certainly they are.

**Socrates**: They have differences of opinion, as you say, about good and evil, just and unjust, honorable and dishonorable: there would have been no quarrels among them, if there had been no such differences —would there be now?

**Euthyphro**: You are quite right.

**Socrates**: Does not every man love that which he deems noble and just and good, and hate the opposite of them?

**Euthyphro**: Very true.

**Socrates**: But, as you say, people regard some things as just and others as unjust, and it is about these things they argue. As a result, wars and fights arise among them.

**Euthyphro**: Very true.

**Socrates**: Then the same things are hated by the gods and loved by the gods, and are both hateful and dear to them?

**Euthyphro**: True.

**Socrates**: And upon this view, the same things, Euthyphro, will be pious and also impious?

**Euthyphro**: So I should suppose.

**Socrates**: Then, my friend, I remark with surprise that you have not answered the question which I asked. For I certainly did not ask you to tell me what action is both pious and impious: but now it would seem that what is loved by the gods is also hated by them. And therefore, Euthyphro, in thus chastising your father you may very likely be doing what is agreeable to Zeus but disagreeable to Cronus or Uranus, and what is acceptable to Hephaestus but unacceptable to Hera, and there may be other gods who have similar differences of opinion.

**Euthyphro**: Yes indeed, Socrates; at least if they will listen to me.

**Socrates**: But they will be sure to listen if they find that you are a good speaker. There was a notion that came into my mind while you were speaking; I said to myself: *Well, and what if Euthyphro does prove to me that all the gods regarded the death of the serf as unjust, how do I know anything more of the nature of piety and impiety? I grant that this action may be hateful to the gods, but piety* *and impiety are still not adequately defined by these distinctions, for that which is hateful to the gods has been shown to be also pleasing and dear to them.*

And therefore, Euthyphro, I do not ask you to prove this; I will suppose, if you like, that all the gods condemn and abominate such an action. But I will amend the definition so far as to say that what all the gods hate is impious, and what they love pious or holy; and what some of them love and others hate is both or neither. Shall this be our definition of piety and impiety?

Euthyphro: Why not, Socrates?

Socrates: Why not! Certainly, as far as I am concerned, Euthyphro, there is no reason why not. But whether this admission will greatly assist you in the task of instructing me as you promised, is a matter for you to consider.

Euthyphro: Yes, I should say that what all the **gods love is pious** and holy, and the opposite which they all hate, impious.

Socrates: Ought we to inquire into the truth of this, Euthyphro, or simply to accept the mere statement on our own authority and that of others? What do you say?

Euthyphro: We should investigate the statement, and I believe that the statement will stand the test of inquiry.

Socrates: We shall know better, my good friend, in a little while. The point which I should first wish to understand is whether the pious or holy is beloved by the gods because it is holy, or holy because it is beloved of the gods.

Euthyphro: I do not understand your meaning, Socrates.

Socrates: I will endeavor to explain: we speak of carrying and we speak of being carried, of leading and being led, seeing and being seen. You know that in all such cases there is a difference, and you know also in what the difference lies?

Euthyphro: I think that I understand.

Socrates: And is not that which is beloved distinct from that which loves?

Euthyphro: Certainly.

Socrates: Well; and now tell me, is that which is carried in this state of carrying because it is carried, or for some other reason?

Euthyphro: No; that is the reason.

## Vocabulary & Annotations

### Hera
The queen of the gods, as well as the goddess of marriage.

### Hephaestus
The god of blacksmiths, metallurgy, and fire in Greek mythology.

### ...gods love is pious
Euthyphro does not realize that ascribing values to the gods and what they love does not solve his dilemma.

### ...not to be holy because it is loved
Something that is pious may be pious *because* it is loved by the gods, or it may already *be* pious and as a result, the gods love it. It seems arbitrary if the gods' love makes an action pious, whereas the gods' love seems irrelevant if an pious action is pious independent of gods' love.

Socrates: And the same is true of what is led and of what is seen?

Euthyphro: True.

Socrates: And a thing is not seen because it is visible, but conversely, visible because it is seen; nor is a thing led because it is in the state of being led, or carried because it is in the state of being carried, but the converse of this. And now I think, Euthyphro, that my meaning will be intelligible; and my meaning is, that any state of action or passion implies previous action or passion. It does not become because it is becoming, but it is in a state of becoming because it becomes; neither does it suffer because it is in a state of suffering, but it is in a state of suffering because it suffers. Do you not agree?

Euthyphro: Yes.

Socrates: Is not that which is loved in some state either of becoming or suffering?

Euthyphro: Yes.

Socrates: And the same holds as in the previous instances; the state of being loved follows the act of being loved, and not the act the state.

Euthyphro: Certainly.

Socrates: And what do you say of piety, Euthyphro—is not piety, according to your definition, that which is loved by all the gods?

Euthyphro: Yes.

Socrates: Because it is pious or holy, or for some other reason?

Euthyphro: No, that is the reason.

Socrates: It is loved because it is holy, not holy because it is loved?

Euthyphro: Yes.

**THE ACROPOLIS / ATHENS**

Socrates: And that which is dear to the gods is loved by them, and is in a state to be loved of them because it is loved of them?

Euthyphro: Certainly.

Socrates: Then that which is dear to the gods, Euthyphro, is not holy, nor is that which is holy loved of God, as you affirm; but they are two different things.

Euthyphro: How do you mean, Socrates?

Socrates: I mean to say that the holy has been acknowledged by us to be loved of God because it is holy, **not to be holy because it is loved**.

Euthyphro: Yes.

Socrates: But that which is dear to the gods is dear to them because it is loved by them, not loved by them because it is dear to them.

Euthyphro: True.

Socrates: But, friend Euthyphro, if that which is holy is the same with that which is dear to God, and is loved because it is holy, then that which is dear to God would have been loved as being dear to God; but if that which is dear to God is dear to him because it is loved by him, then that which is holy would have been holy because it is loved by him. But now you see that the reverse is the case and that they are quite different from one another. For one is of a kind to be loved because it is loved, and the other is loved because it is of a kind to be loved. Thus you appear to me, Euthyphro, when I ask you what is the essence of holiness, to offer an attribute only, and not the essence—the attribute of being loved by all the gods. But you still refuse to explain to me the nature of holiness. And therefore, if you please, I will ask you not to hide your treasure, but to tell me once more what holiness or piety really is, whether dear to the gods or not (for that is a matter about which we will not quarrel), and what is impiety?

Euthyphro: I really do not know, Socrates, how to express what I mean. For somehow or other our arguments, on whatever ground we rest them, seem to turn round and walk away from us.

Socrates: Your words, Euthyphro, are like the handiwork of my ancestor Daedalus; and if I were the sayer or propounder of them, you might say that my arguments walk away and will not remain fixed where they are placed because I am a descendant of his. But now, since these notions are your own, you must find some other gibe, for they certainly, as you yourself allow, show an inclination to be on the move.

Euthyphro: Nay, Socrates, I shall still say that you are the Daedalus who sets arguments in motion; not I, certainly, but you make them move or go round, for they would never have stirred, as far as I am concerned.

Socrates: Then I must be greater than Daedalus: for whereas he only made his own inventions to move, I move those of other people as well. And the beauty of it is, that I would rather not. For I would give the wisdom of Daedalus, and the wealth of Tantalus, to be able to detain them and keep them fixed. But enough of this. As I perceive that you are lazy, I will myself endeavor to show you how you might instruct me in the nature of piety; and I hope that you will not grudge your labor.

**DAEDALUS**

*In Greek mythology, Daedalus was a wise inventor who designed the Labyrinth beneath the palace of King Minos in Crete, as well as a pair of wings he used to escape from the island.*

Tell me, then—Is not that which is pious **necessarily** just?

Euthyphro: Yes.

Socrates: And is, then, all which is just pious? Or is that which is pious all just, but that which is just, only in part and not all, pious?

Euthyphro: I do not understand you, Socrates.

Socrates: And yet I know that you are as much wiser than I am, as you are younger. But, as I was saying, revered friend, the abundance of your wisdom makes you lazy. Please, do not exert yourself, for there is no real difficulty in understanding me. What I mean I may explain by an illustration of what I do not mean. The poet Stasinus sings: *Of Zeus, the author and creator of all these things, You will not tell: for where there is fear there is also reverence.*

Now I disagree with this poet. Shall I tell you in what respect?

Euthyphro: By all means.

Socrates: I should not say that where there is fear

## Vocabulary & Annotations

**Daedalus**
Daedalus was a famous inventor and architect in Greek mythology, credited with building the Labyrinth for King Minos of Crete.

**Tantalus**
Tantalus was a figure in Greek mythology, famously punished in Tartarus with a thirst and hunger he could never satisfy.

**...necessarily**
The word *necessarily* implies that the action could not have been pious otherwise—it *had* to be this way.

there is also reverence; for I am sure that many persons fear poverty and disease, and the like evils, but I do not perceive that they reverence the objects of their fear.

Euthyphro: Very true.

Socrates: But where reverence is, there is fear; for he who has a feeling of reverence and shame about the commission of any action, fears and is afraid of an ill reputation.

Euthyphro: No doubt.

Socrates: Then we are wrong in saying that where there is fear there is also reverence; and we should say, where there is reverence there is also fear. But there is not always reverence where there is fear; for fear is a more extended notion, and reverence is a part of fear, just as the odd is a part of number, and number is a more extended notion than the odd. I suppose that you follow me now?

Euthyphro: Quite well.

Socrates: That was the sort of question which I meant to raise when I asked whether the just is always the pious, or the pious always the just; and whether there may not be justice where there is not piety; for justice is the more extended notion of which piety is only a part. Do you dissent?

Euthyphro: No, I think that you are quite right.

Socrates: Then, if piety is a part of justice, I suppose that we should inquire what part? If you had pursued the inquiry in the previous cases; for instance, if you had asked me what is an even number, and what part of number the even is, I should have had no difficulty in replying, a number which represents a figure having two equal sides. Do you not agree?

Euthyphro: Yes, I quite agree.

Socrates: In like manner, I want you to tell me what part of justice is piety or holiness, that I may be able to tell Meletus not to do me injustice, or indict me for impiety, as I am now adequately instructed by you in the nature of piety or holiness, and their opposites.

Euthyphro: Piety or holiness, Socrates, appears to me to be that part of justice which attends to the gods, as there is the other part of justice which attends to men.

Socrates: That is good, Euthyphro; yet still there is a little point about which I should like to have further information, What is the meaning of 'attention'? For attention can hardly be used in the same sense when applied to the gods as when applied to other things. For instance, horses are said to require attention, and not every person is able to attend to them, but only a person skilled in horsemanship. Is it not so?

Euthyphro: Certainly.

Socrates: I should suppose that the art of horsemanship is the art of attending to horses?

Euthyphro: Yes.

Socrates: Nor is every one qualified to attend to dogs, but only the huntsman?

Euthyphro: True.

Socrates: And I should also conceive that the art of the huntsman is the art of attending to dogs?

Euthyphro: Yes.

Socrates: As the art of the herder of oxen is the art of attending to oxen?

Euthyphro: Very true.

Socrates: In like manner holiness or piety is the art of attending to the gods? Would that be your meaning, Euthyphro?

Euthyphro: Yes.

Socrates: And is not attention always designed for the good or benefit of that to which the attention is given? As in the case of horses, you may observe that when attended to by the horseman's art they are benefited and improved, are they not?

Euthyphro: True.

Socrates: As the dogs are benefited by the huntsman's art, and the oxen by the art of the herder of oxen, and all other things are tended or attended for their good and not for their hurt?

Euthyphro: Certainly, not for their hurt.

Socrates: But for their good?

Euthyphro: Of course.

Socrates: And does piety or holiness, which has been defined to be the art of attending to the gods, benefit or improve them? Would you say that when you do a holy act you make any of the gods better?

Euthyphro: No, no; that was certainly not what I meant.

Socrates: And I, Euthyphro, never supposed that you did. I asked you the question about the nature of the attention, because I thought that you did not.

Euthyphro: You do me justice, Socrates; that is not the sort of attention which I mean.

Socrates: Good: but I must still ask what is this attention to the gods which is called piety?

Euthyphro: It is such, Socrates, as servants show to their masters.

Socrates: I understand—a sort of ministration to the gods.

Euthyphro: Exactly.

Socrates: Medicine is also a sort of ministration or service, having in view the attainment of some object—would you not say of health?

Euthyphro: I should.

Socrates: Again, there is an art which ministers to the ship-builder with a view to the attainment of some result?

## Vocabulary & Annotations

**...person skilled in horsemanship**
Socrates often draws on analogies like this one as part of building his argument.

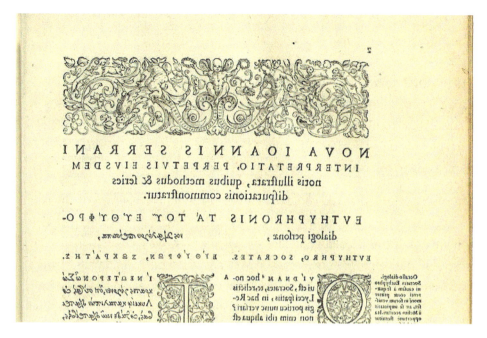

**GREEK AND LATIN TEXT OF PLATO'S *EUTHYPHRO* (1578)**

Euthyphro: Yes, Socrates, with a view to the building of a ship.

Socrates: As there is an art which ministers to the house-builder with a view to the building of a house?

Euthyphro: Yes.

Socrates: And now tell me, my good friend, about the art which ministers to the gods: what work does that help to accomplish? For you must surely know if, as you say, you are of all men living the one who is best instructed in religion.

Euthyphro: And I speak the truth, Socrates.

Socrates: Tell me then, oh tell me—what is that fair work which the gods do by the help of our ministrations?

Euthyphro: Many and fair, Socrates, are the works which they do.

Socrates: Why, my friend, and so are those of a general. But the chief of them is easily told. Would you not say that victory in war is the chief of them?

Euthyphro: Certainly.

Socrates: Many and fair, too, are the works of the husbandman, if I am not mistaken; but his chief work is the production of food from the earth?

Euthyphro: Exactly.

Socrates: And of the many and fair things done by the gods, which is the chief or principal one?

**Euthyphro**: I have told you already, Socrates, that to learn all these things accurately will be very tiresome. Let me simply say that piety or holiness is learning how to please the gods in word and deed, by prayers and sacrifices. Such piety is the salvation of families and states, just as the impious, which is unpleasing to the gods, is their ruin and destruction.

**Socrates**: I think that you could have answered in much fewer words the chief question which I asked, Euthyphro, if you had chosen. But I see plainly that you are not disposed to instruct me—clearly not: else why, when we reached the point, did you turn aside? Had you only answered me I should have truly learned of you by this time the nature of piety. Now, as the asker of a question is necessarily dependent on the answerer, whither he leads I must follow; and can only ask again, what is the pious, and what is piety? Do you mean that they are a sort of science of praying and sacrificing?

**Euthyphro**: Yes, I do.

**Socrates**: And sacrificing is giving to the gods, and prayer is asking of the gods?

**Euthyphro**: Yes, Socrates.

**Socrates**: Upon this view, then, piety is a science of asking and giving?

**Euthyphro**: You understand me capitally, Socrates.

**Socrates**: Yes, my friend; the reason is that I am a votary of your science, and give my mind to it, and therefore nothing which you say will be thrown away upon me. Please then to tell me, what is the nature of this service to the gods? Do you mean that we prefer requests and give gifts to them?

**Euthyphro**: Yes, I do.

**Socrates**: Is not the right way of asking to ask of them what we want?

**Euthyphro**: Certainly.

**Socrates**: And the right way of giving is to give to them in return what they want of us. There would be no meaning in an art that gives to anyone that which he does not want.

**Euthyphro**: Very true, Socrates.

**Socrates**: Then piety, Euthyphro, is an art which gods and men have of doing business with one another?

---

## Vocabulary & Annotations

#### ...to please the gods in word and deed
Notice that Euthphryo's answer comes closer to a broader, more general definition of *piety*.

#### Proteus
Proteus is a Poseidon-like sea god capable of changing his shape and predicting the future, but he only tells people who ask him about future events if they can capture and hold onto him.

#### ...I am in a hurry
The dialogue ends in a moment of *aporia*, with Euthyphro hurrying away from Socrates as quickly as he can.

Euthyphro: That is an expression which you may use, if you like.

Socrates: But I have no particular liking for anything but the truth. I wish, however, that you would tell me what benefit accrues to the gods from our gifts. There is no doubt about what they give to us; for there is no good thing which they do not give; but how we can give any good thing to them in return is far from being equally clear. If they give everything and we give nothing, that must be an affair of business in which we have very greatly the advantage of them.

Euthyphro: And do you imagine, Socrates, that any benefit accrues to the gods from our gifts?

Socrates: But if not, Euthyphro, what is the meaning of gifts which are conferred by us upon the gods?

Euthyphro: What else, but tributes of honor; and, as I was just now saying, what pleases them?

Socrates: Piety, then, is pleasing to the gods, but not beneficial or dear to them?

Euthyphro: I should say that nothing could be dearer.

Socrates: Then once more the assertion is repeated that piety is dear to the gods?

Euthyphro: Certainly.

Socrates: And when you say this, can you wonder at your words not standing firm, but walking away? Will you accuse me of being the Daedalus who makes them walk away, not perceiving that there is another and far greater artist than Daedalus who makes them go round in a circle, and he is yourself; for the argument, as you will perceive, comes round to the same point. Were we not saying that the holy or pious was not the same with that which is loved of the gods? Have you forgotten?

Euthyphro: I quite remember.

Socrates: And are you not saying that what is loved of the gods is holy; and is not this the same as what is dear to them—do you see?

Euthyphro: True.

Socrates: Then either we were wrong in former assertion; or, if we were right then, we are wrong now.

Euthyphro: One of the two must be true.

Socrates: Then we must begin again and ask, What is piety? That is an inquiry which I shall never be weary of pursuing as far as in me lies. I entreat you not to scorn me, but to apply your mind to the utmost and tell me the truth. For, if any man knows, you are he; and therefore I must detain you, like **Proteus,** until you tell me. If you had not certainly known the nature of piety and impiety, I am confident that you would never, on behalf of a serf, have charged your aged father with murder. You would not have run such a risk of doing wrong in the sight of the gods, and you would have had too much respect for the opinions of men. I am sure, therefore, that you know the nature of piety and impiety. Speak out then, my dear Euthyphro, and do not hide your knowledge.

Euthyphro: Another time, Socrates; for **I am in a hurry,** and must go now.

Socrates: Alas! My companion, will you leave me in despair? I was hoping that you would instruct me in the nature of piety and impiety so I might have cleared myself of the charges brought against me. I would have told him that I had been enlightened by Euthyphro and had given up rash innovations and speculations, in which I indulged only through ignorance, and that now I am about to lead a better life.

## Primary Source Questions

1. Why does Socrates argue with the definition that an action is pious if it is loved by the gods? What problems does he see, that Euthyphro does not see?

2. If the gods love an action, does their love make that action pious?

3. If the gods love an action that is already pious, is the gods' love even necessary? Could it have been pious in some other way?

4. How does the dialogue end? Are Socrates or Euthyphro any closer to an understanding of piety?

ACTIVITY

# The First Act of the Mind / Terms

Each row contains a term, the author's use of that term, or a definition of that term suitable for students. If the row contains a quotation, write down a clear, intelligible definition of that term in the box provided. If the term is already defined for you, please find the quotation from the text that supports the appropriate definition.

| Term | Quotations from the Text | Quotations Rephrased as Definitions |
|---|---|---|
| *Piety* | *Piety is doing as I am doing; that is to say, prosecuting anyone who is guilty of murder, sacrilege, or of any similar crime-whether he be your father or mother, or whoever he may be-that makes no difference; and not to prosecute them is impiety.* | |
| *Impiety* | | Suppose *piety* is reverence for the gods and the faithful fulfillment of one's duties towards the gods and, by some extension, to important family members like one's father and mother. In that case, *impiety* is a lack of reverence for the gods and superiors and the neglect of one's duty towards them. |
| *Idea* | *Remember that I did not ask you to give me two or three examples of piety, but to explain the general idea which makes all pious things to be pious. Do you not recollect that there was one idea which made the impious impious, and the pious pious?* | |

CHAPTER 3 The Kinds of Terms ♦ 93

ACTIVITY

# The First Act of the Mind / Terms

Each row contains a term, the author's use of that term, or a definition of that term suitable for students. If the row contains a quotation, write down a clear, intelligible definition of that term in the box provided. If the term is already defined for you, please find the quotation from the text that supports the appropriate definition.

| Term | Quotations from the Text | Quotations Rephrased as Definitions |
|---|---|---|
| Pious | | The word *piety* or *pious* in Greek means *highly favored* or *loved* by the gods; the word can be translated as "holy" or "pious." |
| The gods | *And do you really believe that the gods, fought with one another, and had dire quarrels, battles, and the like, as the poets say, and as you may see represented in the works of great artists?* | |
| Just | | The word in Greek refers to the *observant of custom; see Perseus project.* |

94 ✦ SECTION I Terms & Metaphysics

ACTIVITY

# *The Second Act of the Mind* / Propositions

Each row contains an excerpt from the significant text included in this chapter. These selections include significant points and ideas that the author uses to build his argument and reach a meaningful conclusion, one that was not apparent at the beginning of their work. In the space provided, write a summary of the quotation and try to express it in the form of a proposition. You may express it as one or more propositions, but try to paraphrase the author's ideas in your own words—that way, you can come to a much deeper understanding of the argument the author is advancing.

| Quotations from Text | Quotations rephrased as Propositions |
|---|---|
| *Tell me what is the nature of this idea, and then I shall have a standard to which I may look, and by which I may measure actions, whether yours or those of any one else, and then I shall be able to say that such and such an action is pious, such another impious.* | |
| *We speak of carrying and we speak of being carried, of leading and being led, seeing and being seen. You know that in all such cases there is a difference, and you know also in what the difference lies?* | |

CHAPTER 3 The Kinds of Terms • 95

ACTIVITY

# The Second Act of the Mind / Propositions

Each row contains an excerpt from the significant text included in this chapter. These selections include significant points and ideas that the author uses to build his argument and reach a meaningful conclusion, one that was not apparent at the beginning of their work. In the space provided, write a summary of the quotation and try to express it in the form of a proposition. You may express it as one or more propositions, but try to paraphrase the author's ideas in your own words—that way, you can come to a much deeper understanding of the argument the author is advancing.

| Quotations from Text | Quotations rephrased as a Proposition |
| --- | --- |
| *The point which I should first wish to understand is whether the pious or holy is beloved by the gods because it is holy, or holy because it is beloved of the gods.* | |
| *Then we must begin again and ask, What is piety? That is an inquiry which I shall never be wary of pursuing as far as in me lies; and I entreat you not to scorn me, but to apply your mind to the utmost, and tell me the truth. For, if any man knows, you are he; and therefore I must detain you, like Proteus, until you tell. If you had not certainly known the nature of piety and impiety, I am confident that you would never, on behalf of a serf, have charged your aged father with murder.* | |

ACTIVITY

# The Third Act of the Mind / Inferences

In the space below, create an "argument map", a visual way of representing the premises, assumptions, and ultimately the conclusion that a writer is making in his or her work. You can also use this blank space provided to draw a "conversation map", a visual way of recording the discussion your class had over this text.

WRITING

# Writing Prompt

Remember, writing is thinking. To help us to write and think more clearly, we will spend considerable time this year writing essays based on the texts we read in class. These essays are descriptive in nature and answer one question that arises from the material we are reading in class. In such an essay, the writer wants to explain the meaningful ideas contained in this text by reading and rereading the text under analysis to better explain that author's argument and the consequences of his or her ideas.

**Question**: *What is Euthyphro's dilemma? Why do Socrates and Euthyphro have such trouble understanding what piety actually is?*

## Writing

CANTERBURY CATHEDRAL / ALTAR

*Canterbury Cathedral is most famous for the martyrdom of St. Thomas Becket (1119-1170 AD), who famously quarreled with English King Henry II (1133-1189 AD) and was murdered before the altar pictured here.*

Photo by Alexander Andrews.

SECTION I   Terms & Metaphysics

CHAPTER

# Terms According to Aristotle

### ROADMAP

+ Learn about how Aristotle's categories and predicables.
+ Learn about causation and Aristotle's Four Causes.
+ Practicing writing definitions.
+ Read a selection from Aristotle's *Metaphysics*.

**THALES OUTCOME**

**N⁰ 11**

A person with *Dreams and Aspirations to Change the World* produces plans to accomplish personal and educational aspirations.

A liberal arts education should bring about a certain sense of joy, happiness, and confidence as you come to understand the world and the way it works. One noteworthy exemplar of this kind of joyous intellectual curiosity is the Greek philosopher Aristotle who, like his teacher Plato and Plato's teacher Socrates, went about everywhere asking questions and seeking truth.

# Terms & Aristotle

**Thus far, we've looked at Plato** and two of Plato's works, "The Allegory of the Cave" from Plato's *Republic* and *Euthyphro*. Let us remember that Plato wrote dialogues, a series of script-like extended conversations between Socrates and his interlocutors. Plato was a student of Socrates, and the most famous of Plato's students was the philosopher Aristotle. Whereas Plato wrote dialogues, Aristotle wrote treatises, long, lecture-like texts that examined one particular subject, investigated one particular phenomenon, or sought to solve one problem.

The title of each treatise indicated its subject matter: *Rhetoric* focused on rhetoric, *Politics* on political theory, and *Poetics* on drama, poetry, and literary theory. Aristotle's writing on logic and reasoning comes from six texts compiled into a massive work called the Organon, organized by Aristotle's students, the Peripatetics. The word *organon* comes from a Greek word meaning "tool" or "instrument", since logic is ultimately a tool for constructing and evaluating arguments. The *Organon* is composed of the following six texts:

Categories: *In this work, Aristotle examines all the things that can be said of something or "predicated" of something, with the word "predicate" referring to the ways we can affirm or deny something about a subject.*

On Interpretation: *In this work, Aristotle details how language can reflect and describe reality, principally by way of propositions that can be universal (applying to all things), particular (applying to only some things), affirmative (saying something is), or negative (saying something is not).*

Prior Analytics: *Aristotle focuses on deductive reasoning and the structure—that is, the composition—of syllogisms.*

Posterior Analytics: *Aristotle expounds upon deductive reasoning and syllogisms but focuses on the material or the content of syllogisms.*

Topics: *The Topics focused on ways an orator could discover the best means of arguing for or against a subject.*

On Sophistical Refutations: *Aristotle turns to fallacies, errors in reasoning that arise either because of flaws in the structure of an argument (known as a formal fallacy) or the content of an argument (known as an informal fallacy or a material fallacy).*

*In the* Topics, *Aristotle explains the importance of using clear terms:* It is useful to have examined the number of meanings of a term both for clearness' sake (for a man is more likely to know what it is he asserts, if it has been made clear to him how many meanings it may have), and also with a view to ensuring that our reasonings shall be in accordance with the actual facts and not addressed merely to the term used.

## Vocabulary

### Aristotle
A Greek philosopher whose writings on *Politics, Poetics, Physics, Metaphysics,* and *Rhetoric* form the basis for much of the Western canon.

### Treatise
Lecture-like texts that focus on a particular subject, investigate one particular phenomenon, or solve one particular problem.

### Organon
The title of Aristotle's work on logic and reasoning; the word comes from the Greek word for "tool" or "instrument" in the same way that logic is very much a tool for constructing and evaluating arguments.

### Peripatetics
From Greek for "to walk about", these were the students of Aristotle. The nickname was given because Aristotle habitually walked around while he lectured.

### Predicate
The part of the sentence that follows the verb and *affirms* or *denies* something about the subject.

**ARISTOTLE / 384 - 322 BC**
*Greek philosopher and author of the* Organon, *amongst other texts*

Let us recall that a term brings to the human mind an idea, an idea that has varying degrees of significance and value. The way in which a word may reflect reality is difficult to grasp, and it is easy to dismiss its importance because such intellectual endeavors do not seem as if they are worth the time. After all, we hear the word "apple" or read the word "liberty" and assume we know the meaning of these terms. To Aristotle, the extent to which an idea existed both in the world and in the mind was of great importance.

Accordingly, we will examine three ideas in this section that explore how language reflects being and existence. These ideas include Aristotle's predicables, Aristotle's categories, and the Four Causes. With the exception of the Four Causes, which comes from Aristotle's *Physics*, these ideas come from the texts in the *Organon*. We will end this chapter with a short exercise on writing definitions for abstract words such as knowledge, love, and virtue and conclude with a reading from Aristotle's *Metaphysics*. In this way, we hope to elucidate the significance of terms and cultivate the joy that comes from knowing what a thing is in itself.

## Aristotle's Predicables

The *predicate* is the part of the sentence that affirms or denies something about a subject. Aristotle expands on the nature of predicables at some length in the *Categories*. Predicables (sometimes referred to as *predicate possibilities*) help us

CHAPTER 4  Terms According to Aristotle  ◆  103

to make sense of the substance or the essence of a thing. A **predicable** is a statement that can be said of a subject and either affirms or denies something about that subject. These are called predicables because to *predicate* something is to affirm or deny something about that subject. If we were to use the sentence *man is a rational animal*, as an example, then the predicable, the part of the sentence that describes something about the subject, is *rational animal*. The word *predicable* derives in part from the location of this affirmation or negation in the predicate, that part of the sentence following the verb.

Of these predicables, Aristotle says that there are five possible relationships that a subject and a predicate can have: species, genus, specific difference, property, or accident. Here is how Aristotle begins the idea of predicables in the *Topics*:

> We must now say what are 'definition', 'property', 'genus', and 'accident'. A 'definition' [species] is a phrase signifying a thing's essence. It is rendered in the form either of a phrase in lieu of a term, or of a phrase in lieu of another phrase; for it is sometimes possible to define the meaning of a phrase as well.

As defined by Aristotle, the **species** is the essence of a thing; what that thing is in itself. The species states the whole essence of the subject under discussion. Moreover, the species is identified with the genus and the **specific difference** (or *differentiae*) of a thing so that the species includes both the genus (its general class) and the one factor that distinguishes the species from its genus. The idea of defining something both by its *general class* and the one component that separates that thing from its genus constitutes a good definition of that thing. As an example, Aristotle identified the species, or the essence of man, as his ability to reason: "man is a rational animal". The idea of species is tied to the predicable of specific difference, which is the quality or attribute that separates a thing from its genus. The *specific difference* (or *differentia*) falls outside of the genus so that the species may at once belong to the genus and have the *differentia*. Still, no other member of that genus possesses that *differentia* (Studtmann). As an example, let us consider the proposition *man is a rational animal* again. In this example, *animal* is the *genus*, the general category in which human beings are included, and being *rational* or, in other words, *having the ability to reason* is man's *specific difference*, the attribute that separates man from the rest of his genus. Taking the *genus* and *specific difference* together, *rational animal* constitutes the *species* or the *essence* of man.

Next, Aristotle defines the predicable of property, a quality or an attribute that stems from or derives from the essence of a thing. While a property derives from the essence of that thing, properties are not an attribute that distinguishes that thing from its genus. A property of man might include our capacity for language and creativity. Aristotle writes:

> A 'property' is a predicate which does not indicate the essence of a thing, but yet belongs to that thing alone, and is predicated convertibly of it. Thus it is a property of man to be capable of learning grammar: for if A be a man, then he is capable of learning grammar, and if he be capable of learning grammar, he is a man.

## Vocabulary

### Predicables
Aristotle lists five different types of predicables, the different ways in which we can affirm or deny that something is or is not true about our subject.

### Species
What a thing is in itself, the essence, the fundamental nature of its being; for example, we can take Aristotle's definition of man as a *rational animal* as the species or the essence of man.

### Specific Difference
A quality that separates one thing from its *genus* and thus serves as the defining characteristic that makes a species what it is.

### Property
An essential quality that derives from the species of a thing, from the essence of that thing what that thing is in itself.

**ARISTOTLE TEACHING ALEXANDER THE GREAT**
*Illustration by Charles Laplante* (1866).

Aristotle continues to describe the nature of a *property*:

> *For no one calls anything a 'property' which may possibly belong to something else, e.g. 'sleep' in the case of man, even though at a certain time it may happen to belong to him alone. That is to say, if any such thing were actually to be called a property, it will be called not a 'property' absolutely, but a 'temporary' or a 'relative' property: for 'being on the right hand side' is a temporary property, while 'two-footed' is in point of fact ascribed as a property in certain relations; e.g. it is a property of man relatively to a horse and a dog.*
>
> *That nothing which may belong to anything else than A is a convertible predicate of A is clear: for it does not necessarily follow that if something is asleep it is a man.*

Notice the examples Aristotle gives to illustrate the nature of a *property*: the ability to learn grammar, being two-footed, and sleeping. If the species of man is *rational animal,* then our ability to learn grammatical rules and apply them in communication is a uniquely human function and thus applies to human beings alone. If we consider the sentence *man is a being capable of learning grammar,* we could switch the subject (*man*). The predicate (*thing capable of learning grammar*) and still have the sentence make sense and apply uniquely to human

CHAPTER 4 Terms According to Aristotle ♦ 105

beings: *a thing capable of learning grammar is man*. The idea of *sleeping*, however, is not a property because it does not apply uniquely to man; the subject and predicate terms in the sentence, *man is a sleeping thing*, are not convertible. We will learn more about conversion in later chapters but for now, the idea that the subject and a predicate are *convertible* means that we can interchange the subject and the predicate without any loss of meaning. Other animals sleep, so we cannot distinguish "man" from animals based on this criterion alone.

Aristotle describes the predicable of a *genus* in the following way:

> *A 'genus' is what is predicated in the category of essence of a number of things exhibiting differences in kind. We should treat as predicates in the category of essence all such things as it would be appropriate to mention in reply to the question, 'What is the object before you?'; as, for example, in the case of man, if asked that question, it is appropriate to say 'He is an animal'.*
>
> *The question, 'Is one thing in the same genus as another or in a different one?' is also a 'generic' question; for a question of that kind as well falls under the same branch of inquiry as the genus: for having argued that 'animal' is the genus of man, and likewise also of ox, we shall have argued that they are in the same genus; whereas if we show that it is the genus of the one but not of the other, we shall have argued that these things are not in the same genus.*

A **genus** is a general category to which a thing belongs. If we consider a rose, its *general class* is flowers; an oak, trees; a Yorkshire Terrier, dogs; and so on. The *genus* refers to the general class of things to which the subject generally belongs. As Aristotle states, the genus or the "general category" of man is "animal", but "animal" as a predicable also includes oxen and other creatures.

Then, Aristotle treats the predicable of *accident* last in this section of the *Topics*, where he defines an accident as "something which may possibly either belong or not belong to any one and the self-same thing." That is, an **accident** does not derive from the essence of that thing; instead, an accident is a quality or attribute that could be or could not be present in a subject, and yet that subject remains what it is. An accident is a predicate statement that is not tied to, or derived from, the essence of the subject itself. Such accidental qualities may

## Vocabulary

**Genus**
The general category in which a thing exists.

**Accident**
A characteristic that can be present or be missing from a subject without detracting from or adding to the essence of that particular subject.

**Categories**
Aristotle's *Categories* are ten ways in which language may reflect being and include the ideas of substance, quantity, qualities, relation, place, time, posture, possession, action, and passion.

**Primary Substance**
Something that exists, such as the *individual man* or *horse*.

**Secondary Substance**
The things predicated of a primary substance, including a thing's species, genus, and other predicables.

or may not be present in that subject without radically changing the subject itself, and Aristotle uses the examples of "sitting" versus "not-sitting", and "whiteness" versus "non-whiteness" to illustrate this idea. A characteristic such as *color*, for instance, generally is not tied to any essential quality of the subject. Qualities or attributes that fall under the predicable of accident include hair color, height, and other such distinguishing factors that may apply to one person but do not alter whether or not that individual is a person.

Predicables in logic work to help us understand the sentence or proposition we are examining. Much like grammar, predicables include everything in the sentence except for the subject. It is interesting and perplexing to note, however, that predicables—the idea of species, genus, specific difference (or *differentiae*), property, or accident—do not actually exist. While we can talk about a general category that something exists in—animals, for example—we cannot see some broad, general category of animals; instead, we only see particular animals, individual animals, such as our dogs or cats.

In *De Interpretatione*, or in English, On Interpretation, Aristotle says that of "actual things some are universal, others particular (I call universal that which is by its nature predicated of a number of things, and particular that which is not man; *man*, for instance, is a *universal*, *Callias* [an ancient Greek worthy of being referenced by Aristotle] a *particular*" (Barnes 27; emphasis added).

These particulars Aristotle describes as substance, something that exists as the individual man or horse. Early in the *Categories*, Aristotle turns to this idea of substance, the first of the ten categories. Substance refers to a particular thing that exists in the real world, "individual objects" that possess a certain form and are composed of a certain matter (Robinson). In the Categories, Aristotle defined substance and its relation to secondary substances (like species and genus, of which we will say more in a moment) in the following way:

> *Substance, in the truest and primary and most definite sense of the word, is that which is neither predicable of a subject nor present in a subject; for instance, the individual man or horse.*
>
> *But in a secondary sense those things are called substances within which, as species, the primary substances are included; also those which, as genera, include the species. For instance, the individual man is included in the species 'man', and the genus to which the species belongs is 'animal'; these, therefore—that is to say, the species 'man' and the genus 'animal,'— are termed secondary substances,"* (Edgehill).

That is, there are two kinds of substances, the first kind being **primary substances**, the individual man who at one time or another actually existed. Substance refers to something that does exist, and without that substance, nothing else, namely the predicables, would exist either (Studtmann). The word *predicate* in the passage refers to how an idea can further affirm or deny something is or is not true a substance. For example, imagine that we had a class pet—a Gila monster, for example—named Gil, a real lizard whose real movements we could observe in a real class.

To begin with, Gil would be classified as a *primary substance*. Gil truly exists, but we could say many other things about Gil that do not exist in the real world the way that Gil does. We could say that Gil is a slow-moving, venomous lizard as its species, since that word in Aristotelian terms means "the whole essence of a thing"; yet, we cannot see or experience Gila monsters as an abstract entity but only the real Gila monsters we see in front of us, which we would classify as substance.

We could also talk about the *genus* of Gil, the most

general category in which we may classify Gil. We could classify Gil as a lizard or an animal. Notice, too, that the *genus* of *lizard* is closer to Gil than is the *genus* of *animal*. As a Gila monster, Gil would also have *specific properties* appropriate to and derived from its species (Gila monsters are quite aggressive, for instance). Lastly, we could describe Gil in terms of his size, coloring, and the unique pattern of his scales—*predicables* referred to as *accidents*—but are not connected to the essential characteristics of what makes Gil a substance. Aristotle identifies the predicables as secondary substances in that they are true about the subject—and thus, they truly exist—but they do not exist in the same way that Gil the Gila monster exists.

Recall the "problem of universals" and how one thing may be both one thing and present in other things simultaneously. In *On Interpretation*, Aristotle defines a "universal" as "that which is by its nature predicated of a number of things man, for instance, is a universal, Callias [a contemporary of Aristotle] a particular," (Barnes 27). As a means of helping to elucidate how one thing may be true of and predicated of other things, Aristotle distinguishes between the idea of primary substances and secondary substances. A primary substance is something that exists—the "individual man or the individual horse." In contrast, a secondary substance includes those predicables discussed in this section, "the species in which the things primarily called substances are, are called secondary substances, as also are the genera of these species." These predicables are "either said of the primary substances as subjects", as "animal is predicated of man [man being the species] and therefore also of the individuals individual man [the individual man being a primary substance].

Aristotle also seems to rank secondary substances based on their nearness to primary substances: "the species is more a substance than the genus since it is nearer to the primary substance. For if one is to say of the primary substance what it is, it will be more informative and apt to give the species than the genus." Moreover, if these "primary substances did not exist", neither would the substances that are predicated of those primary substances. Or, conversely, the universal exists in the particular but not apart from that particular (Barns 4-5).

Today, the issue of terms is both more complicated and more important. It is more complicated because we know so much about the world, and thus we have a more challenging time making sense of all that information. It is also more important because of the ease with which we can communicate with each other, and anytime we are communicating, we need to have a solid understanding of the words we use and what they mean.

# Aristotle's Predicables

To help learn this difficult but important material, we have provided the table below as a means of summarizing the information presented in this section—namely, the predicables of *species*, *genus*, *specific difference* (or *differentia*), *property*, and *accident*.

| Aristotle's Predicables | Definition | Example, taken from **Man** |
|---|---|---|
| Species | What a thing is in itself, the essence, the fundamental nature of its being. | The species or very essence of man would be rational animal. |
| Specific Difference (or Differentia) | An essential quality that derives from the species of a thing, from the essence of that thing what that thing is in itself. | Aristotle identified man's specific difference as man's unique ability to reason. |
| Property | An essential quality that derives from the species of a thing, from the essence of that thing what that thing is in itself. | For human beings, our properties include creativity, our rationality, and our ability to make meaningful, rational choices. |
| Genus | The general category in which a thing exists. | Human beings exist in the general category of animals since, like animals, we require food, water, and some form of shelter in order to survive. |
| Accident | A characteristic that can be present or be missing from a subject without detracting from or adding to the essence of that particular subject. | Hair color, skin color, height, weight, etc. all qualify as accidental properties of a human being. |

## Reading Comprehension Questions

1. What are the benefits of knowing the precise definition of a term, according to Aristotle? (see the *Big Idea* at the beginning of this chapter for more information).

2. What is a subject, and what is a predicate? What function does a predicate serve in a sentence?

3. What is a predicable and what are the five predicables?

4. What is a primary substance, and what is a secondary substance?

ACTIVITY

# Aristotle's Predicables

**Instructions**: Continue the exercise from the previous page, identify the *species, genus, specific difference* (or *differentia*), *property*, and *accident* of each term.

Example: *The term man:*

    Genus: *Animal*    Specific Difference: *The ability to reason*    Species: *Rational Animal*

    Property: *The ability to use grammar*    Accident: *Hair color, etc.*

    Note: *The species is often the specific difference combined with the genus of a thing.*

1. The term *bird*:

    Genus: _____    Specific Difference: _____    Species: _____

    Property: _____    Accident: _____

2. The term *penguins*:

    Genus: _____    Specific Difference: _____    Species: _____

    Property: _____    Accident: _____

3. The term *robins*:

    Genus: _____    Specific Difference: _____    Species: _____

    Property: _____    Accident: _____

ACTIVITY

# Aristotle's Predicables

**Instructions**: Continue the exercise from the previous page, identify the *species, genus, specific difference* (or *differentia*), *property*, and *accident* of each term.

4. The term *ostriches*:

   Genus: _____   Specific Difference: _____   Species: _____

   Property: _____   Accident: _____

5. The term *frogs*:

   Genus: _____   Specific Difference: _____   Species: _____

   Property: _____   Accident: _____

6. The term *bullfrogs*:

   Genus: _____   Specific Difference: _____   Species: _____

   Property: _____   Accident: _____

7. The term *poison dart frogs*:

   Genus: _____   Specific Difference: _____   Species: _____

   Property: _____   Accident: _____

ACTIVITY

# Aristotle's Predicables

**Instructions**: Continue the exercise from the previous page, identify the *species, genus, specific difference* (or *differentia*), *property*, and *accident* of each term.

8. The term *government*:

   Genus: _____    Specific Difference: _____    Species: _____

   Property: _____    Accident: _____

9. The term *democracy*:

   Genus: _____    Specific Difference: _____    Species: _____

   Property: _____    Accident: _____

10. The term *republic*:

    Genus: _____    Specific Difference: _____    Species: _____

    Property: _____    Accident: _____

11. The term *tyranny*:

    Genus: _____    Specific Difference: _____    Species: _____

    Property: _____    Accident: _____

ACTIVITY

# Aristotle's Predicables

**Instructions**: Continue the exercise from the previous page, identify the *species, genus, specific difference* (or *differentia*), *property*, and *accident* of each term.

12. The term *flower*:

    Genus: _____  Specific Difference: _____  Species: _____

    Property: _____  Accident: _____

13. The term *tree*:

    Genus: _____  Specific Difference: _____  Species: _____

    Property: _____  Accident: _____

14. The term *tulip*:

    Genus: _____  Specific Difference: _____  Species: _____

    Property: _____  Accident: _____

15. The term *oak tree*:

    Genus: _____  Specific Difference: _____  Species: _____

    Property: _____  Accident: _____

# Aristotle's Categories

IN THE *TOPICS*, ARISTOTLE expands upon the idea of *predicables* by positing how the four orders of *species* (which Aristotle calls *definition*), *genus*, *property*, and *accident* may be further categorized. These are called *categories*, of which there are ten. Aristotle explains the nature of categories, the way in which that language reflects the fundamental nature of being and existence, in the following selection from the *Topics*:

> *Next, then, we must distinguish between the classes of predicates in which the four orders in question are found. These are ten in number: Essence, Quantity, Quality, Relation, Place, Time, Position, State, Activity, Passivity. For the accident and genus and property and definition of anything will always be in one of these categories: for all the propositions found through these signify either something's essence or its quality or quantity or some one of the other types of predicate* (Pickard-Cambridge).

So what are categories? Aristotle called categories the "general classes", the general states of being into which a thing may fall. In Latin, the phrase "general classes" is rendered as *summa genera*. Aristotle said that everything fits into ten categories, broad, general ways we can describe a subject or a predicate. These ways fall into the following categories: substance, quantity, quality, relation, place, time, posture (internal ordering), possession, action, passion.

Here is what Aristotle wrote in the *Categories*:

> *"Of things said without combination, each signifies either substance or quantity or qualification or a relative or where or when or being-in-a-position or having or doing or being-affected. To give a rough idea, examples of substance are man, horse; of quantity: four-foot, five-foot; of qualification: white, grammatical; of a relative: double, half, larger; of where: in the Lyceum, in the market-place; of when: yesterday, last-year; of being-in-a-position: is-lying, is-sitting; of having: has shoes on, has-armor-on; of doing: cutting, burning; of being-affected: being cut, being-burned"* (Barnes 4).

Aristotle's ten categories constitute a broad, general way that language describes being. We categorize things to make sense of them according to their uses, purposes, or other unique property. Categories group different kinds of things into distinct groups of things, and this grouping helps us divide things into manageable and universally recognizable types. These groups are natural ways of making sense of the world around us, and thus categories should help us make sense of the substance of a thing. Categories are a classification of all terms, absolutely or simply in themselves, whether they are in a proposition or not.

On the following page, we have provided a table listing the categories and a brief description of how each category reflects being and existence.

ACTIVITY

# Guided Notes / Aristotle's Categories

**Instructions**: Given the amount of specialized terminology and nuanced definitions in this chapter, we have provided selections from Aristotle's *Categories* in the table below.

| Aristotle's Categories | Part of Speech | Quotation from Categories | Student Definition / Paraphrase |
|---|---|---|---|
| Substance | Noun | A substance—that which is called a substance most strictly, primarily, and most of all—is that which is neither said of a subject nor in a subject, e.g. the individual man or the individual horse. | A thing that exists which we can see or observe, such as the individual man or horse. |
| Quantity | Adjective | Of quantities some are discrete [ex., number and language], others continuous [example, lines, surfaces, etc.]; and some are composed of parts which have position in relation to one another, others are not composed of parts which have position, (Barnes 8). | |
| Quality | Adjective | By a quality I mean that in virtue of which things are said to be qualified somehow: It is what are easily changed and quickly changing that we call conditions, e.g. hotness and chill and sickness and health and the like, (Barnes 14). | |
| Relation | Nouns | We call relatives [that which stands] in some other way in relation to something else. For example, what is larger is called what it is than something else (it is called larger than something); and what is double is called it is of something else.. | |
| Place | Adverb | ...of where: in the Lyceum, in the market-place; of when: yesterday, last-year... | |

ACTIVITY

# Guided Notes / Aristotle's Categories

**Instructions**: Given the amount of specialized terminology and nuanced definitions in this chapter, we have provided selections from Aristotle's *Categories* in the table below.

| Aristotle's Categories | Part of Speech | Quotation from Categories | Student Definition / Paraphrase |
|---|---|---|---|
| Time | Adverb | *of when: yesterday, last-year…* | |
| Posture | Adjective | *…of being-in-a-position: is-lying, is-sitting,* (Barnes 4). | |
| Possession | Adjective | *Having is spoken of in a number of ways: having as a state and condition or some other quality* | |
| Action | Verb | *…of doing: cutting, burning…* | |
| Passion | Verb | *…of being-affected: being cut, being-burned…* | |

ACTIVITY

# Aristotle's Categories

**Instructions**: The categories refer to the ten ways in which a word may reflect some aspect of a subject's being. Read over each term listed below and place it in its most-appropriate category, making note that there will be plenty of disagreement concerning the most appropriate category to which a term may belong.

*Example: The term* Socrates *belongs to the category of* substance *because the word itself refers to the individual man,* Socrates.

1. The term *philosopher* belongs to the category of _____

_____

2. The term *bird* belongs to the category of _____

_____

3. The term *happy* belongs to the category of _____

_____

4. The term *in the garden* belongs to the category of _____

_____

5. The term *sad* belongs to the category of _____

_____

ACTIVITY

# Aristotle's Categories

**Instructions**: Read over each term listed below and place it in its most-appropriate category, making note that there will be plenty of disagreement concerning the most appropriate category to which a term may belong.

6. The term *logician* belongs to the category of _____


_____


7. The term *run* or *running* belongs to the category of _____


_____


8. The term *carried* or *being carried* belongs to the category of _____


_____


9. The term *a cubit in length* belongs to the category of _____


_____


10. The term *at six o'clock* belongs to the category of _____


_____


11. The term *in the Forum* belongs to the category of _____


_____

CHAPTER 4 Terms According to Aristotle ♦ 119

ACTIVITY

# Aristotle's Categories

**Instructions**: Read over each term listed below and place it in its most appropriate category, making note that there will be plenty of disagreement concerning the most appropriate category to which a term may belong.

12. The term *forty* belongs to the category of _____

_____

13. The term *Wake Forest* belongs to the category of _____

_____

14. The term *sitting* belongs to the category of _____

_____

15. The term *outside* belongs to the category of _____

_____

16. The term *in the Lyceum* belongs to the category of _____

_____

17. The term *overjoyed* belongs to the category of _____

_____

ACTIVITY

# Aristotle's Categories

**Instructions**: Read over each term listed below and place it in its most-appropriate category, making note that there will be plenty of disagreement concerning the most appropriate category to which a term may belong.

18. The term *one mile* belongs to the category of _____

19. The term *the best* belongs to the category of _____

20. The term *thrown* or *being thrown* belongs to the category of _____

21. The term *Aristotle* belongs to the category of _____

22. The term *at noon* belongs to the category of _____

23. The term *playing* belongs to the category of _____

# Aristotle's Four Causes

**THE IDEA OF CAUSATION IS CRUCIAL** to our understanding of the world around us. Thales of Miletus, for example, is said to be the first scientist because he was the first to investigate the natural world and try to understand how the world worked without ascribing its mysterious happenings to the gods. Accordingly, *causation* is crucial to our study and practice of science in that empirical observation focuses on elucidating—that is, making clear—the mysterious cause-and-effect relationship governing the world around us. We conduct experiments and carefully control one particular independent variable to determine what effect that variable may have on some other phenomenon we observe in the world. The human mind is relentlessly curious, and we delight in understanding how and why things work the way they do.

Like Thales, Aristotle also investigated the nature of causes. When we understand the cause of something, we believe that we know that thing, as Aristotle argued in *Posterior Analytics* and in *Physics* (Falcon). Here is what Aristotle wrote about the importance of finding and knowing the cause of something. Aristotle states that "knowledge is the object of our inquiry", but people do not think they really know something until they "grasped the 'why' of that thing, as far as the beginning, essence, material, and ultimate purpose of that particular thing. Subsequently, Aristotle differentiated between four different kinds of causes.

The nature of the *Four Causes* appears in Aristotle's *Physics*, Book II, Part 3 (R. P. Hardie and R. K. Gaye). Aristotle outlines the Four Causes as follows:

*In one sense, then, (1) that out of which a thing comes to be and which persists, is called 'cause', e.g. the bronze of the statue, the silver of the bowl, and the genera of which the bronze and the silver are species.*

*In another sense (2) the form or the archetype, i.e. the statement of the essence, and its genera, are called 'causes' (e.g. of the octave the relation of 2:1, and generally number), and the parts in the definition.*

*Again (3) the primary source of the change or coming to rest; e.g. the man who gave advice is a cause, the father is [the] cause of the child, and generally what makes of what is made and what causes change of what is changed.*

*Again (4) in the sense of end or 'that for the sake of which' a thing is done, e.g. health is the cause of walking about. ('Why is he walking about?' we say. 'To be healthy', and, having said that, we think we have assigned the cause.) The same is true also of all the intermediate steps which are brought about through the action of something else as means towards the end, e.g. reduction of flesh, purging, drugs, or surgical instruments are means towards health.*

*All these things are 'for the sake of' the end, though they differ from one another in that some are activities, others instruments. This then perhaps exhausts the number of ways in which the term 'cause' is used.*

## Vocabulary

**Causation**
The idea that one thing, event, person, idea, etc. causes another thing, event, person, idea, etc. to come into being.

**Material Cause**
The composition of a thing and the things from which it is made.

**Formal Cause**
The essence of a thing.

**Efficient Cause**
The agent that brings a thing into being or produces changes in a thing.

**Final Cause**
The purpose or goal for which a thing is made.

Let's describe each of the Four Causes in greater detail, alongside examples to help illustrate this concept.

First Cause / The Material Cause: The material cause refers to the physical, perhaps even biological material out of "which a thing comes to be". Aristotle cites as examples the bronze or silver out of which a metal object is made. If we were to define man solely by our material makeup (i.e., our tissues and organs), then man would be something akin to a biochemical machine.

Second Cause / The Formal Cause: The formal cause is the essence of whatever that thing is. To explain the idea of a formal cause, Aristotle uses like *form*, *archetype*, and the essence of a thing explained in words. The formal cause of a bronze statue would be the man or animal that the sculpture is meant to be in form. If we were to define man solely by our formal cause, man might be best defined as a *rational animal*.

Third Cause / The Efficient Cause: The efficient cause is the agent by which changes are produced in other things, being brought from one state of activity or being to another or being brought to rest. In *Metaphysics*, Aristotle expands upon this definition further, saying that the *efficient cause* is "in general the maker [is the] cause of the thing made and the change-producing of the changing". In other words, the *efficient cause* is the thing that brings something else into being, from one state to another, or into a state of rest (Ross).

The efficient cause implies applying knowledge rightly acquired and rightly applied, as a craftsman needs a certain understanding of how to forge bronze, carve a mold, and then pour the bronze rightly to bring a bronze statue into being (Falcon). In the Judeo-Christian tradition, the *efficient cause* of man is God, who, having created man in his image, also gave to human beings rationality, creativity, and the ability to make meaningful choices.

Fourth Cause / The Final Cause: The final cause is the purpose for which a thing was made. As Aristotle says, it is "the end...that for the sake of which a thing is," (Ross). That is, everything created has a purpose which that thing may one day achieve unless something impedes it and stops its growth. An acorn's "final cause" is an oak tree; a chair, sitting; for a blanket, warmth. Aristotle also includes all the intermediate stages of a thing and all the changes it may go through, providing that these changes contribute to and exist for the sake of that ultimate goal.

ACTIVITY

# Guided Notes / Aristotle's Four Causes

**Instructions**: Write down definitions for *the material cause, the formal cause, the efficient cause,* and the *final cause.* Then, using the original copy of Aristotle's *Organon* as an example, identify the appropriate *cause* of the *Organon*.

| The Four Causes | Definition | The Cause of the Organon |
|---|---|---|
| Material Cause | | |
| Formal Cause | | |
| Efficient Cause | | |
| Final Cause | | |

124 ✦ SECTION I Terms & Metaphysics

ACTIVITY

# Aristotle's Four Causes

**Instructions**: Read over each of the following terms and provide a short description for its *Material Cause, Formal Cause, Efficient Cause,* and *Final Cause*. To help in identifying the appropriate cause for each item, we have provided the picture for the "The Four Causes of Classical Education" below. In completing this exercise, note how much more difficult it is to identify the cause of things which we human beings did not create.

---

Example: *The term* classical education:

Material Cause: *The material makeup of a thing like classical education, would include the Great Books of the Western canon, as well as all the subjects appropriate to a classical education.*

Efficient Cause: *The agent by which an individual might move from ignorance to knowledge, would include the teacher, the student, parents, administrators, and other relevant stakeholders.*

Formal Cause: *The essence of a classical education, would emphasize what is good, true, and beautiful alongside the cultivation of virtue, personal integrity and good character.*

Final Cause: *The purpose of a classical education might be to cultivate students of excellence, to prepare those students to live in a free society, and to contribute to the flourishing of those students and of the societies they live in.*

1. The term *plastic chair:*

Material Cause:_____  Efficient Cause:_____

Formal Cause:_____  Final Cause:_____

2. The term *plastic chair:*

Material Cause:_____  Efficient Cause:_____

Formal Cause:_____  Final Cause:_____

ACTIVITY

# Aristotle's Four Causes

**Instructions**: Continue the exercise from the previous page, identifying the different causes for each term.

3. The term *mahogany table:*

   Material Cause:_____   Efficient Cause:_____

   Formal Cause:_____   Final Cause:_____

4. The term *hammer made of steel and bamboo:*

   Material Cause:_____   Efficient Cause:_____

   Formal Cause:_____   Final Cause:_____

5. The term *stapler:*

   Material Cause:_____   Efficient Cause:_____

   Formal Cause:_____   Final Cause:_____

6. The term *the wheel:*

   Material Cause:_____   Efficient Cause:_____

   Formal Cause:_____   Final Cause:_____

ACTIVITY

# Aristotle's Four Causes

**Instructions**: Continue the exercise from the previous page, identifying the different causes for each term.

7. The term *Printing Press* (1450)*:*

Material Cause: _____   Efficient Cause: _____

Formal Cause: _____   Final Cause: _____

8. The term *Steam Engine:*

Material Cause: _____   Efficient Cause: _____

Formal Cause: _____   Final Cause: _____

9. The term *light bulb:*

Material Cause: _____   Efficient Cause: _____

Formal Cause: _____   Final Cause: _____

10. The term *Ford's Model T:*

Material Cause: _____   Efficient Cause: _____

Formal Cause: _____   Final Cause: _____

ACTIVITY

# Aristotle's Four Causes

**Instructions**: Continue the exercise from the previous page, identifying the different causes for each term.

11. The term *apple tree:*

Material Cause:_____     Efficient Cause:_____

Formal Cause:_____     Final Cause:_____

12. The term *acorn:*

Material Cause:_____     Efficient Cause:_____

Formal Cause:_____     Final Cause:_____

13. The term *tiger:*

Material Cause:_____     Efficient Cause:_____

Formal Cause:_____     Final Cause:_____

14. The term *human being:*

Material Cause:_____     Efficient Cause:_____

Formal Cause:_____     Final Cause:_____

ACTIVITY

# Aristotle's Four Causes

**Instructions**: Continue the exercise from the previous page, identifying the different causes for each term.

15. The term *Scientific Method:*

Material Cause: _____  Efficient Cause: _____

Formal Cause: _____  Final Cause: _____

16. The term *band saw:*

Material Cause: _____  Efficient Cause: _____

Formal Cause: _____  Final Cause: _____

17. The term *Dogwood tree:*

Material Cause: _____  Efficient Cause: _____

Formal Cause: _____  Final Cause: _____

18. The term *cardinal (bird):*

Material Cause: _____  Efficient Cause: _____

Formal Cause: _____  Final Cause: _____

# Metaphysics / By Aristotle

**Description**: In chapter 3, we referenced Aristotle's treatise entitled *Metaphysics*. The title refers to the placement of this text in a manuscript of Aristotle's lectures, coming as it did after Aristotle's Physics and the Greek prefix *meta* means "with" or, in this context, "after". The treatise entitled *Metaphysics* not only comes after *Physics* but continues many of the same discussions of causation Aristotle began in Physics. As the final text in our first section, we will read the first two parts of Book I of Aristotle's *Metaphysics*.

## Aristotle's *Metaphysics:* Book I, Part 1

01 ALL men by nature desire to know. An indication of this is the delight we take in our senses; for even apart from their usefulness they are loved for themselves; and above all others the sense of sight. For not only with a view to action, but even when we are not going to do anything, we prefer seeing (one might say) to everything else. The reason is that this, most of all the senses, makes us know and brings to light many differences between things.

02 By nature animals are born with the faculty of sensation, and from sensation, memory is produced in some of them, though not in others. And therefore the former are more intelligent and apt at learning than those which cannot remember; those which are incapable of hearing sounds are intelligent though they cannot be taught, e.g. the bee, and any other race of animals that may be like it; and those which besides memory have this sense of hearing can be taught.

03 The animals other than man live by appearances and memories, and have but little of connected experience; but the human race lives also by art and reasonings. Now from memory experience is produced in men; for the several memories of the same thing produce finally the capacity for a single experience. And experience seems pretty much like science and art, but really science and art come to men through experience; for 'experience made art', as Polus says, 'but inexperience luck'. Now art arises when from many notions gained by experience one universal judgment about a class of objects is produced. For to have a judgment that when Callias was ill of this disease this did him good, and similarly in the case of Socrates and in many individual cases, is a matter of experience; but to judge that it has done good to all persons of a certain constitution, marked off in one class, when they were sick with some disease—to people burning with fevers—this is a matter of art.

With a view to action experience seems in no respect inferior to art, and men of experience succeed even better than those who have theory without experience. (The reason is that experience is knowledge of individuals, art of universals, and actions and productions are all concerned with the individual; for the physician does not cure man, except in an incidental way, but a man like Socrates or someone else who happens to be a man. If, then, a man has the theory without the experience, and recognizes the universal but does not know the individual included in this, he will often fail to cure; for it is the individual that is to be cured.)

04 But yet we think that knowledge and understanding belong to art rather than to experience, and we suppose artists to be wiser than men of experience (which implies that Wisdom depends in all cases rather on knowledge); and this because the former know the cause, but the latter do not. For men of experience know that the thing is so, but do not know why, while the others

## Vocabulary & Annotations

### ...ALL men by nature
Aristotle grounds his treatise in this premise about human nature: human beings possess reason and because of this unique faculty, take joy in study, observation, reflection, and in learning more and more about the world around them.

### ...little of connected experience
While animals possess certain problem-solving abilities, they generally lack *memory*, the ability to store large amounts of information about themselves, about the past to solve problems in the present.

### Art
The term *art* generally refers to an activity or a skill with a body of knowledge informing its use such as weaving, medicine, farming, etc.

### ...not aim at utility
Aristotle ranks various types of arts or activities by the reasons people pursue such arts. Few individuals pursue an art like *basket-weaving* for the joy of weaving baskets but for the utility (or usefulness) of the basket itself.

### ...at leisure
For an individual or a whole society to pursue the "higher" arts, those not connected with sheer survival, they need considerable amounts of leisure time.

know the 'why' and the cause. Hence we think also that the master workers in each craft are more honorable and know in a truer sense and are wiser than the manual workers, because they know the causes of the things that are done and why events happen as they do. Likewise, we think the manual workers are like certain lifeless things which act but act without knowing what they do, as fire burns, but while the lifeless things perform each of their functions by a natural tendency, the laborers perform them through habit. Thus we view them as being wiser not in virtue of being able to act, but of having the theory for themselves and knowing the causes. And in general it is a sign of the man who knows and of the man who does not know, that the former can teach, and therefore we think art more truly knowledge than experience is; for artists can teach, and men of mere experience cannot.

**05** Again, we do not regard any of the senses as Wisdom; yet surely these give the most authoritative knowledge of particulars. But they do not tell us the 'why' of anything. For example, they do not explain why fire is hot; they only say that it is hot.

**06** At first he who invented any art whatever that went beyond the common perceptions of man was naturally admired by men, not only because there was something useful in the inventions, but because he was thought wise and superior to the rest. But as more arts were invented, and some were directed to the necessities of life, others to recreation, the inventors of the latter were naturally always regarded as wiser than the inventors of the former, because their branches of knowledge did **not aim at utility**. Hence when all such inventions were already established, the sciences which do not aim at giving pleasure or at the necessities of life were discovered, and first in the places where men first began to have leisure. This is why the mathematical arts were founded in Egypt; for there the priestly caste was allowed to be **at leisure**.

**07** We have said in the *Ethics* what the difference is between art and science and the other kindred faculties; but the point of our present discussion is this, that all men suppose what is called Wisdom to deal with the first causes and the principles of things; so that, as has been said before, the man of experience is thought to be wiser than the possessors of any sense-perception whatever, the artist wiser than the men of experience, the master worker than the mechanic, and the theoretical kinds of knowledge to be more of the nature of Wisdom than the productive. Clearly then Wisdom is knowledge about certain principles and causes.

## Book I, Part 2

**08** Since we are seeking this knowledge, we must inquire of what kind are the causes and the principles, the knowledge of which is Wisdom. If one were to take the notions we have about the wise man, this might perhaps make the answer more evident. We suppose first, then, that the wise man knows all things, as far as possible, although he has not knowledge of each of them in detail; secondly, that he who can learn things that are difficult, and not easy for man to know, is wise (sense-perception is common to all, and therefore easy and no mark of Wisdom); again, that he who is more exact and more capable of teaching the causes is wiser, in every branch of knowledge; and that of the sciences, also, that which is desirable on its own account and for the sake of knowing it is more of the nature of Wisdom than that which is desirable on account of its results, and the superior science is more of the nature of Wisdom than the ancillary; for the wise man must not be ordered but must order, and he must not obey another, but the less wise must obey him.

**09** Such and so many are the notions, then, which we have about Wisdom and the wise. Now of these characteristics that of knowing all things must belong to him who has in the highest degree universal knowledge; for he knows in a sense all the instances that fall under the universal. And these things, the most universal, are on the whole the hardest for men to know; for they are farthest from the senses. And the most exact of the sciences are those which deal most with first principles; for those which involve fewer principles are more exact than those which involve additional principles, e.g. arithmetic than geometry. But the science which investigates causes is also instructive, in a higher degree, for the people who instruct us are those who tell the causes of each thing.

**10** And understanding and knowledge pursued for their own sake are found most in the knowledge of that which is most knowable (for he who chooses to know for the sake of knowing will choose most readily that which is most truly knowledge, and such is the knowledge of that which is most knowable); and the first principles and the causes are most knowable; for by reason of these, and from these, all other things come to be known, and not these by means of the things subordinate to them. And the science which knows to what end each thing must be done is the most authoritative of the sciences, and more authoritative than any ancillary science; and this end is the good of that thing, and in general the supreme good in the whole of nature. Judged by all the tests we have mentioned, then, the name in question falls to the

## Vocabulary & Annotations

**...their wonder**
The habit of philosophers to "wonder" about the world and investigate its happenings is the basis of science, philosophy, and other intellectual endeavours.

**...man is free**
By analogy, the free individual exists for himself and not as the tool of some other individual, as in the tragic case of slavery and abuse.

**...first principle**
Later in the *Metaphysics*, Aristotle provides a rational argument for existence of a supreme, divine being, whom later Christian theologians equated with the God of the Bible. The argument is that all events have a prior cause, and we can trace these cause backwards in time, an infinite, backward series of causes is logically impossible. As a result, there must be a "first cause" or an "unmoved mover" who exists outside of the earthly, temporal chain of being but also initiated those movements.

same science; this must be a science that investigates the first principles and causes; for the good, i.e. the end, is one of the causes.

11 That it is not a science of production is clear even from the history of the earliest philosophers. For it is owing to **their wonder** that men both now begin and at first began to philosophize; they wondered originally at the obvious difficulties, then advanced little by little and stated difficulties about the greater matters, e.g. about the phenomena of the moon and those of the sun and of the stars, and about the genesis of the universe.

12 And a man who is puzzled and wonders thinks himself ignorant (whence even the lover of myth is in a sense a lover of Wisdom, for the myth is composed of wonders); therefore since they philosophized in order to escape from ignorance, evidently they were pursuing science in order to know, and not for any utilitarian end.

13 And this is confirmed by the facts; for it was when almost all the necessities of life and the things that make for comfort and recreation had been secured, that such knowledge began to be sought. Evidently then we do not seek it for the sake of any other advantage; but as **the man is free**, we say, who exists for his own sake and not for another's, so we pursue this as the only free science, for it alone exists for its own sake.

14 Hence also the possession of it might be justly regarded as beyond human power; for in many ways human nature is in bondage, so that according to Simonides 'God alone can have this privilege', and it is unfitting that man should not be content to seek the knowledge that is suited to him. If, then, there is something in what the poets say, and jealousy is natural to the divine power, it would probably occur in this case above all, and all who excelled in this knowledge would be unfortunate. But the divine power cannot be jealous (nay, according to the proverb, 'bards tell a lie'), nor should any other science be thought more honorable than one of this sort.

15 For the most divine science is also most honorable; and this science alone must be, in two ways, most divine. For the science which it would be most appropriate for God to have is a divine science, and so is any science that deals with divine objects; and this science alone has both these qualities; for (1) God is thought to be among the causes of all things and to be a **first principle**, and (2) such a science either God alone can have, or God above all others. All the sciences, indeed, are more necessary than this, but none is better.

16 Yet the acquisition of it must in a sense end in something which is the opposite of our original inquiries. For all men begin, as we said, by wondering that things are as they are, as they do about self-moving marionettes, or about the solstices or the fact that the side of diagonal square cannot be measured; for it seems wonderful to all who have not yet seen the reason, that there is a thing which cannot be measured even by the smallest unit. But we must end in the contrary and, according to the proverb, the better state, as is the case in these instances too when men learn the cause; for there is nothing which would surprise a geometer so much as if the diagonal turned out to be commensurable.

17 We have stated, then, what is the nature of the science we are searching for, and what is the mark which our search and our whole investigation must reach.

## Reading Comprehension Questions

1. What do all human beings desire to do, and how is this different from animals and other beings in the created order?

2. How does Aristotle judge some "arts" or activities as being "better" or superior than others? What standard does he use to evaluate the merits of one art or another?

3. What does it mean to "wonder," and how did *wondering* lead to science and philosophy?

4. How is man "free"? How does human freedom help us to understand the value of certain kinds of subjects and activities?

ACTIVITY

# The First Act of the Mind / Terms

Each row contains a term, the author's use of that term, or a definition of that term suitable for students. If the row contains a quotation, write down a clear, intelligible definition of that term in the box provided. If the term is already defined for you, please find the quotation from the text that supports the appropriate definition.

| Term | Quotations from the Text | Quotations Rephrased as Definitions |
|---|---|---|
| Men | | As has been stated throughout this first section, man is a "rational animal"; he may come to know certain things through his senses (like animals), and he comes to know other things through his reason. |
| Experience | *And experience seems pretty much like science and art, but really science and art come to men through experience; for 'experience made art', as Polus says, 'but inexperience luck.'* | |
| Art | | The word used here is *techne*, the Greek word for "art," "craft," or "cunning of hand" the application of specific knowledge towards some meaningful end (see Logeion, an entry in an online Greek dictionary). |

CHAPTER 4 Terms According to Aristotle ✦ 135

ACTIVITY

# The First Act of the Mind / Terms

Each row contains a term, the author's use of that term, or a definition of that term suitable for students. If the row contains a quotation, write down a clear, intelligible definition of that term in the box provided. If the term is already defined for you, please find the quotation from the text that supports the appropriate definition.

| Term | Quotations from the Text | Quotations Rephrased as Definitions |
|---|---|---|
| Universal | | In *On Interpretation*, Aristotle defined the word *universal* as "that which is by its nature predicated of a number of things" like *man*, (Barnes 27). |
| Wisdom | ...but the point of our present discussion is this, that all men suppose what is called Wisdom to deal with the first causes and the principles of things; so that, as has been said before... | |
| ...to philosophize | | The word *philosophy* means the "love of wisdom", so that the action of "philosophizing" would be to engage in rational, meaningful inquiries about the world for the delight and joy that comes from knowing anything at all. |

136 ✦ SECTION I Terms & Metaphysics

ACTIVITY

# The Second Act of the Mind / Propositions

Each row contains an excerpt from the significant text included in this chapter. These selections include significant points and ideas that the author uses to build his argument and reach a meaningful conclusion, one that was not apparent at the beginning of their work. In the space provided, write a summary of the quotation and try to express it in the form of a proposition. You may express it as one or more propositions, but try to paraphrase the author's ideas in your own words—that way, you can come to a much deeper understanding of the argument that the author is advancing.

| Quotations from Text | Quotations rephrased as Propositions |
|---|---|
| ALL men by nature desire to know. ... All men suppose what is called Wisdom to deal with the first causes and the principles of things; so that, as has been said before. | |
| And the science which knows to what end each thing must be done is the most authoritative of the sciences, and more authoritative than any ancillary science; and this end is the good of that thing, and in general the supreme good in the whole of nature." **Note**: "Science" is used of knowledge more generally, not just the empirical sciences like biology, chemistry, etc. | |

CHAPTER 4 Terms According to Aristotle ♦ 137

ACTIVITY

# The Second Act of the Mind / Propositions

Each row contains an excerpt from the significant text included in this chapter. These selections include significant points and ideas that the author uses to build his argument and reach a meaningful conclusion, one that was not apparent at the beginning of their work. In the space provided, write a summary of the quotation and try to express it in the form of a proposition. You may express it as one or more propositions, but try to paraphrase the author's ideas in your own words—that way, you can come to a much deeper understanding of the argument that the author is advancing.

| Quotations from Text | Quotations rephrased as one (or more) Proposition(s) |
|---|---|
| ...since they philosophized in order to escape from ignorance, evidently they were pursuing science in order to know, and not for any utilitarian end... | |
| ...as the man is free, we say, who exists for his own sake and not for another's, so we pursue this as the only free science... | |

138 ✦ SECTION I Terms & Metaphysics

ACTIVITY

# *The Third Act of the Mind* / Inferences

In the space below, create an "argument map", a visual way of representing the premises, assumptions, and ultimately the conclusion that a writer is making in his or her work. You can also use this blank space provided to draw a "conversation map", a visual way of recording the discussion that your class had over this text.

WRITING

# Writing Prompt

Remember, writing is thinking. To help us to write and think more clearly, we will spend considerable time this year writing essays based on the texts we read in class. These essays are descriptive in nature and answer one question that arises from the material we are reading in class. In such an essay, the writer wants to explain the meaningful ideas contained in this text by reading and rereading the text under analysis to better explain that author's argument and the consequences of their ideas.

**Question**: *Why do human beings aspire to know? What is in our nature that moves us to know? What do we hope to accomplish in knowing anything at all?*

# Writing

## WESTMINSTER ABBEY / LATERAL ENTRANCE

*Westminster Abbey is one of the one most famous churches in all of England. Westminster Abbey in its current form was consecrated in 1269 and almost every English monarch has been crowned, beginning with the coronation of William the Conqueror in 1066.*

Photo by Zaymuel

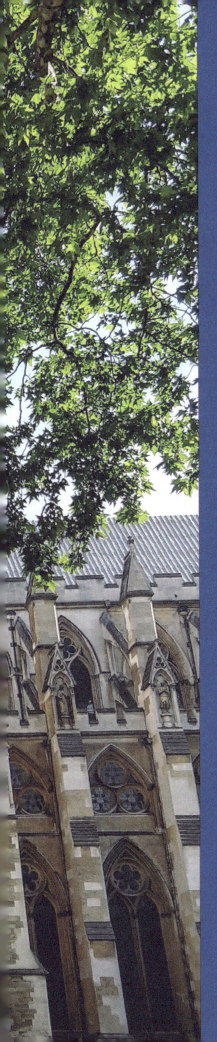

# Section II
# Propositions & Epistemology

**CHAPTERS**

05  The Medieval Consensus

06  Epistemology & Truth

07  Categorical Propositions

08  Relationships of Equivalence

09  The Square of Opposition

WESTMINSTER ABBEY / NAVE
*Photo by K. Mitch Hodge*

CHAPTER 5

# The Medieval Consensus

## ROADMAP

✦ Learn about how the philosophers and thinkers of the medieval world refined and integrated the ideas of Socrates, Plato, and Aristotle.

✦ Reflect on the nature and beauty of truth—and what it means for an idea to be true.

✦ Learn about the lives of Augustine of Hippo and Thomas Aquinas and read selections from the works of these two noteworthy philosophers.

### THALES OUTCOME Nº 6

A *Continuous Learner* implements continual informal and/or formal learning using mentors, texts, the Internet, and experience.

Logic aims at truth, and we delight in knowing what is true, good, and beautiful. But what is truth? How do we know that an idea truly corresponds to reality? What methods of inquiry might we use to determine what is true? In this chapter, we will consider these questions and more as we continue our study of logic and the great ideas of the Western tradition.

# The Medieval Consensus

**WE DIVIDED OUR TEXTBOOK** into four sections, with each section focusing on a different act of the mind. The first section of our textbook focused on the *First Act of the Mind*, the act of simple apprehension and the importance of using clear terms. To illustrate the importance of terms and the difficulty of knowing what a term is in itself, we read selections from Plato, Euclid, and Aristotle. We also studied the philosophical field known as *metaphysics*, which investigates questions concerning the underlying nature of reality and the very nature of being.

This particular section, Section II, focuses on the *Second Act of the Mind*, the mental act of **judgment**, an act that operates on propositions. A **proposition** is an indicative statement that asserts that something is true or is not true about the world. Accordingly, we have paired the topics in this section with **epistemology**, a branch of philosophy that focuses on the nature of knowledge and the means by which we may know anything at all. We have paired this section with epistemology, the study of knowledge and how we know what we know. Below is our table of contents for this book, including the topics we will study and the works we will read.

## The Structure of *Logic and Writing*

| Section | Act of the Mind | Philosophical & Academic Field | Significant Authors |
|---|---|---|---|
| Section I | 1st Act of the Mind: Apprehension | Metaphysics | Plato, Euclid, Plato, and Aristotle |
| Section II | 2nd Act of the Mind: Judgment | Epistemology | Augustine, Aquinas, René Descartes, John Locke, David Hume |
| Section III | 3rd Act of the Mind: Inference / Deductive Reasoning | Political Theory | Thomas Hobbes, John Locke, Montesquieu, Jean-Jacques Rousseau, James Madison, and Alexander Hamilton |
| Section IV | 3rd Act of the Mind: Inference / Inductive Reasoning | Economics | Noteworthy economists including David Ricardo, Frédéric Bastiat, and Friedrich Hayek |

## Vocabulary

**Judgment**
The second act of the mind is the mental act of connecting one term with another to form a proposition.

**Proposition**
A sentence that joins together a term with another term in order to communicate some idea about reality. Only propositions can be true or false.

**Epistemology**
The study of how we know what we know.

| LIBRARY OF ALEXANDRIA

We will read works by authors from the medieval period, such as Augustine and Aquinas, and from the modern period, including René Descartes, John Locke, and David Hume. Logic aims at truth and it is only propositions, and the extent to which a proposition may or may not correspond to reality, that convey truth (Kreeft 138-139). As a result, the study of both propositions and epistemology may be one of the most important topics that we examine this year since we, as logicians, want to know things that are true, good, and beautiful. But what is truth?

The means by which we determine whether or not a proposition is true depends on the nature of the proposition. As Socrates said in the *Euthyphro*, certain controversies can be resolved through empirical means like testing, weighing, measuring, experimenting, and the like (remember that empirical means experience). Whether or not one student can jump higher or lift more weight than another can be easily determined through such methods. In a similar way, if we wondered about the effects of sunlight on plants (or other scientific questions), we could devise an experiment to see how much a plant may or may not grow depending on the amount of sunlight it receives. Such methods are "empirically verifiable" because a proposition like "plants grow better in sunlight" or "student $x$ can lift more weight than student $y$" can be proven or disproven based on evidence that we can see, hear, touch, and experience. These questions are not necessarily easy, but they are, perhaps, more straightforward problems to solve.

**JACQUES-LOUIS DAVID, *THE DEATH OF SOCRATES* (1787)**

Or, perhaps the proposition is of some mathematical nature. We could revisit Euclid's *Elements* and Thales' Theorem, for example, and construct a mathematical proof to support the proposition that "a triangle inscribed inside a circle, with one side being diameter, always forms a right triangle". Mathematics can be verified not only by reason as we think through mathematical proofs but also by experience. We can draw out shapes and build from definitions that we know to be true until we reach conclusions not readily apparent from the information available to us. This step-by-step process was the case with Thales' Theorem, as we used our knowledge of circles and triangles until we reached Proposition 31, in that all triangles inscribed within a circle, with one side being the diameter of that circle, will always be a right triangle. Mathematical propositions may be empirically verified as we literally draw them on the page in front of us. In this way, mathematical propositions are true in a way independent of human experience. Such propositions are still relatively easy to evaluate since we can see the evidence, the data, or the mathematical steps needed to support (or disprove) that proposition.

But what about questions of value? We may want to evaluate a proposition such as "Justice is in the interest of the stronger party" (a scary notion, to be sure, one expressed by Thrasymachus in Plato's *Republic*). Or, the proposition that "the mark of good character is how well one treats individuals they do not have to treat well", a statement original to the present author. How might we define what is just and unjust, good and evil, honorable and dishonorable, values that Socrates identified in the *Euthyphro* as important but difficult to define?

Recall that **Platonism**, the philosophical system derived from the writings of Plato and the teachings of Socrates, teaches that ideas like truth and beauty exist independently of human experience. Such ideas exist in what Plato and Socrates called the World of Forms, and everything good, true, and beautiful in our world is good in as much as it derives from the Forms. However, this view is still not without its problems.

Plato outlines such issues in the *Euthyphro* in what is commonly known as **Euthyphro's Dilemma**: either something is pious and then it is loved by the gods, or it is pious because the gods love it and in that sense,

## Vocabulary

### Platonism
A philosophical school of thought that, following the influence of Socrates and Plato, holds as its central idea the existence of ideas such as truth, beauty, and goodness in the World of Forms.

### Euthyphro's Dilemma
*Euthyphro's Dilemma* refers to the difficulty of defining and understanding the meaning of an abstract term like goodness and piety. If something is pious because the gods love it, the piety of that thing may be arbitrary and unfair; if it is pious and then the gods love it, then the love of the gods seems irrelevant and unnecessary.

### Jesus of Nazareth
A 1st-century itinerant preacher and teacher from the Roman province of Judea whose teachings, miraculous acts of healing, and accounts of his resurrection from the dead led to the founding of Christianity, whose adherents believe Jesus to be the Son of God.

### Christianity
A religion that grew out of 1st century Judaism, centered on the life, death, and resurrection of Jesus Christ, whom Christians believe to be the Messiah and the Son of God.

### Logos
A Greek word that means "reason", "reckoning", or "account", a word that John uses to describe Jesus himself.

**JESUS WITH PONTIUS PILATE**
*The painting is entitled* Ecce Homo *by Antonio Cisari (1871)*

the pious thing became pious because of the gods' love. If something is pious, holy, or good and it is then loved by the gods, then the gods' love is irrelevant and unnecessary (and we are back where we started). If it is pious because it is loved by the gods, then the fact that it is pious seems arbitrary and dependent on the gods' favor. The gods, moreover, do not always display the best character and often quarrel on even the simplest of matters. How do we know what a term means in such a way that we could actually base our actions on that understanding? So again, what is truth?

The Roman governor Pontius Pilate asked the same question of Jesus at his trial. "What is truth?" Pilate asked **Jesus of Nazareth**, a wandering preacher and teacher who lived in first-century Judea. Today, Christians believe Jesus to be a figure of inestimable importance because of the miraculous events surrounding his life and death, a death that came in the form of crucifixion by the Romans. Jesus' immediate followers, called the disciples, even claimed that they had seen Jesus three days after Jesus was crucified and buried in a tomb. They carried this news with them throughout the ancient world, proclaiming that Jesus had died to save people from condemnation for their sins, a message that formed the foundation of this new, upstart religion called **Christianity**.

Initially, the Romans persecuted the followers of this new religion. They barred their meetings and executed their followers, but the fact that its adherents kept dying for the message of Jesus Christ rather than renouncing this new faith only made the faith more attractive to outsiders. The religion of Christianity grew in popularity until 312 AD when Constantine, embroiled in a life-or-death struggle over who would be the next Roman Emperor, painted the Greek letters *chi* and *rho*, the first two letters of the Greek word *Christos*, onto the shields of his soldiers before the Battle of the Milvian Bridge.

After winning that battle, Constantine converted to Christianity, and the religion formerly targeted for annihilation enjoyed a new privileged, elevated status in Roman society. The popularity of Christianity grew for the next century while the Roman Empire weakened both from without and from within. When barbarians sacked the city of Rome first in 410 and later in 476 and the Roman empire fell, the Christian church was one of the few institutions to survive the destruction. The faith tradition of Christianity provided the answers to many questions of values circulating in the twilight of the Roman Empire. The Romans in general grounded questions of value in terms of swords, shields, and soldiers, so that whoever had the most of these could impose its will upon the vanquished.

"Woe to the conquered", a phrase the Romans picked up in 390 BC after they suffered a humiliating defeat at the hands of the Gauls. From that point forward, the Romans took care they would never again be on the losing side of such a conflict. The Romans lived in a world where power and might counted for everything, but Roman virtue and hardiness decayed over time. By the mid-first century AD, the Roman people seemingly lived only for the bread and circuses available at the Roman Colosseum. Such an existence did not resemble the "good life" extolled by Socrates, Plato, and Aristotle.

In contrast, the answers Christianity provided concerning the overarching questions of life proved reasonable and compelling for members of Rome's highly-stratified society. First, to the poor, enslaved, and marginalized

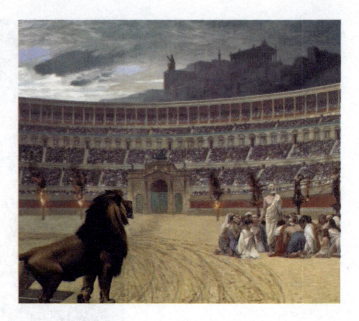

**ROMAN COLOSSEUM & MARTYRDOM**
*Jean-Léon Gérôme (1883)*

members of the Roman world, Christianity emphasized the inherent dignity and value of all human beings. Whereas masters and local magistrates might denigrate such groups, Christianity taught that God not only created them but had also given them unique attributes and abilities. More importantly, God loved them. Then, for Roman soldiers and noblemen, Christianity provided a new avenue to cultivate virtue and fulfill public duties that had seemingly disappeared from Roman culture generations ago.

And for Rome's philosophers, they saw that Christianity could answer some, but not all, of the questions that were as perennial as the human condition itself:

> *In the beginning was the Word, and the Word was with God, and the Word was God. The same was in the beginning with God. All things were made through him. Without him, nothing was made that has been made. In him was life, and the life was the light of men. The light shines in the darkness, and the darkness hasn't overcome it (John 1:1-4).*

What is justice? What is goodness? What is the purpose of life? What is truth? Furthermore, well-educated individuals took note of the prologue to the gospel of John, whose author John described Jesus as the **Logos**. The opening verses read:

The word *Word* John uses here is the Greek term **logos**. John's choice of words has numerous points of implication, beginning with its allusion to the account of creation in Genesis, the first book of the Hebrew and Christian Bible. That book's opening chapter describes God creating the world by speaking and commanding something like light, the days, or the animals to come into being, and they did so in a peaceful and orderly way. Moreover, the word *logos* has philosophical overtones relevant to the ancient Greeks; the word means a "rational account" of a historical event or a field of study, like a history book that tries to portray some historical event as it really happened. Greek philosophers like the Platonists used the word *logos* to refer to the *divine mind,* a kind of nebulous, impersonal force that bound the whole universe together. John's use of the word *logos* to describe Jesus implied that the perennial issues in the human condition could be resolved by turning to Jesus, who was not an impersonal force but, being both man and God, was not unlike themselves. In this way, John identifies the purpose or goal of all philosophical study with the person of Jesus, the *logos* who holds together the entirety of the universe and gives it meaning.

To investigate this question further, we will now examine two philosophers from the medieval period, the thousand or so years between the fall of the Roman Empire and the rise of Renaissance Italy. The writings of these two thinkers established many of the contours of philosophical discussion during the Middle Ages: Augustine of Hippo (AD 354-430) and Thomas Aquinas (AD 1225-1274). In this way, we hope to deepen our knowledge of what is good, true, and beautiful, and better understand the nature and beauty of truth.

## Reading Comprehension Questions

1. Why are questions of a "scientific nature" more straightforward and perhaps even easier to settle than questions of value?

## Reading Comprehension Questions

2. How might we prove mathematical propositions using both reason and experience?

3. How did the Romans (generally) settle questions of value?

4. How did Christianity change this mindset?

# Plato, Augustine, & Truth

THE ROMAN PHILOSOPHER Augustine (AD 354 to 430) was born in Tagaste (sometimes spelled Thagaste), a town in the Roman province of North Africa. The years of his life coincided with the end of the Roman Empire: Augustine was alive when the Visigoths first sacked Rome in AD 410 and when the Vandals besieged and conquered Augustine's city of Hippo in 430, the year of Augustine's death. When Augustine died, he was one of the most widely-known and respected figures in the Catholic church, an individual who wrote on practically every issue surrounding Christian theology, philosophy, and ethics. Augustine is most famous for two works: *The City of God*, written soon after the Visigoths sacked Rome, and The Confessions, a kind of spiritual autobiography detailing Augustine's upbringing and conversion to Christianity. Now, Augustine occupies a special place in the Western tradition, but his youth and upbringing did not show much of this promise.

As described in *The Confessions*, Augustine was something of a wild and unruly teenager who rejected the Christian faith of his mother, Monica, in favor of the kind of hedonism—the pursuit of physical pleasures (i.e., partying) as one of the chief ends in life—practiced by many wealthy Roman youths. Augustine explains his selfish disposition in *The Confessions* through the following story: one day, he and his friends snuck into a neighbor's garden to steal some pears. They were not particularly interested in eating the pears (that would be the sin of gluttony), nor were they interested in selling them (that might be the sin of greed), nor were they even impressed with the quality of the pears they wanted to steal (that might be the sin of jealousy, and Augustine's own garden had better pears). Instead, Augustine and his friends simply took delight in doing

|| AUGUSTINE / AD 354 - 430

wrong (indulging in sin more generally, as a way of living), a moment that illustrated Augustine's own twisted and selfish disposition, a state that, once he became a Christian, Augustine would call sin. They later threw the pears to some pigs.

Augustine's teenage years and early career illustrate a man trying to find meaning and purpose in life via professional achievements, worldly ambitions, and intermittent hedonism, albeit mixed with philosophical reflection and study. Augustine studied and taught rhetoric in Carthage, Rome, and later Milan, but Augustine found teaching at first to be thankless and difficult, since his students tried to avoid paying him. Augustine persevered in part because of his overwhelming ambition to be a successful and noteworthy scholar and teacher. But then Augustine read Cicero's *Hortensius*, a dialogue that is now lost, but which inspired Augustine to take questions in philosophy and ethics more seriously. Augustine then embarked on a quest to answer those perennial, meaningful questions in life: what is the meaning of life? Why am I here? How should I live my life and fulfill my obligations to the people about whom I care?

To answer these questions, Augustine moved from one philosophical school to another, particularly the schools of Manichaeism and later Platonism. Augustine said that Platonism spurred him "to seek for immaterial truth," while Manichaeism's belief in an eternal, dualistic struggle between good and evil sounded plausible at first but contained numerous contradictions (Chadwick 129). Augustine kept up his search for what made life meaningful while he pursued his worldly ambitions as a teacher of rhetoric in Rome and Milan. All the while, Augustine felt a pull towards Christianity which, in the late 4th century, had continued to grow in popularity throughout the Roman Empire. Augustine's mother Monica also kept praying for him and urging him to take matters of faith more seriously. While in Milan, Augustine became friends with a man named Ambrose (340 to 397 AD), the bishop of that city, who talked with him further about the Christian faith.

Finally, one day, in the midst of these personal struggles, Augustine heard a voice urging him to "*tolle lege*", to "take up and read", the Bible (Chadwick 152). This he did, and he felt his desire for worldly success and physical pleasures begin to slip away. Augustine would cite this moment as the starting point for his Christian faith. Before his conversion, Augustine had received a premier professorship in the city of Milan, teaching rhetoric. This position was one for which Augustine had worked to achieve for most of his life. After becoming a Christian, Augustine may have given up this lucrative teaching, or he may have lost his position. Either way, Augustine made his way back to North Africa.

En route, his mother Monica died at Ostia, a port city near Rome, and his son Adeodatus also died around the same time. These losses, coupled with the decision to return home to North Africa, compelled Augustine to devote the rest of his life to the church. It probably helped matters that, upon his arrival in the city of Hippo, the townspeople practically forced him to become a junior clergyman and later a bishop. Augustine would devote the rest of his time and his talents to serving the church, giving long speeches called sermons on books of the Bible, and writing books on the intersection of the Christian faith and philosophy. In this way, Augustine used his training in rhetoric and his expert knowledge of Latin to write works that have since become among the most influential in the Western canon. Augustine became ill in the spring of 430 while the Vandals, one of many Germanic barbarian tribes tearing down the Roman

## Vocabulary & Annotations

### Augustine
Augustine was a North African philosopher and theologian who lived near the fall of the Roman Empire. His most famous books include *The Confessions* and *City of God*, and among his most notable accomplishments were integrating ideas of Platonism with elements of Christian faith and doctrine. He lived from 354 to 430 AD.

### The Confessions
The spiritual autobiography of the Roman philosopher and theologian Augustine.

### ...yet are corrupted
Augustine ranks things that are good in their relation to God, who is incorruptible. Earthly goods, meanwhile, spoil, rot, and change over time.

Empire, lay siege to the city of Hippo. He passed away shortly before the Vandals took Hippo and razed much of the city to the ground, sparing only Augustine's home and his library.

Remember *Euthyphro's Dilemma*? That, if the gods love something because it is pious, well, it is already pious and the influence of the gods is not necessary. But, if the gods love something, and that thing becomes pious because of the gods' love, then the fact that it is pious seems arbitrary and severed from any real meaningful metaphysical connection between ideas and the real world. The gods could love something bad and their love could make that thing pious, something that could very easily happen since the gods rarely demonstrated moral virtue and steadfast love. Augustine saw that the faith tradition of Christianity, and its belief in one personal, merciful God could reconcile much of the inherent tension left unresolved by Socrates and Euthyphro in their conversation on the way to the Athenian court of law. Augustine, in addition to writing several of the Great Books of the Western canon, is famous for reconciling one of the most significant philosophical traditions in the Western tradition, namely Platonism and the influence of Socrates, with that of Christianity. As far as truth, the existence of ideas, and understanding what a term means in itself, Augustine rooted these transcendental convictions in the character of God.

# The Confessions / By Augustine of Hippo

01 And I learned, that you, oh God, discipline man for iniquity, and you made my soul to consume away like a spider. And I said, "Is Truth therefore nothing because it is not diffused through space finite or infinite?"

02 1 And you cried to me from afar: *"Yet truly, I AM that I AM."* And I heard, as the heart hears, nor had I room to doubt, and I should sooner doubt that I live than that Truth is not, which is clearly seen, being understood by those things which are made. And I beheld the other things below you, and I perceived that they neither altogether are, nor altogether are not, for they are, since they are from you, but are not, because they are not what you are. For that truly is which remains unchangeably. It is good then for me to hold fast unto God; for if I remain not in Him, I cannot in myself; but He remaining in Himself, renews all things. And you are the Lord my God, since you do not stand in need of my goodness.

03 And it was shown to me, that those things be good which yet are corrupted; which neither were they sovereignly good, nor unless they were good could be corrupted: for if sovereignly good, they were incorruptible, if not good at all, there were nothing in them to be corrupted. For corruption injures, but unless it diminished goodness, it could not injure. Either then corruption injures not, which cannot be; or which is most certain, all which is corrupted is deprived of good. But if they be deprived of all good, they shall cease to be.

04 For if they shall be, and can now no longer be corrupted, they shall be better than before, because they shall abide incorruptibly. And what more monstrous than to affirm things to become better by losing all their good? Therefore, if they shall be deprived of all good, they shall no longer be. So long therefore as they are, they are good: therefore whatsoever is, is good. That evil then which I sought, whence it is, is not any substance: for were it a substance, it should be good. For

either it should be an incorruptible substance, and so a chief good: or a corruptible substance; which unless it were good, could not be corrupted. I perceived therefore, and it was manifested to me that you, O God, made all things good, nor is there any substance at all, which you made not; and for that you made not all things equal, therefore are all things; because each is good, and altogether very good, because our God made all things very good.

## Reading Comprehension Questions

1. Describe the events of Augustine's life. How are his life and his struggles perhaps similar to our own?

2. How did Augustine become a Christian? What was his life like before and after this event?

3. How does Augustine define what is good? How are earthly goods different from spiritual goods?

WRITING

# Writing Prompt

Remember, writing is thinking. To help us to write and think more clearly, we will spend considerable time this year writing essays based on the texts we read in class. These essays are descriptive in nature and answer one question that arises from the material we are reading in class. In such an essay, the writer wants to explain the meaningful ideas contained in this text by reading and rereading the text under analysis to better explain that author's argument and the consequences of their ideas.

**Question**: *Read over the selection from Augustine's* Confessions. *How does this text attempt to solve (as much as that is possible) Euthyphro's Dilemma?*

# Writing

# Aristotle & Aquinas, Faith & Reason

**THE FALL OF THE ROMAN EMPIRE** introduced immense changes to Western Europe. We call this period the Middle Ages, the thousand or so years between the fall of the Roman Empire in AD 476 (when tribes known as the Scirians and Ostrogoths sacked Rome) and the fall of Constantinople, the capital of the Eastern Roman Empire, in 1453 (that great city fell to the Ottoman Turks). We use the words **Middle Ages** or "Medieval Europe" to refer to this period since they are a kind of "middle" period between the fall of the Roman Empire and the rise of Renaissance Italy in the late-14th and early-15th centuries.

When the Roman Empire fell, many new institutions arose to take its place. Trade routes collapsed, institutions to educate people disappeared, and the Roman bureaucracy failed to manage the former provinces of the Roman Empire. Institutions such as the Catholic Church, monasteries (close-knit communities of Christian believers), and a new system of organizing society called manorialism based on self-supporting farms developed in the wake of the fall of Rome. A new hybrid civilization formed from the remnants of the Roman world and the new barbarian kingdoms that had carved up that world for themselves such as the Anglo-Saxons in Roman Britain and the Franks in Roman Gaul. The Catholic Church was one of the few institutions to survive Rome's collapse largely intact. In time, the teachings of the Christian faith and the influence of the Catholic Church would become the most significant cultural influences in medieval Europe.

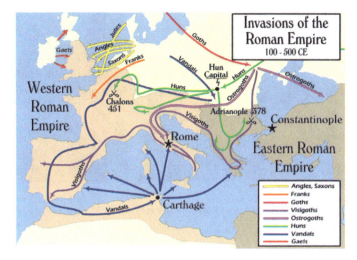

**FALL OF THE ROMAN EMPIRE**

For example, the Catholic Church and its literate bishops and priests provided administrative support to kings across medieval Europe. The bishop of Rome, called by the name Pope, derived from the Italian for *father*, served so many different functions in the city of Rome that he was almost the mayor of the city as well as the overseer of its churches. Many people also flocked to monasteries, old Roman villas converted into Christian communities.

The individuals who took vows and lived as monks spent each day engaged in hard farm labor, fellowship with other Christian monks, and reading the Bible. These monasteries and cathedral schools also helped educate youth across medieval Europe. That way, monks could fulfill their most important task: copying manuscripts of significant books that included not only the Bible but also all the other books worth preserving from the ancient world.

**A LECTURE AT A MEDIEVAL UNIVERSITY**

Local cathedral schools became the basis for the world's first universities founded in places like Bologna, Paris, Oxford, and Cambridge. As these universities gained a foothold and increased in number, a class of scholars known as the Scholastics emerged, Christian theologians well-trained in both Christian doctrine and Western philosophy. We will learn more about the accomplishments of the Scholastics, who developed many of the concepts in logic that we are studying this year. For our purposes, we'll look in depth at one of the most significant theologians amongst the Scholastics: Thomas Aquinas (1225-1274).

St. Thomas Aquinas (1225-1274) was born in Roccasecca, Italy, a town then located in the Kingdom of Naples. The youngest of four boys, Thomas was born into a noble Italian family, and Thomas' father had decided that Thomas should become a member of the clergy. He attended school at the relatively new University of Naples (it was founded in 1224) and completed his coursework in the medieval trivium of grammar, logic, and rhetoric. He then moved on to the more advanced subject matter, the quadrivium, of arithmetic, music, astronomy, and geometry. In addition to the normal curriculum of a medieval university student, Thomas had the opportunity to study the writings of Aristotle, which had only recently been translated into Latin. Aquinas would go on to teach theology at the University of Paris for most of his life.

Thomas' study of Aristotle prepared him for his most significant work, the *Summa Theologiae*. In this work, Aquinas "reconciled", to the extent that anyone could do such a thing, the tenets of the Christian faith with the ratio-

# Vocabulary

### Middle Ages
The approximately thousand-year period between the fall of the Roman Empire in 476 AD to the fall of Constantinople in 1453, whose worldview was shaped mainly by the influence of Christianity and the Catholic Church.

### The Scholastics
A movement amongst well-educated professors, bishops, and priests that arose in European universities during the Middle Ages.

### Thomas Aquinas
A philosopher and theologian from Italy, author of the *Summa Theologiae*, and amongst the most noteworthy members of the Scholastics; among his accomplishments are integrating the ideas of Aristotle with elements of Christian faith and doctrine (1225-1274 AD).

### *Summa Theologiae*
The great work of Thomas Aquinas wherein he attempts to reconcile the philosophy of Aristotle with the worldview of Christianity. Aquinas' great work was unfinished at the time of his death.

### Faith and Reason
A formula derived from Thomas Aquinas that helps to define the relationship between faith, the truths we find revealed to man in religious writings like the Bible, and reason, the truths that we primarily find through our intellect and our senses.

nal and logical framework of the Greek philosopher Aristotle. The rediscovery of Aristotle's writings in the High Middle Ages caused immense controversy in Western Europe. Aristotle seemed to possess an accurate, methodical, and comprehensive view of the world, including a powerful argument for God's existence that he may have derived independently of the Bible—and yet Aristotle was not a Christian. How could Aristotelian philosophy be reconciled with the teachings of the Christian faith?

Much of this reconciliation focuses on the relationship between **faith and reason**. God gave reason to man, Aquinas argued, and reason can solve certain problems and discover some truths with certainty. For instance, there is a rational argument for the existence of God—in fact, Aquinas took Aristotle's argument for an *Unmoved Mover*, adapted it for the Middle Ages, and composed five proofs of his own for God's existence. But reason has its limits, and one cannot discover everything about God. Subjects like the personality of God, the mercy of Jesus Christ, and other tenets of Christianity could only be received by faith and cannot be proved by reason alone. The *Summa Theologiae* covers numerous topics in philosophy, each one mimicking the format of a Scholastic debate. Each section begins with a question on a topic of great significance, then covers the arguments for and against each position on that topic. (We've provided an excerpt from the *Summa*

|| THOMAS AQUINAS / 1225 - 1274

appropriately focused on the nature of truth.) Aquinas cites the leading authorities on the subject, drawing from the Bible, Augustine, Boethius, and Aristotle.

Aquinas had been working on the *Summa Theologiae* since his time in Rome in 1265-1268, but he stopped working on this massive theological tome in 1273. Aquinas explained that he had undergone a religious experience that led him to stop working on the book right in the middle of a section on the nature of the sacraments. Aquinas wrote of this experience, "Everything I have written seems like straw compared to what I have seen and what has been revealed to me." Then, while journeying to a church council in Lyon, Thomas Aquinas died in the town of Fossanova, Italy on March 7, 1274. He was canonized as a saint and declared a Doctor of the Church in 1567.

*The Middle Ages are often derided as a time of superstition and ignorance, but in reality, it was a time of great courage, resilience, and fortitude. People in the Middle Ages overcame challenges ranging from the Vikings to the Black Death, and they introduced meaningful intellectual and academic advancements we still enjoy today.*

## Reading Comprehension Questions

1. Describe the world of the Middle Ages. How did Christianity come to exert so much influence over the medieval world?

2. What were the major events of Thomas' life? What do you think was the most significant moment in his time as a philosopher and a writer? Explain your reasoning.

# Summa Theologiae / By Thomas Aquinas

In this particular section of the *Summa Theologiae*, Aquinas explores the relationship between truth and the Christian worldview. Recall that each section in the *Summa* begins with a question on a topic of great significance, then covers the arguments for and against each position on that topic. We will read this selection of the *Summa* on three fronts.

One, we want to learn how we should engage with ideas with which we do not altogether agree. Two, we want to get a sense of how we should do an activity called *active reading*. And three, we want to become more familiar with the worldview that has in turn influenced so much of the Western tradition and the kind of Classical education we strive to teach.

# On Truth

### First Part, Question 16, Article 1: *Of Truth*

Since knowledge is of things that are true, after the consideration of the knowledge of God, we must inquire concerning truth. About this there are eight points of inquiry. Whether truth resides **only in the intellect**?

**Objection 1**: It seems that truth does not reside only in the intellect, but rather in things. For Augustine (*Soliloq.* ii, 5) condemns this definition of truth, "That is true which is seen"; since it would follow that stones hidden in the bosom of the earth would not be true stones, as they are not seen. He also condemns the following, "That is true which is as it appears to the knower, who is willing and able to know", for hence it would follow that nothing would be true, unless someone could know it. Therefore he defines truth thus: "That is true which is." It seems, then, that truth resides in things, and not in the intellect.

**Objection 2**: Further, whatever is true, is true by reason of truth. If, then, truth is only in the intellect, nothing will be true except in so far as it is understood. But this is the error of the ancient philosophers, who said that whatever seems to be true is so. Consequently **mutual contradictories** seem to be true as seen by different persons at the same time.

**Objection 3**: Further, "that, on account of which a thing is so, is itself more so", as is evident from **the Philosopher**. But it is from the fact that a thing is or is not, that our thought or word is true or false, as the Philosopher teaches (*Praedicam* iii). Therefore truth resides rather in things than in the intellect.

**On the contrary**, The Philosopher says (*Metaphysics* vi), "The true and the false reside not in things, but in the intellect".

*I answer that*, As the good denotes that towards which the appetite tends, so the true denotes that towards which the intellect tends. Now there is this difference between the **appetite and the intellect**, or any knowledge whatsoever, that knowledge is according as the thing known is in the knower, while appetite is according as the desirer tends towards the thing desired. Thus the term of the appetite, namely good, is in the object desirable, and the term of the intellect, namely truth, is in the intellect itself.

Now as good exists in a thing so far as that thing is related to the appetite—and hence the aspect of goodness passes on from the desirable thing to the appetite, in so far as the appetite is called good if its object is good; so, since the true is in the intellect in so far as it is conformed to the object understood, the aspect of the true must needs pass from the intellect to the object understood, so that also the thing understood is said to be true in so far as it has some relation to the intellect.

Now a thing understood may be in relation to an intellect either **essentially or accidentally**. It is related essentially to an intellect on which it depends as regards its essence; but accidentally to an intellect by which it is knowable; even as we may say that a house is related essentially to the intellect of the architect, but accidentally to the intellect upon which it does not depend.

Now we do not judge of a thing by what is in it accidentally, but by what is in it essentially. Hence, everything is said to be true absolutely, in so far as it is related to the intellect from which it depends; and thus it is that artificial things are said to be true as being related to our intellect. For a house is said to be true that expresses the likeness of the form in the architect's mind; and words are said to be true so far as they are the signs of truth in the intellect. In the same way natural things are said to be true insofar as they express the likeness of the species that are in the divine mind. For a stone is called true, which possesses the nature proper to a stone, according to the preconception in the divine intellect. Thus, then, truth resides primarily in the intellect, and secondarily in things according as they are related to the intellect as their principle.

Consequently there are various definitions of truth. Augustine says (*Of True Religion* xxxvi), "Truth is that whereby is made manifest that which is"; and Hilary says (*On the Trinity* v) that "Truth makes being clear and evident" and this pertains to truth according as it is in the intellect. As to the truth of things in so far as they are related to the intellect, we have Augustine's definition (*Of True Religion*. xxxvi), "Truth is a supreme likeness without any unlikeness to a principle": also Anselm's definition (*On Truth* xii), "Truth is rightness, perceptible by the mind alone"; for that is right which is in accordance with the principle; also Avicenna's definition (*Metaphysics* viii, 6), "The truth of each thing is a property of the essence which is immutably attached to it." The definition that "Truth is the equation of thought and thing" is applicable to it under either aspect.

## Reply to Objection 1
Augustine is speaking about the truth of things, and excludes from the notion of this truth, relation to our intellect; for what is accidental is excluded from every definition.

# Vocabulary & Annotations

### ...only in the intellect
Aquinas asks whether or not truth is objective (and thus exists outside the mind, as in the mind of God), or if truth is subjective (and thus exists only in the minds of the subject, a human being).

### ...mutual contradictories
Aquinas' insight here is similar to the Scholastic formulation of the *law of non-contradiction*, that something *x* cannot simultaneously be *non-x* at the same time.

### ...the Philosopher
Aquinas refers to Aristotle simply as the *Philosopher*.

### ...appetite and the intellect
Aquinas distinguishes between two different faculties of human beings, namely, their appetite and its desire for food and other physical things, and the intellect and its desire for truth.

### ...essentially or accidentally
Following Aristotle, Aquinas distinguishes between qualities that are essential to the subject, and must always be in that subject, and those that are merely accidentally. For human beings, we may consider reason as an *essential* faculty and a particular hair color as *accidental*.

**Reply to Objection 2**: The ancient philosophers held that the species of natural things did not proceed from any intellect, but were produced by chance. But as they saw that truth implies relation to intellect, they were compelled to base the truth of things on their relation to our intellect. From this, conclusions result that are inadmissible, and which the Philosopher Aristotle refutes (*Metaph*. iv). Such, however, do not follow, if we say that the truth of things consists in their relation to the divine intellect.

**Reply to Objection 3**: Although the truth of our intellect is caused by the thing, yet it is not necessary that truth should be there primarily, any more than that health should be primarily in medicine, rather than in the animal: for the virtue of medicine, and not its health, is the cause of health, for here the agent is not univocal. In the same way, the being of the thing, not its truth, is the cause of truth in the intellect. Hence the Philosopher says that a thought or a word is true "from the fact that a thing is, not because a thing is true."

## Reading Comprehension Questions

1. Why does it matter if truth exists "only in the intellect" but not also in the world?

2. Is the knowledge inside our minds like that of the plan of a house inside the mind of an architect?

3. Must truth be grounded in the "divine intellect," or in the mind of God? Why or why not?

ACTIVITY

# The First Act of the Mind / Terms

Each row contains a term, the authors use of that term, or a definition of that term suitable for students. If the row contains a quotation, write down a clear, intelligible definition of that term in the box provided. If the term is already defined for you, please find the quotation from the text that supports the appropriate definition.

| Term | Quotations from the Text | Quotations Rephrased as Definitions |
| --- | --- | --- |
| Knowledge | Since knowledge is of things that are true … | |
| Intellect | | The word *intellect* refers to our ability to reason, solve problems, and comprehend truth, although not in its entirety. |
| Accidental *versus* Essential | It is related essentially to an intellect on which it depends as regards its essence; but accidentally to an intellect by which it is knowable; even as we may say that a house is related essentially to the intellect of the architect, but accidentally to the intellect upon which it does not depend. | |

166 · SECTION II Propositions & Epistemology

ACTIVITY

# The Second Act of the Mind / Propositions

Each row contains an excerpt from the significant text included in this chapter. These selections include significant points and ideas that the author uses to build his argument and reach a meaningful conclusion, one that was not apparent at the beginning of their work. In the space provided, write a summary of the quotation and try to express it in the form of a proposition.

| Quotations from Text | Quotations rephrased as one (or more) Proposition(s) |
|---|---|
| ...The true and the false reside not in things, but in the intellect...Thus, then, truth resides primarily in the intellect, and secondarily in things according as they are related to the intellect as their principle... | |
| In the same way, the being of the thing, not its truth, is the cause of truth in the intellect. Hence the Philosopher says that a thought or a word is true 'from the fact that a thing is, not because a thing is true.' | |
| In the same way natural things are said to be true in so far as they express the likeness of the species that are in the divine mind. For a stone is called true, which possesses the nature proper to a stone, according to the preconception in the divine intellect. Thus, then, truth resides primarily in the intellect, and secondarily in things according as they are related to the intellect as their principle. | |

CHAPTER 5  The Medieval Consensus  ✦  167

ACTIVITY
# The Third Act of the Mind / **Inferences**

In the space below, create an "argument map", a visual way of representing the premises, assumptions, and ultimately the conclusion a writer is making in his or her work. You can also use this blank space provided to draw a "conversation map", a visual way of recording the discussion that your class had over this text.

WRITING

# Writing Prompt

Remember, writing is thinking. To help us to write and think more clearly, we will spend considerable time this year writing essays based on the texts we read in class. These essays are descriptive in nature and answer one question that arises from the material we are reading in class. In such an essay, the writer wants to explain the meaningful ideas contained in this text by reading and rereading the text under analysis to better explain that author's argument and the consequences of his or her ideas.

**Question**: *Based on the reading from the* Summa Theologiae, *how might one have certainty of the propositions that we think are true?*

**WESTMINSTER ABBEY / EXTERIOR**
*Photo by Charles Postiaux*

CHAPTER

# Epistemology & Truth

**ROADMAP**

- Learn about epistemology, the study of how we know what we know.
- Discover the difference between rationalism and empiricism.
- Read a selection from René Descartes' *Discourse on Method*.

**THALES OUTCOME Nº 4**

*A Truth Seeker* critiques a variety of truth statements and/or observations through research and scientific methodology.

The study of epistemology focuses on how we know what we know, and whether or not what we know is actually true. In this chapter, we will look at two of the main theories of epistemology: rationalism, that we come to know things through reason, and empiricism, that we come to know things through sense experience.

# Introduction to Epistemology

**EPISTEMOLOGY IS THE STUDY** of how we know what we know. The word **epistemology** comes to us from two Greek words: *episteme* meaning "knowledge" and "understanding," derived from the Greek word *pisteo* meaning "faith" and the word *logos* referring a "reason," a "reckoning," an "account," or "the study of" some important subject. The word *logos* is the basis of the common suffix *-logy* referring to the study of something. The study of how we know what we know and how we come to know it is an important subject. For there are always more things to discover, and the human mind is limited in its ability to gain, evaluate, and hold onto meaningful pieces of information. In short, epistemology focuses on these significant questions about how we come to know anything at all, and how we know whether or not such things are (or are not) true. But how does epistemology relate to the second act of the mind, that of judgment, and of propositions?

First, a **proposition** is an indicative statement that says something about the world, an affirmation that is either true or false. Remember that the first act of the mind is simple apprehension and focuses on terms, and that the second act of the mind is judgment and focuses on propositions. The mental act of judgment resides in evaluating the truth content of a propositional statement and judging whether or not that proposition is true. The process of evaluating a proposition is an act of the mind's personal, private inner judgments, and these are expressed in sensible, linguistic terms as a sentence. These sentences are formed according to the vocabulary and the grammatical structure of the language in which these propositions are expressed, so that the resulting proposition can be expressed in a variety of languages with the same overall meaning. For terms can be clear or unclear, and arguments valid and invalid, but only propositions are either true or false—and logic aims at truth.

Propositions are important because logic and reasoning aim towards truth, and propositions are the vehicles by which we convey truth, meaning, and value. We can only identify the difference between what is objectively stated (and its truth value) and how you subjectively feel upon hearing such-and-such a proposition. We want to try and separate what we feel in order to figure out what is said and what truth claims (if any) are found therein, and there are three significant theories of how a proposition corresponds to something in the world. They are as follows: the Correspondence Theory of Truth, the Pragmatic Theory of Truth, and the Coherence Theory of Truth (which we do not cover in this book). Let's examine the Correspondence Theory of Truth, a theory that derives from the writings of Aristotle.

The **Correspondence Theory of Truth** is formulated most clearly in Aristotle's *Metaphysics*. There, Aristotle states:

> *To say of what is that it is not, or of what is not that it is, is false, while to say of what is that it is, and of what is not that it is not, is true; so that he who says of anything that it is, or that it is not, will say either what is true or what is false; but neither what is nor what is not is said to be or not to be.*

## Vocabulary

*Write down this vocabulary in your notebook. These terms will help you better learn and understand the material in this chapter.*

### Epistemology
The study of how we know what we know.

### Proposition
A sentence that describes something about reality and in effect, asserts that something that is either true or false.

### The Correspondence Theory of Truth
A proposition is true in as much as that statement corresponds to reality (or the best evidence we have available).

### The Pragmatic Theory of Truth
A proposition is true in as much as that statement works--in short, truth is what works.

**ARISTOTLE & PLATO IN CONVERSATION**
*A relief made by Luca della Robbia in Florence, Italy (1437-1439)*

If we substitute the word *exists* for the word *is*, Aristotle's definition becomes much more clear: "he who says of anything that it [exists], or that it [does not exist], will say either what is true or what is false." That is, if we say that a certain state of affairs exists, and that state of affairs in fact does exist, then we can say that it is true. Thus, the word correspondence in the name *Correspondence Theory of Truth*: a proposition is true in as much as that proposition corresponds to reality. A state of affairs is true in as much as that thing exists, and a proposition is true inasmuch as that proposition corresponds to reality.

Moreover, the fact that such a thing is true is true independent of human experience—that state of affairs already exists whether we assent to it or not. Truth, in that sense, is outside ourselves, and we discover things or ideas to be true. If we investigate some proposition to see if it corresponds to reality, and we find that it does exist in some meaningful way, it existed before we investigated it. For example, if we say, *it is raining outside*, that statement is true in and as much as it is actually raining outside. The state of affairs encapsulated in the proposition *it is raining* either does or does not exist in the world outside our window—and it began raining before we happened to look outside. Such propositions are empirically verifiable and can be investigated through the means of observation, testing, weighing, measuring, and other similar methods, the kind of which Socrates identified to Euthyphro.

But, other propositions cannot be verified with the senses. Instead, they require the use of logical argumentation, the methods of inquiry that we are learning in this book. The veracity of such a proposition is easy enough to test with one's senses, for we can see, we can hear, we can even feel the real, physical presence of raindrops falling through the air. It is harder to verify the veracity of a statement like *all humans have free will* or *all humans are animals*, or propositions that are themselves the conclusions of rational arguments like *all created things have a cause*. These propositions require us to create arguments that verify these ideas, arguments supported by extensive evidence and sound, logical reasoning. If the terms of an argument are clear, its premises are true, and its structure is valid, then the conclusion of that argument must necessarily be true as well.

Another, more contemporary theory concerning what is true and what is not true comes from the philosophical school known as Pragmatism. The **Pragmatic Theory of Truth** states that a proposition is true in as much as that statement is useful to believe and works—in short, truth is what has utility and thus works. Three American philosophers at the turn of the 20th century are credited with inventing the Pragmatist school. They include Charles Sanders Peirce (1839-1914), a professor of mathematics and logic at Johns Hopkins University in Baltimore, the Harvard psychologist William James (1842-1910), and the Progressive, educational reformer and philosopher John Dewey (1859-1952). The most concise and formulaic definition of the pragmatist theory comes from the psychologist William James in his aptly-titled book, *The Problem of Knowledge*:

> *Pragmatism asks its usual question. Grant an idea or belief to be true, it says, what concrete difference will its being true make in any one's actual life? What experiences [may] be different from those which would obtain if the belief were false? How will the truth be realized? What, in short, is the truth's cash-value in experiential terms? The moment pragmatism asks this question, it sees the answer. True ideas are those that we can assimilate, validate, corroborate, and verify.*
>
> *False ideas are those we cannot. That is the practical difference it makes to us to have true ideas; that therefore is the meaning of truth, for it is all that truth is known as.*
>
> *The truth of an idea is not a stagnant property inherent in it. Truth happens to an idea. It becomes true, is made true by events. Its verity is in fact an event, a process, the process namely of verifying itself, its verification. Its validity is the process of its validation.... Any idea that helps us to deal, whether practically or intellectually, with either the reality or its belongings, that doesn't entangle our progress in frustrations, that fits, in fact, and adapts our life to the reality's whole setting, will agree sufficiently to meet the requirement. It will be true of that reality.*

When James (and other Pragmatists like Dewey) state that "truth happens to an idea", they mean that such an idea is proven to be true by the consequences that result from that idea. Human beings, in effect, prove a proposition is true by demonstrating that this idea works. For example, the laws of motion and thermodynamics are true in as much as those ideas help planes to fly and cannons to fire projectiles. Those ideas are true because they do, in reality, work. As James says, true ideas are those ideas "that we can assimilate, validate, corroborate, and verify". We verify such ideas through the methods of empirical science, a process that makes some intuitive sense when we focus on propositions that are empirically verifiable. Such principles work in as much as they correspond to the reality that govern the natural world, and the application of such principles allows human beings to manipulate those laws to

**JOHN DEWEY / 1859-1952**

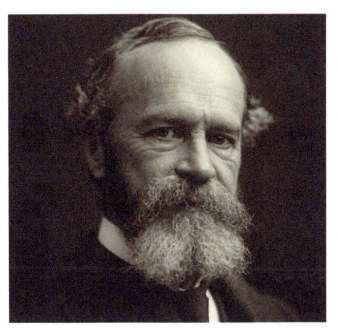

**WILLIAM JAMES / 1842 - 1910**

our benefit and demonstrate that such ideas work. But how might we know that an idea or an abstract term like truth, beauty, and goodness actually *work*? How long do we have to evaluate whether or not the idea work? Who gets to decide whether that idea really works, anyhow? The confirmation of whether or not an idea works resides in people arguing over the effects of such an idea, so that the basis for whether or not an idea is true or false resides in people. And people, like the gods, often quarrel.

At first glance, the correspondence theory and the pragmatic theory seem eerily similar to each other. The fact that a proposition corresponds to reality or if such a proposition works seems to be more of a word game. The chief difference between these two theories lies in the arbiter—the judge in the mental act of judgment—of who decides what is and what is not true. Under the correspondence view, a state of affairs exists, and this state of affairs exists outside of human experience. Truth in this sense exists outside of ourselves, and we human beings come to discover that truth in the same way we might discover the phases of the moon, the parts of a cell, or mathematical propositions.

We discover such things to be true in the same way in which Socrates taught Meno's servant in the *Meno* how to formulate the Pythagorean Theorem: Socrates asked questions that spurred a chain of reasoning in the servant until the servant discovered that theorem for himself; and the Pythagorean Theorem, moreover, was true whether or not the servant happened to discover it. In this way, we say that truth, and propositions that are true, exists outside ourselves, and we come to discover such things. And if a proposition is true, it is true whether or not we agree with it.

To its credit, the pragmatic theory emphasizes the role of human beings investigating and testing propositions. We should not take for granted whether or not a proposition is true, but subject it to testing and analysis. But the source of truth is not in ideas or things outside of human experience but in the very human beings evaluating these propositions. "Truth", as James described it, "is not a stagnant property", but something inherent to the idea or the thing itself, in direct contradiction to the *correspondence theory*. In contrast, the Pragmatists argued that an idea becomes true as human beings determine that this particular proposition is useful to believe, has utility, and thus works in a way that helps human beings. As James states, such true ideas "deal, whether practically or intellectually", with the affairs of this world and do not "entangle our progress in frustrations", perhaps even the same frustrations that spurred Euthyphro to hurry away from Socrates at the conclusion of *Euthyphro*. The source of truth is in the human beings who continually evaluate ideas and propositions in light of the usefulness of that particular idea, so that truth becomes subjective and relative to each person, not something objective, real, and existing outside of that person. To paraphrase Protagoras (490-420 BC), "man [becomes] the measure of all things" because only man can determine what works. This theory is, unfortunately, not a good foundation upon which to build one's life.

In this section, we will attempt to explain the epistemological gap between Aristotle and the Correspondence Theory and Pragmatists like Dewey and James and the Pragmatist Theory. We have almost two thousand years of history to cover, which we will attempt to do through the analysis of three significant texts in the Western canon: René Descartes' *Discourse on Method* (1637), John Locke's *An Essay Concerning Human Understanding* (1690), and David Hume's *An Enquiry Concerning Human Understanding* (1748), each of which interacts with and builds off the ideas presented in the earlier works and in other works of the time. We hope that by reading through these significant texts, we may have a better understanding of the world in which we live and a deeper appreciation for truth, beauty, and goodness. For now, let us turn from what we can know to how we come to know anything at all, and whether we know things through our senses (empiricism) or through our reason (rationalism).

## The Ways We Know What We Know: Rationalism & Empiricism

Recall that epistemology is the study of how we know what we know. The problem of knowledge becomes much harder when we consider how it is we know anything at all. There are two ways in which we come to gain knowledge about ourselves and the world around us: rationalism and empiricism. **Rationalism** is the idea that it is through reason— our unique ability to solve problems and create arguments—that we come to know anything at all about the world. We may have ideas within us that are so deeply ingrained within us and self-evident to us that we might consider these ideas to be innate, and it is by our reason that we know anything at all. Rationalism comes from the Latin *ratio*, *rationis* and refers to an "account", "judgment", or "reasoning", and rationalism argues that we gain knowledge through our reason, independently of what we perceive with our senses.

**Empiricism**, meanwhile, is the thesis that if we know anything at all about the world, we come to know it through our senses. The word *empiricism* comes to us from the Greek word for *experience*, and empiricists would argue that it is through our experience of the world that we come to have any knowledge of it. We have to see something, feel something, and hear something before we

# Vocabulary

**Rationalism**
From the Latin word for "reason or account," this is the belief that all knowledge comes in and through the powers of man's reason.

**Empiricism**
From the Greek word for "experience," this is the belief that all knowledge comes through the senses.

**Francis Bacon**
English philosopher and government official who is credited with inventing the Scientific Method. He lived from 1561 to 1626.

**Rene Descartes**
A French philosopher and mathematician who wanted to ground logic in the same sort of rigorous chain-of-reasoning found in geometry. He is most famous for his practice of *methodological skepticism* and the phrase, "I think; therefore, I am." He lived from 1596 to 1650.

**Methodological Skepticism**
In his philosophical works, Descartes famously described subjecting each and every belief he had to rigorous testing to make sure each belief was, in fact, true.

**FRANCIS BACON / 1561 - 1626**

**RENÉ DESCARTES / 1596 - 1650**

can really know anything about whatever that thing is. Some empiricists would argue that an idea that seems so deeply ingrained within us is only there because we experienced it. If we consider a moral axiom like "stealing is bad" and uncover the origins of that idea, we may find that our parents whispered it to us when we were much younger and that such an axiom is no more than our parents' opinion.

One of the earliest and most significant empiricists was Francis Bacon (1561-1626), an English civil servant and amateur scientist. In his most famous work, the *Novum Organum*, Bacon argued that the systematic study of the natural world through observation and testing could radically increase not only the knowledge we had of the world but also our understanding of the mysterious ways and processes of the natural world. We have an insight about the world and the way it works, and then by testing that insight through observation, reflection, and experimentation, we can devise "axioms, and from established axioms again new experiments", and from those experiments an ever-increasing body of knowledge.

Still, it is not so easy to make sure that our thoughts about the world truly correspond to what happens in the world. To see all the ways that the propositions we might form about the world fail to match up with the world itself, let's turn to René Descartes (1596-1650), a French mathematician and philosopher. Descartes loved the kind of certainty that is inherent to geometry, and Descartes applied the strict, straightforward chain of logical reasoning that one finds in mathematics to the conduct of philosophy and the acquisition of new knowledge. As geometry begins with simple, well-established axioms and builds upon these to form conclusions that, because they are grounded in true premises, must also be true, so Descartes wanted to ground his beliefs in propositions that he was absolutely sure were true. The following excerpt is from the *Discourse on Method*, where he proposes this rigorous method by which he jettisons the beliefs he cannot be certain are true. Descartes called such an approach methodological skepticism, wherein he subjected his beliefs to rigorous testing to make sure each belief was, in fact, true.

René Descartes was a rationalist, and in the following text, Descartes grounds all knowledge and all certainty about the world in his ability to reason. Let's read this text, draw out his argument, and evaluate it in light of the "Three Acts of the Mind." Then we will use Descartes' reasoning to examine all the ways in which a proposition may or may not correspond to reality and how we might have certainty of the ideas we have.

CHAPTER 6 Epistemology & Truth ◆ 179

## Reading Comprehension Questions

1. What is a proposition? Why is a proposition so important?

2. What is epistemology? rationalism? empiricism? Why is it so hard to really know anything at all?

3. What are the strengths and weaknesses of the *Pragmatic Theory of Truth*?

4. Who was Descartes, and how did he contribute to the study of epistemology?

# Discourse on Method / By René Descartes

## Part I

01 Good sense is, of all things among men, the most **equally distributed**; for every one thinks himself so abundantly provided with it, that those even who are the most difficult to satisfy in everything else, do not usually desire a larger measure of this quality than they already possess. And in this it is not likely that all are mistaken. The conviction is rather to be held as testifying that the power of judging aright and of distinguishing truth from error, which is properly what is called good sense or reason, is by nature equal in all men; and that the diversity of our opinions, consequently, does not arise from some being endowed with a larger share of reason than others, but solely from this, that we conduct our thoughts along different ways, and do not fix our attention on the same objects.

02 For to be possessed of a vigorous mind is not enough; the great need is rightly to apply it. The greatest minds, as they are capable of the highest excellences, are open likewise to the greatest aberrations; and those who travel very slowly may yet make far greater progress, provided they keep always to the straight road, than those who, while they run, forsake it...

## Part IV

03 I am in doubt as to the propriety of making my first meditations in the place above mentioned matter of discourse; for these are so metaphysical, and so uncommon, as not, perhaps, to be acceptable to every one. And yet, that it may be determined whether the foundations that I have laid are sufficiently secure, I find myself in a measure constrained to advert to them. I had long before remarked that, in relation to practice, it is sometimes necessary to adopt, as if above doubt, opinions which we discern to be highly uncertain, as has been already said; but as I then desired to give my attention solely to the search after truth, I thought that a procedure exactly the opposite was called for, and that I ought to reject as absolutely false all opinions in regard to which I could suppose the least ground for doubt, in order to ascertain whether after that there remained aught in my belief that was wholly indubitable.

04 Accordingly, seeing that our senses **sometimes deceive us**, I was willing to suppose that there existed nothing really such as they presented to us; and because some men err in reasoning, and fall into paralogisms, even on the simplest matters of geometry, I, convinced that I was as open to error as any other, rejected as false all the reasonings I had hitherto taken for demonstrations; and finally, when I considered that the very same thoughts (presentations) which we experience when awake may also be experienced when we are asleep, while there is at that time not one of them true, I supposed that all the objects (presentations) that had ever entered into my mind when awake, had in them no more truth than the **illusions of my dreams**.

05 But immediately upon this I observed that, whilst I thus wished to think that all was false, it was absolutely necessary that I, who thus thought, should be somewhat; and as I observed that this truth, **I think, therefore I am,** was so certain and of such evidence that no ground of doubt, however extravagant, could be alleged by the sceptics capable of shaking it, I concluded that I might, without scruple, accept it as the first principle of the philosophy of which I was in search.

06 In the next place, I attentively examined what I was and as I observed that I could suppose that I had no body, and that there was no world nor any place in which I might be; but that I could not therefore suppose that I was not; and that, on the contrary, from the very circumstance that I thought to doubt of the truth of other things, it most clearly and certainly followed that I was; while, on the other hand, if I had only ceased to think, although all the other objects which I had ever imagined had been in reality existent, I would have had no reason to believe that I existed; I thence concluded that I was a substance whose whole essence or nature consists only in thinking, and which, that it may exist, has need of no place, nor is dependent on any material thing; so that "I", that is to say, the mind by which I am what I am, is wholly distinct from the body, and is even more easily known than the latter, and is such, that although the latter were not, it would still continue to be all that it is.

07 After this I inquired in general into what is essential to the truth and certainty of a proposition; for since I had discovered one which I knew to be true, I thought that I must likewise be able to discover the ground of this certitude. And as I observed that in the words *I think, therefore I am*, there is nothing at all that gives me assurance of their truth beyond this, that I see very clearly that in order to think it is necessary to exist, I concluded that I might take, as a general rule, the principle, that all the things which we very clearly and distinctly conceive are true, only observing, however, that there is some difficulty in rightly determining the objects which we distinctly conceive.

*Descartes lived through tumultuous times in European history when people began to question the beliefs and ideas people had long simply assumed to be true. Thus, Descartes wants to have certainty of his beliefs, and he tries to ground the practice of philosophy in the straightforward chain of reasoning one finds in mathematics. Descartes wants to find one truth so self-evident and irrefutable on which to build a firm intellectual foundation for the rest of his life. This practice may be called* methodological skepticism, *but Descartes hopes to help others ward off skepticism by grounding the cultivation of knowledge in man's unique ability to reason.*

# Vocabulary & Annotations

### ...equally distributed
That is, all people possess common sense, the ability to work out problems, even if they are not as formally educated as an individual like Descartes.

### ...sometimes deceive us
Think of the way a straw "bends" when it is placed in a glass of water. The straw does not bend, but the interplay of light and water play a trick on your eyes. At times, our senses can mislead us and thus, information taken from sense perception and experience cannot serve as a ground for truth.

### ...illusions of my dreams
Some dreams can seem so real that we think as if we are awake when we are actually dreaming. Imagine, then, that we think we are awake, when we are actually dreaming?

### ...I think, therefore I am
The Latin phrase *cogito, ergo sum* is more famous and well-known. In this short sentence, Descartes finds evidence for his own existence based on his ability to reason and think: as long as he is thinking, he must also be existing.

## Reading Comprehension Questions

1. Why does Descartes doubt the knowledge gained through his senses?

2. How does Descartes go about deciding whether or not a belief he has is, in fact, true?

3. Explain the meaning of the quotation, "I think; therefore, I am," or in Latin, "cogito ergo sum."

4. How does Descartes gain certainty about the truth or falsity of a proposition?

ACTIVITY

# The First Act of the Mind / Terms

Each row contains a term, the authors use of that term, or a definition of that term suitable for students. If the row contains a quotation, write down a clear, intelligible definition of that term in the box provided. If the term is already defined for you, please find the quotation from the text that supports the appropriate definition.

| Term | Quotations from the Text | Quotation Rephrased as a Definition |
|---|---|---|
| Reason | ...that the power of judging aright and of distinguishing truth from error, which is properly what is called good sense or reason. | |
| Metaphysical | | *Metaphysical* refers to a branch of philosophy that examines the fundamental nature of being and non-being, and of certain unresolvable issues in philosophy like the nature of reality, the existence of universals, whether or not man's will is free, among other issues. |
| Proposition | ...I inquired in general into what is essential to the truth and certainty of a proposition. | |
| Thoughts, Objects, & Presentations | | The images that enter into the mind, a process Descartes says can happen whether he is awake or asleep. |

184 ✦ SECTION II Propositions & Epistemology

ACTIVITY

# The Second Act of the Mind / Propositions

Below are several quotations from the text. Rewrite each quotation as a proposition, according to the format in our textbook. Remember that in formulating arguments, we have to judge (the second act of the mind) whether or not a proposition is true.

| Quotations from Text | Quotation rephrased as one (or more) Proposition(s) |
|---|---|
| *And in this it is not likely that all are mistaken the conviction is rather to be held as testifying that the power of judging aright and of distinguishing truth from error, which is properly what is called good sense or reason, is by nature equal in all men.* | |
| *…when I considered that the very same thoughts (presentations) which we experience when awake may also be experienced when we are asleep, while there is at that time not one of them true, I supposed that all the objects (presentations) that had ever entered into my mind when awake, had in them no more truth than the illusions of my dreams.* | |
| *But immediately upon this I observed that, whilst I thus wished to think that all was false, it was absolutely necessary that I, who thus thought, should be somewhat; and as I observed that this truth, I think, therefore I am (cogito ergo sum), was so certain and of such evidence that no ground of doubt, however extravagant, could be alleged by the sceptics capable of shaking it, I concluded that I might, without scruple, accept it as the first principle of the philosophy of which I was in search* | |

ACTIVITY

# The Third Act of the Mind / Inferences

In the space below, create an "argument map," a visual way of representing the premises, assumptions, and ultimately the conclusion a writer is making in their work. You can also use this blank space provided to draw a "conversation map," a visual way of recording the discussion your class had over this text.

WRITING

# Writing Prompt

Remember, writing is thinking. To help us to write and think more clearly, we will spend considerable time this year writing essays based on the texts we read in class. These essays are descriptive in nature and answer one question that arises from the material we are reading in class. In such an essay, the writer wants to explain the meaningful ideas contained in this text by reading and rereading the text under analysis to better explain that author's argument and the consequences of their ideas.

**Question**: *Descartes famously removed from his understanding all of the beliefs of which he did not have absolute certainty. What particular kinds of beliefs did he remove and why? What was the only belief of which he could have any certainty? What implications might this have for the course of Western philosophy which will follow after?*

# Writing

WESTMINSTER ABBEY / INTERIOR
*Photo by Cajeo Zhang*

CHAPTER

# Categorical Propositions

## ROADMAP

- Learn about Categorical Propositions and their importance to the study of logic.

- Identify the forms of categorical propositions like A, E, I, and O Statements.

- Complete exercises to help you master taking long, complex statements and putting them into logical form.

**THALES OUTCOME**

**Nº 5**

*A Critical Thinker* analyzes a variety of truth statements and/or observations through a dialectic examination of facts and assumptions.

This chapter focuses on simplifying categorical propositions, the ability to take a long, complicated sentence and reduce it down to its simplest components. That way, it becomes easier to evaluate whether or not a sentence expresses a true proposition.

CHAPTER 7 Categorical Propositions ✦ 191

# Introduction to Categorical Propositions

**THE SECOND ACT OF THE MIND** is the mental act of **judgment**, with its logical expression being a proposition. A **proposition** will appear in the form of a declarative sentence, a kind of sentence that joins a subject to a predicate and affirms or denies something about the world. These kinds of sentences describe something about reality. Such sentences may or may not be true, and it is your job to determine whether or not they are true—that is, after all, what judgment is. The act of judging is the act by which the mind relates two concepts and determines whether or not such a proposition indeed corresponds to reality. In this chapter, we will examine a kind of logic called **categorical logic**, which focuses on terms that represent categories of things. For this reason, in order to be in proper categorical form, the subject and predicate must be in the form of a noun or a noun phrase, which is why they are often referred to as subject-terms and predicate-terms. And for that, we take a relatively long and difficult sentence and reduce it down to its simplest component parts. Such a simple, formulaic sentence is called a **categorical proposition**.

A categorical proposition is made up of four parts: a word like *all, some,* or *no*, which is known as a **quantifier**, the subject, the predicate, and a linking verb known as a **copula** that joins the subject to the predicate. The copula will typically be a linking verb like *is* or *are*. The simplicity of these categorical propositions makes it easier to evaluate whether or not such a proposition is true or false. We should include one helpful tip about the copula. We do not use the copula as a helping verb (such as *the birds are flying*). Instead, the copula should always be a linking verb to join the subject to the predicate, and it is the predicate that affirms or denies something about that subject (such as *birds are animals*).

Let's examine the idea of a subject and a predicate in a categorical proposition more closely.

## Subjects and Predicates

A **subject** is the principal actor of the sentence and refers to what we are talking about. The **predicate**, meanwhile, is the part of the sentence that describes the

*The second act of the mind is "judgment," the act of looking at a proposition and determining whether or not it is true or false. As apprehension dealt with terms, so judgment deals with propositions. The logic behind categorical propositions is that if we can reduce a sentence down to a simple formula, we can more easily evaluate that proposition for its truth content.*

## Vocabulary

**Judgment**
The second act of the mind, which connects one term with another to form a proposition.

**Proposition**
A sentence that joins together a term with another term in order to communicate some idea about the world, an idea that could either be true or false.

**Categorical Proposition**
The particular arrangement of terms in a proposition.

**Categorical Logic**
The kind of logic that focuses on the relationship between categories of things.

**Copula**
The linking verb that joins together the subject and the predicate in a categorical proposition; most often, it is a form of the verb *to be*.

**Quantifiers**
These are words such as *all, no, some, some...not* that indicate the *quantity* and the *quality* of a given proposition.

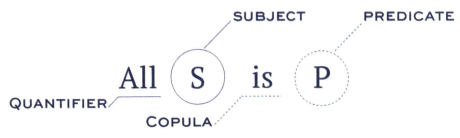

## THE PARTS OF A PROPOSITION

subject's state of being or what the subject is doing. In short, the predicate is what we are saying about the subject, what we affirm or deny about the subject. In logic, the subject and predicate are identical to the grammatical subject and predicate. Such propositions are only talking about one thing—the subject—and they are only making one assertion about that subject—the predicate.

A categorical proposition is further distinguished by two elements: that proposition's quality and its quantity. The **quality** of a proposition refers to whether or not a proposition is affirmative or negative. An **affirmative** proposition affirms something is true about the subject, whereas a **negative** proposition denies something about the subject and thus says that it is false.

Then, propositions are distinguished by their **quantity**. Typically, when we use the word *quantity*, we refer to the number of things that exist in the world. In logic, the word *quantity* refers to how much of the subject we are talking about, and there are two options for quantity: universal and particular. The term **universal** would refer to all of the subject, and the term **particular** would refer to only part of the subject. When we say *all men are mortal*, we mean that the idea of being *mortal* is predicated, or true, of *all men* everywhere. Meanwhile, when we use a word like *some*, as in *some birds are flying creatures*, we refer to only a particular group of birds—that is, those birds that are capable of flight, whereas not all birds actually can fly.

Amongst the ideas of affirmative and negative and universal and particular, we can make four different combinations. That is, we can have four different statements: universal and affirmative, universal and negative, particular and affirmative, and particular and negative. Each statement is identified by a quantifier, one of four words — *some*, *some not*, *no*, and *all*—that tells us how much of the subject the predicate describes. **Quantifiers** provide the quantity and quality of a proposition. In order to easily categorize types of positions, beginning with Aristotle, logicians gave a vowel to represent each type of proposition. *A* is used for the universal affirmative, *E* for the universal negative, *I* for the particular affirmative, and *O* for the particular negative. The vowels come from the Latin verbs *affirmo*, meaning "I affirm," and *nego*, meaning "I deny." The *a* in *affirmo* gives us the *A* in *A Statements*, the *i affirmo* the *I* in *I Statements*, and the *e* in *nego* the *E* in *E Statements*, and the *o* in *nego* the *O* in *O Statements*.

See the diagram and the chart on the following page as a visual means of summarizing this information and the four different types of statements: *A Statements*, *E Statements*, *I Statements*, and *O Statements*.

| Statement | Quantifier | From the Latin... | Quality | Quantity |
|---|---|---|---|---|
| *A Statement* / All S is P | A / All | *Affirmo* | Affirmative | Universal |
| *E Statement* / No S is P | E / No | N*e*go | Negative | Universal |
| *I Statement* / Some S is P | I / Some | Aff*i*rmo | Affirmative | Particular |
| *O Statement* / Some S is not P | O / Some...not | Neg*o* | Negative | Particular |

These are the *forms* you will need to reduce those long, declarative sentences down to. They are like molds for unformed clay or mathematical formulas for which you plug in the appropriate values. The idea is that if we take a sentence and remove all of its modifiers to make that sentence read as clearly and succinctly as we can, we can understand the truth content of that sentence in a more straightforward and logical fashion and determine if that proposition is true.

Put another way, if we are to take a more complicated declarative sentence and reduce it down to its simplest possible components, it will look something like one of the four different categorical propositions listed above. The elements that compose a proposition include its quantifier, the copula (the linking verb joining the subject and the predicate together), and the subject and predicate.

Let's examine categorical propositions more closely. We only have four forms, which makes it easier to create clear, concise definitions. This is all the more important in philosophical thinking and logical argumentation because we want to make our arguments as clear and concise as possible.

## A Statements: All S is P.

This type of categorical proposition is known as an **A statement**, with the designation A coming from the first vowel of the Latin verb *affirmo*, meaning "I affirm." An *A statement* is a *universal affirmative* proposition, in that it affirms something is true (and is always true) about the entirety of the subject. If we are to state the claim that *All men are mortal*, we mean all *men* at all times and

# Vocabulary

**Subject**
The main actor in the sentence; the principal person, place, or thing that the sentence is about.

**Predicate**
This part of the sense includes the verb and everything following the verb; this part of the sentence either affirms or denies the subject of the sentence.

**Quality**
The notion that a predicate may affirm or deny something about the subject.

**Quantity**
The notion that a subject is either universal or particular.

**Affirmative**
When the proposition affirms something about the subject.

**Negative**
When the proposition denies something about the subject.

**Universal**
The notion that the propositions discuss or encompasses the entire category of a subject.

**Particular**
The notion that the subject of a proposition only discusses or touches upon one particular, undefined group within that subject.

**Quantifiers**
These are words such as "all," "some," or "no" that indicate the quantity and the quality of a given proposition.

in all places are *mortal* (and all women, too, as the word *man* is inclusive of both men and women). An A statement is phrased so that whatever the predicate says about the subject, it applies to the whole of the subject at all times and at places. The form for an A statement is *All S is P*. (At times and in other logic textbooks, brackets are put around the subject *S* and the predicate *P* to help distinguish those parts of a categorical proposition).

## E Statements: No S is P

This type of categorical proposition is known as an E statement, with the designation E coming from the first vowel of the Latin verb *nego*, meaning "I deny." An E statement denies something is entirely and universally true about a subject. That is, an E statement is a universal negative proposition, in that it denies something is true (and it is always not true) about the entirety of the subject. The form for an E statement is *No S is P*, with the subject represented by S and the predicate going represented by P.

As an example, let's consider the phrase, *No men are angels*. This statement implies that of all *men* everywhere and at all times, are not *angels*. That is, there is something fundamentally wrong with human nature (this assertion is one of the propositions in the Federalist Papers, for instance), that keeps all of us from acting like angels. As a result, we can deny that all *men* everywhere are in fact *angels*—or, more simply, that *no men are angels*. Human beings are human beings, and human beings are not angels.

To review, A statements and E statements are both universal in what they affirm or deny about the subject. Whatever the subject is, the predicate says that either all of the subject is always this or that all of the subject is never under any circumstances joined together or associated with that predicate.

**Note on Singular Terms** The subjects of some propositions may refer to a real person. This, in philosophical terms, is known as a *particular*, or a real, extant thing which can be seen in the real world. One example of that a proposition is the statement, *Socrates is a man* in the famous syllogism, *All men are mortal; Socrates is a man; therefore, Socrates is a mortal*. Treat any proposition that contains a singular, particular subject as a universal proposition—either an A statement or an E statement. These are treated under the quantity of universal propositions because you cannot really divide someone or something that is already a singular whole.

## I Statements: Some S is P

This type of categorical proposition is known as an I statement, with the designation I coming from the second vowel of the Latin verb *affirmo*, meaning "I affirm." An I statement affirms something is true of the subject, but only for a select (but undefined group) within that subject. In logic, the quantifier *some* means "at least one." The form for an I statement is *Some S is P*.

As an example, let's consider the categorical proposition, *Some birds are flying creatures*. In this example, we are affirming that of all the *birds* in existence, only *some* of them, an undefined-group of them, are also *flying creatures*. Such birds would include storks, blue jays, hummingbirds, and condors.

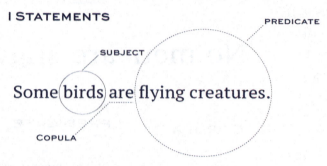

## O Statements: Some S is not P

The last categorical proposition is an **O Statement**, with the designation O coming from the second vowel of the Latin verb *nego*, meaning "I deny." An O statement denies something is true in some instances but not necessarily in all circumstances where that subject exists. Put another way, an O statement says an undefined-group within that subject is not identified with or joined to its corresponding predicate. The formula for an O statement is Some S is not P.

As an example, let's consider the categorical proposition *Some birds are not flying creatures*. In this example, we are denying that of all the *birds* in existence, only *some* of them, an undefined-group of them, are *flying creatures*. Such birds would include penguins, ostriches, and emus. These birds (and others) are not flying creatures.

In conclusion, there are four types of categorical propositions, four ways we can affirm or deny something about all or part of the subject. When we speak of anything, we are speaking about either *all* or *part* of something, and we are saying that something either *is true* or *false* of whatever that thing is. In logic, we simplify the act of evaluating propositions by reducing longer sentences into shorter, formulaic statements. That way, we can more easily evaluate whether or not that statement is *true* or *false*.

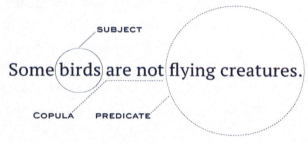

## Vocabulary

**A Statement**
A universal affirmative proposition that affirms something is true (and is always true) about the entirety of the subject. A Statements take the form, "A [S] is [P]".

**E Statement**
A universal negative proposition that denies something is true (and it is always not true) about the entirety of the subject. E Statements take the form, "No [S] is [P]".

**I Statement**
A particular affirmative proposition that affirms something is sometimes true, or is true part of the time, about a certain undefined part of the subject. I Statements take the form, "Some [S] is [P]".

**O Statement**
A particular negative proposition that denies something is true, or is not true part of the time, about a certain undefined part of the subject. O Statements take the form, "Some [S] is not [P]".

ACTIVITY

# Guided Notes / Categorical Propositions

**Instructions**: Given the amount of vocabulary in this chapter, take a moment to fill in the blank for each of the four categorical propositions in the space below.

| Statement | Formula | Quantifier | From the Latin... | Quality | Quantity |
|---|---|---|---|---|---|
| A Statement | All S is P | | | | |
| E Statement | | E / No | | | |
| I Statement | | | I affirmo | | |
| O Statement | | | | Negative | |

CHAPTER 7 Categorical Propositions ✦ 197

ACTIVITY

# Guided Notes / Categorical Propositions

**Instructions:** Given the amount of vocabulary in this chapter, take a moment to write down a definition for each term in the table provided below as they appear in the reading.

| Vocabulary Word | Definition |
|---|---|
| Quantifier | |
| Quality | |
| Quantity | |
| Subject | |
| Predicate | |
| Affirmative | |
| Negative | |
| Universal | |
| Particular | |
| Copula | |

ACTIVITY

# Recognizing Categorical Propositions

**Instructions**: Read over each of the following categorical propositions and identify whether it is an example of an A statement, an E statement, an I statement, or an O statement.

Example: *All animals are creatures who rule by force.*

*This categorical proposition is an example of an* A statement, *marked by the quantifier* all. *Moreover, this categorical proposition is affirming something is true—creatures who rule by force—of all the subject, in that all animals are creatures who rule by force.*

1. All human beings are beings who desire to know.

    _____ Statement

2. No human beings are irrational animals.

    _____ Statement

3. Some birds are creatures capable of swimming.

    _____ Statement

4. Some snakes are not poisonous.

    _____ Statement

5. No monarchies are democracies.

    _____ Statement

6. All animals are creatures who learn through experience.

    _____ Statement

7. All philosophers are people who love wisdom.

    _____ Statement

8. No doctors are people who are uneducated.

    _____ Statement

9. No snakes are creatures with legs.

    _____ Statement

ACTIVITY

# Recognizing Categorical Propositions

**Instructions**: Read over each of the following categorical propositions and identify whether it is an example of an A statement, an E statement, an I statement, or an O statement.

10. Some monkeys are curious creatures.

    _____ Statement

11. Some monkeys are not curious creatures.

    _____ Statement

12. All virtues are habits of moral excellence.

    _____ Statement

13. No vices are habits worth pursuing.

    _____ Statement

15. All monarchies are ruled by one person.

    _____ Statement

14. Some animals are more equal than others.

    _____ Statement

15. Some birds are not colorful creatures.

    _____ Statement

15. Some spiders are creatures who can dance.

    _____ Statement

16. All insects are creatures with six legs.

    _____ Statement

17. No creatures with six legs are spiders.

    _____ Statement

18. All water is wet.

    _____ Statement

19. All scientists are people who examine causes.

    _____ Statement

# Translating Statements

**WE SEE THAT REGULAR,** ordinary sentences assert something to be true about the world. To make it easier to determine if these propositions are true, we can rearrange these sentences with all their modifiers and descriptive words into a strict, straightforward logical form. That is, we take an ordinary sentence and reformat it so that it fits one of the four forms of categorical propositions. That way, we can better understand what these sentences are actually saying and evaluate the truth content of these propositions.

To do this, we have to carefully evaluate what the sentence is actually saying. Then, we have to identify the categorical proposition that this sentence matches up with. Is the sentence making a universal claim about a subject, that either something always is or is always not true about that subject? In that case, we should use an A statement or an E statement. Is it making a claim about a small, particular, undefined group? In that case, we should use either an I or an O statement—an I statement if it affirms something about the subject, or an O statement if it denies something about a particular group within that subject. Once we have figured out how much of a subject we are talking about, then we have to turn the predicate into a noun or a noun phrase.

Let's take an example from the wonderful world of birds. The declarative sentence *All birds can fly* seems true enough at face value. One would even be tempted to say that a bird is defined by its ability to fly. But if we reduce this sentence down to the categorical proposition *All birds are flying creatures*, we see this definition falls apart. All we need are a few birds that cannot fly—emus, for instance—to see that the A statement *All birds are flying creatures* is false and does not actually correspond to reality. Other birds would include ostriches, penguins, puffins, and emus. The ordinary sentence, *Many birds cannot fly* seems to be true at face value as well. The word *many* as with many other indefinite pronouns, refers to a certain, undefined number within a much larger group, and would imply that this statement matches with a *particular* categorical proposition of an O statement. We can rearrange that ordinary sentence, *Many birds cannot fly* to *Some birds cannot fly* and then to *Some birds are flightless creatures*, so that the meaning of the sentence fits into the formula of an O statement.

**BIG IDEA**

*At its heart, logic is the art of right thinking and the ability to distinguish truth from error. The skill of taking a sentence and translating it into categorical form is important to the study of logic because a proposition, once reduced to its simplest component parts, becomes easier to evaluate whether it is true or false.*

## Table / Steps for Translating Categorical Propositions

| Step | Explanation |
|---|---|
| Step 1 | Read over the sentence to determine what the sentence is actually saying. |
| Step 2 | Identify the subject and the predicate—who is the main actor in the sentence, and what is he/she/it doing? |
| Step 3 | Ask yourself, "Is the sentence talking about all members of that subject [universal], or only a certain group [particular]?" |
| Step 4 | Ask yourself, "What is being affirmed or denied about the subject? Is the predicate already a noun?" Remember that a term can only be a noun, so you have to turn the predicate into a noun phrase. To do so, use a relative pronoun like who, which, that which, or that; or use the word one, ones, creatures, things, etc. |
| Step 5 | Identify the correct categorical proposition that best fits this sentence. |
| Step 6 | Rewrite the sentence in the form of a categorical proposition. |

## Table / Categorical Propositions

| Statement | Formula | Quantifier | From the Latin… | Quality | Quantity |
|---|---|---|---|---|---|
| A Statement | All S is P | A / All | *Affirmo* | Affirmative | Universal |
| E Statement | No S is P | E / No | *Nego* | Negative | Universal |
| I Statement | Some S is P | I / Some | *Affirmo* | Affirmative | Particular |
| O Statement | Some S is not P | O / Some…not | *Nego* | Negative | Particular |

ACTIVITY

# Translating Categorical Propositions

**Instructions**: Read over each sentence, translate that sentence into its appropriate categorical proposition, and indicate the type of statement it is in the blank provide (A, E, I, or O).

1. Animals settle their disputes by fighting.

   _____

   _____ Statement

2. Stronger animals rule over weaker animals.

   _____

   _____ Statement

3. Many birds can fly.

   _____

   _____ Statement

4. A handful of superheroes get their powers through technology.

   _____

   _____ Statement

5. Happiness is based in virtue.

   _____

   _____ Statement

6. Human beings act in order to be happy.

   _____

   _____ Statement

ACTIVITY

# Translating Categorical Propositions

**Instructions**: Read over each sentence, translate that sentence into its appropriate categorical proposition, and indicate the type of statement it is in the blank provide (A, E, I, or O).

7. A friend is someone who wants your good (paraphrased from Aristotle's *Rhetoric*).

_____

_____ Statement

8. Under no circumstances can we trust the information we gain from our senses.

_____

_____ Statement

9. We do not have any innate ideas.

_____

_____ Statement

10. All knowledge comes through the senses.

_____

_____ Statement

11. The human mind is a blank slate.

_____

_____ Statement

12. Truth happens to an idea.

_____

_____ Statement

ACTIVITY

# Translating Categorical Propositions

**Instructions**: Read over each sentence, translate that sentence into its appropriate categorical proposition, and indicate the type of statement it is in the blank provide (A, E, I, or O).

13. All of humanity is chained in a cave, watching shadows flicker on a wall.

   _____

   _____ Statement

14. Most men don't lead lives of quiet desperation (paraphrased from Henry David Thoreau)

   _____

   _____ Statement

15. No thing exists in the understanding which did not come to it from the senses.

   _____

   _____ Statement

16. We can have no knowledge of anything beyond sense experience.

   _____

   _____ Statement

17. All moral values are ideas, albeit complicated ones.

   _____

   _____ Statement

18. Not all superheroes wear capes.

   _____

   _____ Statement

WESTMINSTER ABBEY / EXTERIOR
*Photo by Hulki Okan Tabak*

CHAPTER

# Relationships of Equivalence

### ROADMAP

✦ Learn about relationships of equivalences—that is, the kinds of inferences that can be drawn from only one premise. These include the ideas of *obversion*, *conversion*, and *contraposition*.

✦ Learn about the distribution of terms, and how a term in a proposition may be fully identified with or excluded from a corresponding term in that proposition.

✦ Read a selection from John Locke's *Essay Concerning Human Understanding*.

### THALES OUTCOME
### Nº 4

*A Critical Thinker* analyzes a variety of truth statements and/or observations through a dialectic examination of facts and assumptions.

We will continue our focus on being a "Critical Thinker" because knowing how much of a term is distributed, or how much of a term is identified with, equated to, or has knowledge of its corresponding term, is crucial to knowing whether or not an idea corresponds to reality.

# Relationships of Equivalence

IN THIS CHAPTER, we will discuss **relationships of equivalence**, ways that we can alter propositions and still convey the same truth-content. That is, we can make changes to a proposition, but that proposition still makes a meaningful, logically-identical truth claim. For example, we can change a proposition's quantity and quality or interchange the subject with the predicate or the predicate with the subject, all of which allow us to analyze these propositions from different viewpoints. The rules around relationships of equivalence allow us to make changes like these without altering the facts of the sentence. This is often called a **direct inference** or an *immediate inference*; a direct inference is the act of drawing a conclusion from only one premise.

In this chapter, we will discuss three relationships of equivalence known as conversion, obversion, and contraposition. We will begin with conversion, the process of interchanging the subject and the predicate, but to help understand this concept, we will begin with a concept you have most likely never heard of before: the distribution of terms.

The word **distribution** in logic relates to how that term is used in a sentence. A term is **distributed** in a proposition if that term refers to all that is in its category. A term is **undistributed** in a proposition when it refers to only some of that category. We can think of distribution as one term being equated with another term. A subject and a predicate each belong to their own class of things, and the idea of distribution refers to whether or not we can equate a subject to a general class of things found in the predicate and vice versa—or if we can be certain that the term is most certainly not identified with that corresponding term. In logic, we say that a term is distributed if we know a term is fully and wholly identified with the class of that corresponding term, or if we know that it is most certainly not fully and wholly identified with such a class. For instance, the term *man* is distributed in the proposition *all men are mortal* since all *men* are identified with the category of being *mortal*. On the other hand, the term *birds* in *some birds are flying creatures* is undistributed since we are unsure of how many *birds* are also those *flying creatures* to which the subject refers.

The idea of being distributed or undistributed is important in logic. The extent to which a subject or a predicate is distributed or undistributed is one way to determine whether or not the argument is valid or invalid. Moreover, the idea of a term's distribution factors

*The idea of whether or not a term is "distributed" may not seem very relevant to our lives today but if you create an argument with an undistributed term, that argument will not make sense. Moreover, your ability to identify whether or not a term is distributed will help become a quicker and more critical thinker.*

208 • SECTION II Propositions & Epistemology

## Vocabulary

**Relationships of Equivalence**
These are ways to alter a proposition to create ones that have the same meaning.

**Direct Inference**
The act of drawing a conclusion from only one premise. Direct inference is also called *immediate inference*.

**Inference**
The act of drawing a conclusion from one or more premises.

**Distribution**
The idea of "distribution" and the "distribution of terms" refers to how much of one term is identified with, or found in, the corresponding term it is joined to in a proposition. In negative propositions, distribution refers to the extent to which a term is excluded from its corresponding term.

**Distributed**
A term is *distributed* if it refers to all of the things that are in its category.

**Undistributed**
A term is undistributed if it refers to only some of the things that are in its category.

into whether or not that statement can be converted. As a helpful analogy, if a term is distributed in the premise in which it initially appears, then that term will be strong enough to bear the "weight" that the conclusion will place upon that term. A term is a fundamental unit of meaning and when a term is used in a proposition, it can be either a subject or a predicate. The extent to which a term is "distributed" depends on the type of categorical proposition in use.

Let's go over the rules for what terms are distributed and what implications we can draw from this relationship. The rules governing the distribution of terms are as follows:

*The subject term is always distributed in universal propositions—that is, A statements and E statements.*

*The predicate term is always distributed in negative propositions—that is, E statements and O statements.*

## A Statements: All S is P

In an A statement, the subject term is always distributed, but the predicate is undistributed. That is, the subject is always equated with and subsumed within the predicate term with which it is joined together. Let's consider the proposition, *All men are mortal*. The subject *man* is found within the predicate of mortal. *Man* can be wholly identified with and found within the concept of being *mortal*, so that for all *men* everywhere, they are all *mortal*. That's what it means that the subject is distributed in a categorical proposition.

But it is not true that the idea of being mortal is confined to just men—in fact, there are many more mortal things out there than just human beings, for all living things are subject to death and thus mortal. The predicate term, then, is not distributed—that is, it is not equated with or found within the idea of mankind. The predicate term is by definition a "larger" or more "general" class of things than the subject; in fact, the predicate has to be larger or else the subject could not be found within that predicate.

Let's consider one more proposition: *All stars are beautiful*. It would be hard to contest this statement, for certainly stars are objects of great beauty and wonder. As in an A statement, the subject-term is distributed so that the subject *stars* is found within and identified with the predicate of *beautiful things*. The predicate term *beautiful things* is not, however, distributed because we cannot wholly identify *beautiful things* with *stars*. We know intuitively that there are many more *beautiful things* in the world around us that are, in fact, not *stars*.

CHAPTER 8 Relationships of Equivalence ♦ 209

## E Statements: No S is P

The predicate is always distributed in a negative statement such as an E or O statement. Since an E statement is both universal and negative, both the subject term and the predicate term are distributed. That is because the way an E statement is constructed, we can be certain that both subject and predicate are fully, wholly, and absolutely separated from each other. As a result, we can be certain the subject and predicate are distributed: we know that neither subject nor predicate are identified with, equated to, or have any knowledge of their corresponding term. Let's take a look at an example: *No monkeys are rational beings*.

That is, *monkeys* have not demonstrated the ability to reason and work out problems on a scale commensurate with human beings— although great science fiction movies have been made on the premise that one day monkeys will develop mental powers rivaling that of humans (i.e., *Planet of the Apes*).

As with the previous example, this E statement and the distribution of terms within that statement imply that of all the *monkeys* observable in the world, none of them display the kind of rational powers human beings do. We can see that of the subject-term *monkeys*, no monkey is identified with, equated to, or has any knowledge of being *rational beings*.

## I Statements: Some S is P

An I statement is both particular and affirmative, and so neither the subject nor the predicate term are distributed in an I statement. In an I statement, both the subject and the predicate are undistributed. The subject is distributed only in a universal statement, such as A and E, and the predicate is only distributed in a negative statement, such as E and O.

That is, neither the subject nor the predicate are fully identified with or separated from their corresponding term. Instead, there will always be some overlap between the two, and because of that overlap, we cannot say that these terms are distributed. We can never be sure of how much of the subject the proposition is referring to, and as a result, we say that the subject is undistributed.

Let's consider some examples: *Some birds are flying creatures*. The way this categorical propositional is written is that of all the *birds* extant in the world, a certain number of them are most certainly *flying creatures*. This statement we know to be true at face value because we have seen many birds which can fly, but we also know of birds that lack the unique ability to soar to the heavens.

## Vocabulary

**Copula**
The linking verb that joins together the subject and the predicate in a categorical proposition; most often, it is a form of the verb *to be*.

**Subject**
The main actor in the sentence; the principal person, place, or thing that the sentence is about.

**A Statement**
A universal affirmative proposition that affirms something is true (and is always true) about the entirety of the subject. A Statements take the form, "All S is P".

**E Statement**
A universal negative proposition that denies something is true (and it is always not true) about the entirety of the subject. E Statements take the form, "No S is P".

**I Statement**
A particular affirmative proposition that affirms something is sometimes true, or is true part of the time, about a certain undefined part of the subject. I Statements take the form, "Some S is P.".

**O Statement**
A particular negative proposition that denies something is true, or is not true part of the time, about a certain undefined part of the subject. O Statements take the form, "Some S is not P".

## Chart / Distribution of Terms

| Statement | Quality | Quantity | Subject | Predicate |
|---|---|---|---|---|
| A Statement / All S is P | Affirmative | Universal | Distributed | Undistributed |
| E Statement / No S is P | Negative | Universal | Distributed | Distributed |
| I Statement / Some S is P | Affirmative | Particular | Undistributed | Undistributed |
| O Statement / Some S is not P | Negative | Particular | Undistributed | Distributed |

Because the subject does not state which birds fly and which do not, we say that the term is "undistributed." Moreover, because we know that there are other types of *flying creatures* out there such as insects and bats, we cannot fully equate our predicate term with its subject, either. Neither the subject term nor the predicate can be fully identified within the general class that the other belongs to, and so we would say that both the subject and the predicate are undistributed.

## O Statements: Some S is not P

O statements are negative, so the predicate is distributed; but they are also particular, so the subject is not distributed. An O Statement is particular in its quantity and negative in its quality, so an O Statement's subject is undistributed and its predicate is undistributed. Consider the proposition *Some birds are not flying creatures*. We can think of many *birds* that lack the ability to fly such as penguins and ostriches, and we can think of many *flightless creatures* which are not birds such as pigs, hippos, and a host of other animals incapable of getting off the ground. As with the previous example, because neither the subject nor the predicate can be fully identified with, equated to, the class to which the other term belongs, we can say that the subject is undistributed and the predicate is distributed.

As we will see in later chapters, O statements are "tricky" in that we cannot be sure of how many *flying creatures* are not *birds* since the subject itself is particular and thus indefinite.

To recap, the subject term is distributed in universal propositions—namely, A and E statements. The predicate term, meanwhile, is only distributed in negative statements—E and O statements. While the idea of whether or not a term is "distributed" may not seem very relevant to our lives today but if you create an argument with an undistributed term, that argument will not make sense. Moreover, your ability to identify whether or not a term is distributed will help become a quicker and more critical thinker. The table on the following summarizes which terms are and are not distributed for each categorical proposition.

ACTIVITY

# The Distribution of Terms

**Instructions**: Examine the following propositions and, in the space provided, write down whether the subject or the predicate is distributed or undistributed.

*Example: All animals are living creatures.*

*Since this is an A statement, the subject term* animals *is distributed—that is,* animals *is wholly found in and identified with the predicate term* living things. *But* living creatures, *being the predicate term, is not distributed.*

1. All human beings are beings who desire to know.

   The subject term is _____, and the predicate term is _____.

2. No human beings are irrational animals.

   The subject term is _____, and the predicate term is _____.

3. Some birds are creatures capable of swimming.

   The subject term is _____, and the predicate term is _____.

4. Some snakes are not poisonous.

   The subject term is _____, and the predicate term is _____

5. No monarchies are democracies.

   The subject term is _____, and the predicate term is _____.

ACTIVITY

# The Distribution of Terms

**Instructions**: Examine the following propositions and, in the space provided, write down whether the subject or the predicate is distributed or undistributed.

6. All animals are creatures who learn through experience.

    The subject term is _____, and the predicate term is _____.

7. All philosophers are people who love wisdom.

    The subject term is _____, and the predicate term is _____.

8. No doctors are people who are uneducated.

    The subject term is _____, and the predicate term is _____.

9. No snakes are creatures with legs.

    The subject term is _____, and the predicate term is _____.

10. Some monkeys are curious creatures.

    The subject term is _____, and the predicate term is _____

11. Some monkeys are not curious creatures.

    The subject term is _____, and the predicate term is _____.

ACTIVITY

# The Distribution of Terms

**Instructions**: Examine the following propositions and, in the space provided, write down whether the subject or the predicate is distributed or undistributed.

12. All virtues are habits of moral excellence.

    The subject term is _____, and the predicate term is _____.

13. No vices are habits worth pursuing.

    The subject term is _____, and the predicate term is _____.

14. All monarchies are ruled by one person.

    The subject term is _____, and the predicate term is _____.

15. Some animals are more equal than others.

    The subject term is _____, and the predicate term is _____.

16. Some birds are not colorful creatures.

    The subject term is _____, and the predicate term is _____.

17. Some spiders are creatures who can dance.

    The subject term is _____, and the predicate term is _____.

ACTIVITY

# The Distribution of Terms

**Instructions**: Examine the following propositions and, in the space provided, write down whether the subject or the predicate is distributed or undistributed.

18. All insects are creatures with six legs.

   The subject term is _____, and the predicate term is _____

19. No creatures with six legs are spiders.

   The subject term is _____, and the predicate term is _____

20. All water is wet.

   The subject term is _____, and the predicate term is _____

21. All scientists are people who examine causes.

   The subject term is _____, and the predicate term is _____

22. All life is that which is valuable.

   The subject term is _____, and the predicate term is _____

# Relationships of Equivalence: Conversion

**IN ITS SIMPLEST FORM**, an argument is made up of three propositions, and these three propositions are two premises and a conclusion. The movement from premises to a conclusion is known as an <u>inference</u>, and an inference is a synonym for reasoning or arguing. This particular type of inference—moving from two premises to the conclusion—is known both as a syllogism and also as a mediate inference (Kreeft 166-167). A syllogism has two premises, with one premise serving as a mediator between the first premise and the conclusion.

However, we can also move from just one premise to a conclusion. This is known as a <u>direct inference</u> or an immediate inference, presumably because the argument makes an immediate jump from that one premise to its conclusion. A direct inference does not introduce a third term that helps equate one term to another. Since an immediate inference deals with one premise and one conclusion, it is merely a way of rephrasing the initial premise. There are three ways of making immediate inferences: conversion, obversion, and contraposition. Let's look at each of these ways of making an immediate inference, beginning with conversion.

## Conversion

<u>Conversion</u> is the process of interchanging the subject and predicate. To switch the terms in a sentence and have it still make sense (i.e., a valid immediate inference), the terms you switch have to be equally distributed. Since the subject and the predicate in E statements and I statements are equally distributed, we can interchange those terms without any loss of meaning.

In E statements, both the subject and the predicate are equally distributed, while in I statements neither the subject nor the predicate is distributed, so you can swap

| Statement | Quality | Quantity | Subject | Predicate |
|---|---|---|---|---|
| A Statement / All S is P | Affirmative | Universal | Distributed | Undistributed |
| E Statement / No S is P | Negative | Universal | Distributed | Distributed |
| I Statement / Some S is P | Affirmative | Particular | Undistributed | Undistributed |
| O Statement / Some S is not P | Negative | Particular | Undistributed | Distributed |

## Vocabulary

**Inference**
The third act of the mind, a process that takes information we already know and uses that information to reach a new conclusion.

**Direct Inference**
The act of drawing a conclusion from only one premise. Direct inference is also called *immediate inference*.

**Conversion**
The process of interchanging the subject and predicate in a sentence to create an equivalent statement; conversion only works on E and I statements.

**A Statement**
All S is P.

**E Statement**
No S is P.

**I Statement**
Some S is P.

**O Statement**
Some S is not P.

**Partial Conversion**
Because the subject and predicate terms in an A statement are not evenly distributed, A statements convert to I statements.

them around without problems. *No monkeys are rational beings* makes as much sense as *No rational beings are monkeys*, as does the statement, *No snakes are creatures with legs* to *No creatures with legs are snakes*. The subject and the predicate in both these examples are wholly separated from each other, so we could consider them to be evenly distributed. We can interchange the subject and predicate in E and I statements without making any other changes and still have a proposition that makes a meaningful, logically identical truth claim. (On a related note, E statements can convert to O statements since the truth of a universal proposition implies the truth of the particular proposition.)

The same is true of I statements, even though its subject and the predicate are undistributed. The statement, *Some birds are flying creatures* makes as much sense as *Some flying creatures are birds*. We know some birds can fly, and some flying creatures (but not all) are also birds. The same is also true of a proposition about flightless birds: *Some birds are flightless creatures*. We know that some birds, like penguins and ostriches, cannot fly; we also know of animals like pigs and elephants which cannot fly (although it is delightful to think of them doing so). Thus, E statements and I statements can be converted without any apparent loss of meaning.

### Partial & Unconvertible Statements

However, we should be careful to note that A statements and O statements are not subject to conversion. That is because their respective subject and predicate terms are not evenly distributed. In fact, if you switch the subject and predicate around in an A Statement or an O Statement, the resulting sentence will not make sense.

If one considers the structure of an A statement, the subject term is always grouped together and found within the predicate term and, as a result, the predicate term must always be a larger category of things than the subject term. Logicians would say that the terms in an A statement are unevenly distributed, which prevents us from creating a logically equivalent statement. Let us consider an example: *All elephants are mammals*. This proposition implies that all of the subject term *elephants* is found in, and identified with, the predicate term *mammals*; for every *elephant* that exists, that *elephant* is also a *mammal*. But if we switch the subject and predicate to read, *All mammals are elephants*, we recognize this proposition is patently false. That is, we know of many more examples of *mammals* than just *elephants*.

Instead, we must first convert an A statement converts to an I statement. This process is known as **partial conversion**. The proposition, *All elephants are mammals*, converts to *Some mammals are elephants*. That is, an indefinite number of mammals that exist in the world are also elephants. As a second example, the proposition *All men are mortal* does not carry the same truth content as *All mortals are men*. We know, intuitively, that many creatures other than people are mortal. In the same way, the proposition *All men are mortal* converts to *Some mortals are men*—that is, of all the mortals in the world, a certain, undefined group of them are also human beings.

O Statements do not convert because the subject and predicate terms in an O statements are not evenly distributed, either. When we convert an O statement, we can determine right away that the sentence is nonsensical. The reason is that you cannot tell where the subject ends and the predicate begins, and thus you cannot draw any adequate conclusions from switching the terms. For instance, when converted, the statement *Some birds are not flying creatures* becomes *Some flying creatures are not birds*. At face value, they look the same. But, if you look closer, we see that these two statements refer to entirely different categories of things. The statement *Some birds are not flying creatures* refers to birds that cannot fly such as penguins, ostriches, and emus. The statement *Some flying creatures are not birds* refers to a class of flying creatures that are not birds such as bats and insects. The fact that these statements refer to entirely-different classes of things implies that these statements do not carry the same truth value and thus are not logically equivalent (Kreeft 169). For this reason, we say that the terms in an O statement cannot be interchanged.

Consider, as a second example, a failed science experiment. When a science experiment fails, we do not necessarily know anything more—only what we do not know. The reasoning behind the inconvertibility of O statements is the same as that of such a failed science experiment. Because we only know what some birds are not, we cannot conclude anything. If we devise a science experiment and the experiment fails, we still have not proved anything. All we know is that our initial hypothesis was incorrect. Because all we know is that some birds do not fly, we cannot make a conclusion about flying creatures in general.

To recap, relationships of equivalence are the ways that we can alter propositions and still convey the same truth-content. The first relationship of equivalence we have covered is known as conversion, the act of interchanging the subject and the predicate terms in a categorical proposition. E statements and I statements are *convertible* because we can interchange their subject and predicate terms and still have a logically-equivalent sentence. Both the subject and the predicate terms in an E statement are equally distributed so we can interchange them without any apparent loss of meaning.

Meanwhile, the subject and predicate terms in an I statement are equally undistributed, so we can interchange them as well. In a process known as partial conversion, A statements become I statements when they are converted. To help remember this, recall that "All men are mortal" but only "some mortals are men". Lastly, O statements are not convertible because we do not know what part of the subject about which we are denying something. Whether or not a categorical proposition is convertible depends upon whether or not the terms are distributed or undistributed. Here is a recap of the rules of conversion:

*E Statements are convertible; E Statements can also convert to O Statements.*

*I Statements are convertible.*

*A Statements actually convert to I Statements.*

*O Statements do not convert at all.*

RELATIONSHIPS OF EQUIVALENCE / CONVERSION

# Review of Conversion

**AS A SUMMARY**, here is a review of *Conversion* and the steps needed to convert a categorical proposition.

| Step | Distribution of Terms | Convertible | Converts to . . . | Example |
|---|---|---|---|---|
| **A Statement** *All S is P* | The subject is distributed, but the predicate is undistributed. | **Partially-Convertible**: Because the subject and the predicate terms are unequally distributed, A statements only partially convert. A statements convert to I statements. | A statements convert to I statements | *All men are mortal* becomes *Some mortal things are men.* |
| **E Statement** *No S is P* | Both the subject and the predicate are distributed. | **Convertible**: Because the subject and the predicate term are equally distributed, the terms in an E statement are interchangeable. | E statements are convertible | *No men are angels* becomes (and is logically equivalent to) *No angels are men.* |
| **I Statement** *Some S is P* | Both the subject and the predicate are undistributed. | **Convertible**: Because the subject and the predicate terms are equally distributed, the terms in an I statement are interchangeable. | I statements are convertible | *Some birds are flying creatures* becomes (and is logically equivalent to) *Some flying creatures are birds.* |
| **O Statement** *Some S is not P* | The subject is undistributed, but the predicate is distributed. | **Unconvertible**: Because the subject and the predicate terms are unequally distributed, O statements do not convert. | O statements are not convertible. | *Some birds are not flying creatures (such as penguins)* is not logically equivalent to the statement *Some flying creatures are not birds (such as bats).* |

CHAPTER 8 Relationships of Equivalence ♦ 219

ACTIVITY

# Conversion

**Instructions**: Convert the following sentences. Some propositions are not in categorical form and may need to be translated first. If the statement cannot be converted, explain why. The first proposition has been done as an example.

*Example*: Some propositions are true statements.

Conversion: The I statement *Some propositions are true statements* can be converted to *Some true statements are propositions*.

1. All human beings are beings who desire to know.

Conversion: _____

_____

2. No human beings are irrational animals.

Conversion: _____

_____

3. Some birds are creatures capable of swimming.

Conversion: _____

_____

4. Some snakes are not poisonous.

Conversion: _____

_____

5. No monarchies are democracies.

Conversion: _____

_____

ACTIVITY

# *Conversion*

**Instructions**: Convert the following sentences. Some propositions are not in categorical form and may need to be translated first. If the statement cannot be converted, explain why.

6. All animals are creatures who learn through experience.

Conversion: _____

_____

7. All philosophers are people who love wisdom.

Conversion: _____

_____

8. No doctors are people who are uneducated.

Conversion: _____

_____

9. No snakes are creatures with legs.

Conversion: _____

_____

10. Some monkeys are curious creatures.

Conversion: _____

_____

11. Some monkeys are not curious creatures.

Conversion: _____

_____

ACTIVITY

# Conversion

**Instructions**: Convert the following sentences. Some propositions are not in categorical form and may need to be translated first. If the statement cannot be converted, explain why.

12. All virtues are habits of moral excellence.

Conversion: _____

_____

13. No vices are habits worth pursuing.

Conversion: _____

_____

14. All monarchies are ruled by one person.

Conversion: _____

_____

15. Some animals are more equal than others.

Conversion: _____

_____

16. Some spiders are creatures who can dance.

Conversion: _____

_____

17. All insects are creatures with six legs.

Conversion: _____

_____

ACTIVITY

# Conversion

**Instructions**: Convert the following sentences. Some propositions are not in categorical form and may need to be translated first. If the statement cannot be converted, explain why.

18. All scientists are people who examine causes.

Conversion: _____

_____

19. No creatures with six legs are spiders.

Conversion: _____

_____

20. All water is wet.

Conversion: _____

_____

# Relationships of Equivalence: Obversion

**OBVERSION IS THE PROCESS** of taking a proposition and negating both its copula and its predicate and because two negatives make a positive, we can create an immediate inference that is true (Kreeft 170).

We will carry out the steps for obversion on the following proposition: *Some birds are flying creatures*.

First Step: Read the original proposition, figure out what it is actually saying, and make sure the sentence has a quantifier and a copula. Then, if necessary, we should put that proposition into logical form.

The original sentence reads *Some birds are flying creatures*, an I statement. The sentence already has the quantifier *some*, so the statement is *particular* in its quality, and being an I statement, is *affirmative* in its quality. It is not necessary to translate this sentence into logical form.

Moreover, it is helpful to think of some examples of *birds* that are also *flying creatures*. Such examples would include robins, wrens, and blue jays, amongst other birds also capable of flying. That way, we have a test we can run to see if we have obverted this statement correctly.

Second Step: Change the quality of the proposition. If the statement was affirmative, change it to negative and vice versa. In doing so, be sure that you do not change the quantity. If the proposition is universal, the proposition must stay universal, and if the proposition is particular, it must stay particular. In other words, an A proposition becomes an E proposition and vice versa, and an I proposition becomes an O proposition and vice versa.

Our original example is changed from *Some birds are flying creatures* to *Some birds are* not *flying creatures*. Effectively, what was originally an I statement has now become an O statement.

Third Step: The step in obversion focuses on the predicate. Whatever the predicate is, take it and negate it—that is, turn the predicate into its opposite, or its complement. If your predicate is *P*, then your predicate is now *non-P* and if your predicate was originally *non-P*, the predicate is now *P*. The predicate in our original statement was *flying creatures*, and our new predicate is *non-flying creatures* or *flightless creatures*. Our original example *Some birds are flying creatures* has now changed in obversion to *Some birds are not non-flying creatures* or *Some birds are not flightless creatures*.

This process also applies to words that may have a prefix that turns that word into its complement. One can think of the word *mortal* and its complement, *immortal*; or *moral* and its complement, *immoral* or *amoral*. When choosing a complement, it is essential that it is a true complement. For example, *big* is not the complement of *small*. Just because something is *not big* does not make it *small*. Whatever that thing is, it could be a variety of other sizes. When a true complement cannot be determined, it is acceptable to use *non-* or *not-* in

## Vocabulary

**Obversion**
The process of negating the predicate of a proposition and changing the quality of that statement to create an equivalent statement. These work for all statement types.

**Affirmative**
When the proposition affirms something about the subject.

**Negative**
When the proposition denies something about the subject.

front of the subject or predicate, as in *non-big* or *non-small*. This technique is also useful when the subject or predicate is more complex, as in our current example.

When a proposition has a proper noun as its subject, obversion becomes a little trickier. In that case, there is no quantifier. We remember that propositions with a proper noun as the subject are always universal. For example, *Plato is a writer about morality* is an A statement. When we obvert it, we first change it to an E statement (*Plato is not a writer about morality*) before we negate the predicate (*Plato is not a non-writer about morality*) When you negate the predicate, be sure you negate the entire predicate, not just part of it Notice that we negated the entire predicate here, not just the word *morality*. It would not be equivalent to saying *Plato is not a writer about immorality*. Almost all of Plato's dialogues focus on some aspect of morality. Although a bit unwieldy, changing the A statement to an E statement then negating the predicate is the only accurate way to obvert this statement.

Let's return to our original statement about birds and their ability to fly. Our original I statement *Some birds are flying creatures* was obverted to *Some birds are not flightless creatures*. As an example, *birds* that were also *flying creatures* included robins, wrens, and blue jays, whereas the obverted statement *Some birds are not flightless creatures*, or *birds* that did not lack the ability to fly, also included robins, wrens, and blue jays. This gives us a sense that we correctly obverted the original statement, and that the statement in its original form carries the same truth content.

### Examples of Obverted Statements

| Example | Original Proposition | In Obversion |
|---|---|---|
| *A Statement* / All S is P | All men are mortal | No men are immortal. |
| *E Statement* / No S is P | No monkeys are rational. | All monkeys are irrational. |
| *I Statement* / Some S is P | Some birds are flying creatures. | Some birds are not flightless creatures. |
| *O Statement* / Some S is not P | Some birds are not flying creatures. | Some birds are flightless creatures. |

RELATIONSHIPS OF EQUIVALENCE / CONVERSION

# Review of Obversion

**AS A SUMMARY,** here is a review of *Obversion* and the steps needed to obvert a categorical proposition with the proposition "Treat others as you wish to be treated," (the Golden Rule).

| Step | Quality | Quantity | Final Product |
|---|---|---|---|
| **Step #1** — *Read the original proposition, figure out what it is actually saying, and then put that proposition into logical form.* | The predicate of this proposition seems to be affirming something about the subject. As a result, this sentence is either an A statement or an I statement. | The proposition seems to refer to all the members of the subject, not an undefined particular group within this subject, so it is an A statement. | *Treat others as you wish to be treated* really means, *All the ways I would treat myself are the ways I should treat others.* |
| **Step #2** — *Change the quality of the proposition.* | The quality of the original proposition affirmed something about the subject, so we need to change it so that it denies something about that subject. In this case, we change this A statement to an E statement. | We do not change the quantity. | *All the ways I would treat myself are the ways I should treat others* becomes *No way I would treat myself is a way I should treat others.* |
| **Step #3** — *Take the predicate and negate it—that is, turn the predicate into its opposite, or its complement.* | We do not make any changes to the quality of the proposition. | We do not make any changes to the quantity of the proposition. | *No way I would treat myself is a way I should treat others* becomes *No way I would treat myself is a non-way I should treat others.* |

ACTIVITY

# *Obversion*

**Instructions**: Obvert the following sentences. Some propositions are not in categorical form and may need to be translated first. The first sentence has been done as an example.

*Example*: Some propositions are true statements.

> Obversion: The I statement *Some propositions are true statements* can be obverted to *Some propositions are not false statements*.

1. All human beings are beings who desire to know.

Obversion: _____

2. No human beings are irrational animals.

Obversion: _____

3. Some birds are creatures capable of swimming.

Obversion: _____

4. Some snakes are not poisonous.

Obversion: _____

5. No monarchies are democracies.

Obversion: _____

## ACTIVITY

# Obversion

**Instructions**: Obvert the following sentences. Some propositions are not in categorical form and may need to be translated first.

6. All animals are creatures who learn through experience.

Obversion: _____

_____

7. All philosophers are people who love wisdom.

Obversion: _____

_____

8. No doctors are people who are uneducated.

Obversion: _____

_____

9. No snakes are creatures with legs.

Obversion: _____

_____

10. Some monkeys are curious creatures.

Obversion: _____

_____

11. Some monkeys are not curious creatures.

Obversion: _____

_____

ACTIVITY

# *Obversion*

**Instructions**: Obvert the following sentences. Some propositions are not in categorical form and may need to be translated first.

12. All virtues are habits of moral excellence.

Obversion: _____

_____

13. No vices are habits worth pursuing.

Obversion: _____

_____

14. All monarchies are ruled by one person.

Obversion: _____

_____

15. Some animals are more equal than others.

Obversion: _____

_____

16. Some spiders are creatures who can dance.

Obversion: _____

_____

17. All insects are creatures with six legs.

Obversion: _____

_____

ACTIVITY

# Obversion

**Instructions**: Obvert the following sentences. Some propositions are not in categorical form and may need to be translated first.

18. All scientists are people who examine causes.

Obversion: _____

_____

19. No creatures with six legs are spiders.

Obversion: _____

_____

20. All water is wet.

Obversion: _____

_____

# Epistemology, Empiricism, and John Locke

**THIS SECTION FOCUSES ON** both propositions and epistemology. Recall that epistemology is the study of how we know what we know, and whether or not what we know is true. Propositions are especially important in logic because only propositions can be true or false. Thus far we have looked at Rene Descartes, the founder of modern philosophy, a noted mathematician, and a rationalist. Descartes believed that human beings know things primarily through the faculty of reason, and he grounded his confidence in his own existence in his discovery that he, himself, was a thinking, reasoning thing. The other significant school of epistemology is that of **empiricism**, and to better understand empiricism, we turn now to the life and writings of the British philosopher John Locke.

John Locke (1632-1704) has cast a long shadow over the entire Western tradition. Thomas Jefferson prominently displayed a small statue of Locke at Monticello, and every political theorist has in some way, shape, or form argued for or against Locke ever since the publication of his works back in the 17th century. Those works range from contract theory, property rights, and ideas about human nature and human potential, all of which have had a profound impact on British and American political institutions. John Locke even wrote the "Fundamental Constitutions of Carolina", the original founding documents for both North and South Carolina.

John Locke came from a politically well-connected family, whose members had served in Parliament. Locke attended the best public school in England: Westminster School in London and later Christ College, Oxford, the

| **THE EMPIRICIST JOHN LOCKE**

best college at Oxford University. You may be interested to know Locke did not enjoy the school's heavy emphasis on Aristotle and Aristotelian logic, which he found did not correspond to how he believed people came to know information. Then, John Locke lived during not one, but two of the most tumultuous times in English history: the English Civil War of 1642 to 1651 and the Glorious Revolution of 1688.

**The English Civil War** was particularly brutal. The battle lines were drawn between the supporters of King Charles I, individuals who often were Catholic in their religious identity, and the supporters of Parliament, who most often had converted to Protestantism. Thus, the English Civil War was not merely a conflict between the will of the King and the rights of Parliament, but also a religious war in which Catholics and Protestants fought each other over the religious future of England. **The Glorious Revolution**, meanwhile, was a bloodless coup in which the Protestant William of Orange replaced an unpopular King James II as king, a regime change so successful and nonviolent that it is often described as the starting date for the Enlightenment. Locke and his family played significant roles in both of these conflicts, and they served to help shape Locke's thinking. One can see some influence of the century's religious strife in Locke's *Essay Concerning Human Understanding*, if one reads carefully enough.

Locke's *Essay Concerning Human Understanding* was published in 1689-90. In this work, Locke examined epistemology, the science of how we as human beings know things and have any certainty of the knowledge we possess. As has been noted in this chapter, Locke argued for empiricism, in that we human beings are born as a **tabula rasa**, a "white paper" or a "blank slate" without any real "innate ideas" inscribed upon it. We only come to know the world through our sense experience, and our knowledge comes from acts of reflecting on what we see, hear, feel, and experience. Contra Descartes, John Locke does not believe that we are born with innate ideas or that we fundamentally understand the world through reason. Instead, if we know anything about the world or even about ourselves, we come to know it through the senses. Let's turn now to Locke's work, evaluate his argument, and above all understand how Locke's work comes to shape the philosophical conversation that follows after him.

## Vocabulary

### Empiricism
From the Greek word for "experience", the belief that all knowledge comes through the senses.

### John Locke
The "father of Liberalism", this political theorist said that all human beings have natural rights, chief amongst them being life, liberty, and property; He lived from 1632 to 1704.

### The English Civil War
Lasting from 1642 to 1651, the English Civil War was fought between the forces of King Charles I and the New Model Army of the English Parliament. The English Civil War ended in the victory of Parliament over King Charles I.

### Tabula Rasa
Latin for *blank slate*, John Locke used this metaphor to describe the human mind at birth: a blank slate, upon which information and knowledge is inscribed through experience.

### The Glorious Revolution
In 1688, the English Parliament successfully (and without bloodshed) replaced the unpopular King James II with the Dutch Prince William of Orange. William and his English wife Mary supported the goals of Parliament, which included increased support for Protestant Christianity, a national bank, and protections for freedom of expression and other liberties.

## Reading Comprehension Questions

1. Who was John Locke? For what accomplishments is he most famous?

2. Describe the tumultuous century in which John Locke lived. What events happened during his lifetime?

3. How did those events shape his thinking and writing?

4. Explain the term *tabula rasa*. What does this Latin term mean?

# Essay Concerning Human Understanding / By John Locke

## Idea is the Object of Thinking.

01 Every man being conscious to himself that he thinks; and that which his mind is applied about whilst thinking being the IDEAS that are there, it is past doubt that men have in their minds several ideas,—such as are those expressed by the words whiteness, hardness, sweetness, thinking, motion, man, elephant, army, drunkenness, and others: it is in the first place then to be inquired, HOW HE COMES BY THEM?

02 I know it is a received doctrine, that men have native ideas, and original characters, stamped upon their minds in their very first being. This opinion I have at large examined already; and, I suppose what I have said in the foregoing Book will be much more easily admitted, when I have shown whence the understanding may get all the ideas it has; and by what ways and degrees they may come into the mind;—for which I shall appeal to everyone's own observation and experience.

## All Ideas Come From Sensation or Reflection.

03 Let us then suppose the mind to be, as we say, white paper, void of all characters, without any ideas: How comes it to be furnished? Whence comes it by that vast store which the busy and boundless fancy of man has painted on it with an almost endless variety? Whence has it all the MATERIALS of reason and knowledge? To this I answer, in one word, from EXPERIENCE. In that all our knowledge is founded; and from that it ultimately derives itself. Our observation employed either, about external sensible objects, or about the internal operations of our minds perceived and reflected on by ourselves, is that which supplies our understandings with all the MATERIALS of thinking. These two are the fountains of knowledge, from whence all the ideas we have, or can naturally have, do spring.

## The Objects of Sensation: One Source of Ideas.

04 First, our Senses, conversant about particular sensible objects, do convey into the mind several distinct perceptions of things, according to those various ways wherein those objects do affect them. And thus we come by those IDEAS we have of yellow, white, heat, cold, soft, hard, bitter, sweet, and all those which we call sensible qualities; which when I say the senses convey into the mind, I mean, they from external objects convey into the mind what produces there those perceptions. This great source of most of the ideas we have, depending wholly upon our senses, and derived by them to the understanding, I call SENSATION.

## The Operations of Our Minds, The Other Source of Them.

05 Secondly, the other fountain from which experience fills the understanding with ideas is,—the perception of the operations of our own mind within us, as it is employed about the ideas it has got;—which operations,

## Vocabulary & Annotations

**IDEAS**

Locke looks at ideas, the images we have in our minds, to determine if they exist apart from experience, or if we come to know such ideas through our senses. In that way, ideas are like impressions left on wax.

**...received doctrine**

In Locke's day, people believed in certain innate ideas, ideas that an individual could come to by reason alone.

**...yellow, white, heat**

The ideas that we have of colors, temperature, and the like can only come about through our experience of things that are of such a color, such a temperature, etc.

**...mind gets by reflecting**

The mind makes use of the information it takes in through the senses to reach new conclusions.

**...nothing in our minds**

Locke argues that we come to know things about the world through our senses while the mind in its "operations" reflects upon that information to reach new conclusions.

**...superstition of a nurse**

Ideas concerning religion and morality were taught to us when we were so young, we assumed they were innate ideas.

**...grow up to the dignity**

Overtime, certain principles become so widely-accepted by society that these ideas are thought to be innate.

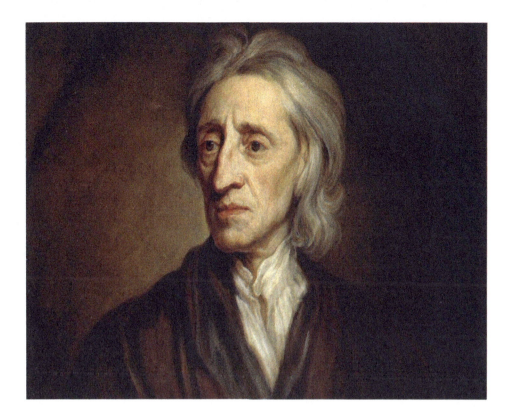

**JOHN LOCKE / 1632 - 1704**
*Portrait by Godfrey Keller*

when the soul comes to reflect on and consider, do furnish the understanding with another set of ideas, which could not be had from things without. And such are perception, thinking, doubting, believing, reasoning, knowing, willing, and all the different actings of our own minds;—which we being conscious of, and observing in ourselves, do from these receive into our understandings as distinct ideas as we do from bodies affecting our senses. This source of ideas every man has wholly in himself; and though it be not sense, as having nothing to do with external objects, yet it is very like it, and might properly enough be called INTERNAL SENSE.

06 But as I call the other Sensation, so I call this REFLECTION, the ideas it affords being such only as the **mind gets by reflecting** on its own operations within itself. By reflection then, in the following part of this discourse, I would be understood to mean, that notice which the mind takes of its own operations, and the manner of them, by reason whereof there come to be ideas of these operations in the understanding. These two, I say, viz. external material things, as the objects of SENSATION, and the operations of our own minds within, as the objects of REFLECTION, are to me the only originals from whence all our ideas take their beginnings. The term OPERATIONS here I use in a large sense, as comprehending not barely the actions of the mind about its ideas, but some sort of passions arising sometimes from them, such as is the satisfaction or uneasiness arising from any thought.

## All Our Ideas are of the One or of the Other Of These.

**07** The understanding seems to me not to have the least glimmering of any ideas which it doth not receive from one of these two. EXTERNAL OBJECTS furnish the mind with the ideas of sensible qualities, which are all those different perceptions they produce in us; and THE MIND furnishes the understanding with ideas of its own operations.

**08** These, when we have taken a full survey of them, and their several modes, and the compositions made out of them we shall find to contain all our whole stock of ideas; and that we have nothing in our minds which did not come in one of these two ways. Let any one examine his own thoughts, and thoroughly search into his understanding; and then let him tell me, whether all the original ideas he has there, are any other than of the objects of his senses, or of the operations of his mind, considered as objects of his reflection. And how great a mass of knowledge soever he imagines to be lodged there, he will, upon taking a strict view, see that he has not any idea in his mind but what one of these two have imprinted;—though perhaps, with infinite variety compounded and enlarged by the understanding, as we shall see hereafter.

## Contrary Principles in the World.

**09** I easily grant that there are great numbers of opinions which, by men of different countries, educations, and tempers, are received and embraced as first and unquestionable principles; many whereof, both for their absurdity as well oppositions to one another, it is impossible should be true. But yet all those propositions, how remote soever from reason are so sacred somewhere or other, that men even of good understanding in other matters, will sooner part with their lives, and whatever is dearest to them, than suffer themselves to doubt, or others to question, the truth of them.

## How Men Commonly Come by Their Principles.

**10** This, however strange it may seem, is that which every day's experience confirms; and will not, perhaps, appear so wonderful, if we consider the ways and steps by which it is brought about; and how really it may come to pass, that doctrines that have been derived from no better origin than the superstition of a nurse, or the authority of an old woman, may, by length of time and consent of neighbors, grow up to the dignity of PRINCIPLES in religion or morality. For such, who are careful (as they call it) to principle children well, (and few there be who have not a set of those principles for them, which they believe in,) instill into the unwary, and as yet unprejudiced, understanding, (for white paper receives any characters,) those doctrines they would have them retain and profess.

**11** These being taught them as soon as they have any apprehension; and still as they grow up confirmed to them, either by the open profession or tacit consent of all they have to do with; or at least by those of whose wisdom, knowledge, and piety they have an opinion, who never suffer those propositions to be otherwise mentioned but as the basis and foundation on which they build their religion and manners, come, by these means, to have the reputation of unquestionable, self-evident, and innate truths.

## Reading Comprehension Questions

1. What is an "idea"? How do we come to have such ideas?

2. What are the "operations of the mind"?

3. Do we come to know anything apart from our senses? Why or why not?

4. What are the drawbacks to empiricism? Do we really only "know" ideas about morality because we hear them from our parents, guardians, and other members of society??

ACTIVITY

# The First Act of the Mind / Terms

Each row contains a term, the author's use of that term, or a definition of that term suitable for students. If the row contains a quotation, write down a clear, intelligible definition of that term in the box provided. If the term is already defined for you, please find the quotation from the text that supports the appropriate definition.

| Term | Quotations from the Text | Quotations Rephrased as Definitions |
|---|---|---|
| Idea | Idea is the Object of Thinking | |
| Native Ideas | | Ideas that are found in the mind independent of sense of experience. |
| White Paper | Let us then suppose the mind to be as... white paper, void of all characters, without any ideas:-How comes it to be furnished? | |
| Objects of Sensation | | These are things we see, hear, and experience in the real world which then forms an *impression* upon our minds. |

SECTION II Propositions & Epistemology

ACTIVITY

# The Second Act of the Mind / Propositions

Each row contains a term, the author's use of that term, or a definition of that term provided by the editors of this book. If the row contains a quote, write down a clear, intelligible definition of that term in the box provided. If the term is already defined for you, please find the quote from the text that supports the appropriate definition. Remember that if you do not know or understand the terms an author is using to build his or her argument, you cannot understand that argument.

| Quotations from Text | Quotation rephrased as one (or more) Proposition(s) |
|---|---|
| *Let us then suppose the mind to be, as we say, white paper, void of all characters, without any ideas:—How comes it to be furnished? Whence comes it by that vast store which the busy and boundless fancy of man has painted on it with an almost endless variety? Whence has it all the MATERIALS of reason and knowledge? To this I answer, in one word, from EXPERIENCE. In that all our knowledge is founded; and from that it ultimately derives itself. Our observation employed either, about external sensible objects, or about the internal operations of our minds perceived and reflected on by ourselves, is that which supplies our understandings with all the MATERIALS of thinking.* | |
| *First, our Senses, conversant about particular sensible objects, do convey into the mind several distinct perceptions of things, according to those various ways wherein those objects do affect them.* | |
| *...the other fountain from which experience furnishes the understanding with ideas is,—the perception of the operations of our own mind within us, as it is employed about the ideas it has got;—which operations, when the soul comes to reflect on and consider, do furnish the understanding with another set of ideas, which could not be had from things without.* | |

ACTIVITY

# The Third Act of the Mind / Inferences

In the space below, create an "argument map", a visual way of representing the premises, assumptions, and ultimately the conclusion that a writer is making in their work. You can also use this blank space provided to draw a "conversation map", a visual way of recording the discussion your class had over this text.

WRITING

# Writing Prompt

Remember, writing is thinking. To help us to write and think more clearly, we will spend considerable time this year writing essays based on the texts we read in class. These essays are descriptive in nature and answer one question that arises from the material we are reading in class. In such an essay, the writer wants to explain the meaningful ideas contained in this text by reading and rereading the text under analysis to better explain that author's argument and the consequences of his or her ideas.

**Question**: *Drawing from John Locke's* Essay Concerning Human Understanding, *examine the role of the senses in receiving and evaluating information from the world around us. How exactly do we come to know anything at all? Can we trust the dictates of traditional morality if we just "heard" such ideas, the way we might hear the wind? Why or why not? Explain your reasoning.*

# Writing

WESTMINSTER ABBEY / INTERIOR
*Photo by Evan Buchholz*

SECTION II Propositions & Epistemology

CHAPTER

# The Square of Opposition

**ROADMAP**

- Learn about the Square of Opposition.
- Learn about the relationships of equivalence including contradictions, contrariety, subcontrariety, superalternation, and subalternation.
- Read a selection from David Hume's *Enquiry Concerning Human Understanding*.

THALES OUTCOME
№ 8

Someone with *Astute Problem Solving* plans the best possible solutions to challenges to achieve optimal success.

In this chapter, we will learn about the Square of Opposition. The Square of Opposition and the ideas on which it is based will help you to quickly and thoroughly evaluate propositions, draw inferences from those propositions, and determine more quickly and efficiently whether or not a proposition is true or false.

CHAPTER 9  The Square of Opposition  ✦  245

# The Square of Opposition

AS MIGHT BE EXPECTED, we can take what we know about categorical propositions and examine the relationships between different kinds of statements. If we affirm that one kind of categorical proposition is true, then another corresponding categorical proposition—one with the same subject and predicate—could be true, false, or undefined. Aristotle explained these relationships in his work, *De Interpretatione*, in that the truth of one particular kind of proposition necessitated that another statement with the same predicate might be true or false.

Let's look at an example sentence to test out this observation. If we look at the statement, *All birds are flying creatures* and we affirm that this statement is true, then it implies that the particular statement, *Some birds are not flying creatures* is, by necessity, false. If all birds can fly, then it is impossible that there is species of *bird* living on planet Earth that is *not* also a *flying creature*.

Obviously, the statement *All birds are flying creatures* is as false as the statement *No birds are flying creatures*. This is the insight behind the idea that all categorical propositions stand in relationship to one another, and if we correctly identified the kind of categorical proposition we are dealing with, whether it is an A, E, I, or O statement, we can also make inferences about whether or not another categorical proposition with the same subject or predicate is also either true, false, or undefined.

There are four relationships between different categorical propositions: contradictions, contrariety, subcontrariety, subalternation, and the related relationships of superimplication and subimplication. Lastly, these relationships can be represented visually in a diagram known as the Square of Opposition. We will now examine each of these relationships beginning with contradictions and concluding with the Square of Opposition at the end.

## Contradictions

A **contradiction** involves one categorical proposition being directly contradicted (or made to be false) by another categorical proposition. Contradictions entail that if one statement is true, then the other statement must be false. Each categorical proposition is contradicted by another categorical proposition that is paired with it, provided they both have the same subject and the same predicate. Contradictions exist between all four kinds of categorical propositions: A statements are contradicted by O statements (and vice-versa), and E statements are contradicted by I statements (and vice-versa).

Let's explain this further using universal propositions. For a universal claim to be true, it must be true in each and every instance in which that claim could apply. Accordingly, universal claims (like A statements and E statements) are contradicted or proven false in the following ways.

Let's consider the subject *birds* and the predicate *flying things*. We often think of *birds* as *flying things*, so much so that we can express this idea as an A statement *All birds are flying things*. However, this proposition is contradicted by the O statement, *Some birds are not flying things,* and by the very existence of real, particular birds out there in the world that cannot fly, such as emus and ostriches. One can think of the word *contradiction* as

## Vocabulary

**The Square of Opposition**

As formulated by Aristotle, this illustration is a visual way of showing the relationships between categorical propositions, providing that they all have the same subject and predicate terms.

**Contradictions**

The relationship between A and O statements, and between E and I statements. These pairs of statements cannot be both true or both false at the same time; an A statement is proven false by an O statement (and vice-versa), and an E statement is proven false by an I statement (and vice-versa).

**Contrariety**

The relationship between A and E statements, in that two universal propositions with the same subject and the same predicate can both be false, but they cannot both be true.

meaning "proven wrong by," so that if one were to find one example disproving the universal claim, that universal claim is made false.

For example, medieval European thinkers believed that all swans were white, a proposition that can be reformatted into the A statement *All swans are white birds*. They held onto this belief until Dutch and English explorers discovered the continent of Australia where they found large numbers of black swans. The existence of even one black swan disproved (or contradicted) the universal proposition, *All swans are white birds.*

On the other hand, an E statement is contradicted by an I Statement, and an I statement is contradicted by an E statement. Let's take the proposition *All birds are flying creatures* and obvert it into the E statement *No birds are non-flying creatures* or *No birds are flightless creatures*. This statement is easily proven false (contradicted) by the I statement, *Some birds are flightless creatures*, of which we can think of penguins and puffins. Such birds are still birds despite the fact that they cannot fly.

## Contrariety

<u>Contraries</u> cannot both be true, but they can both be false, and this relationship applies to universal propositions like A statements and E statements. Let's look at an example: *All birds are flying creatures* and the E statement, *No birds are flying creatures*. If one of those statements were true, it would by necessity imply the other was false—if *all birds can fly*, then it follows that *no birds are flying creatures* must be false. But both of these statements can be false—and in fact, both of them are false. Some birds can fly, and there are some birds that lack the unique ability to fly. This is the case with all A statements and E statements: they can both be false, but they cannot both be true.

## Subcontrariety

There is a similar relationship between I statements and O statements called subcontrariety. **Subcontrariety** means that an I statement and an O statement that contain the same subject and the same predicate can both be true, but they cannot both be false. We can immediately determine the veracity of the I statement, *Some birds are flying creatures,* and the O statement, *Some birds are not flying creatures,* and recognize that no illogical, irrational contradiction has been made. This is because the subject in an I statement and an O statement

*Teachers and parents*: You may want to consider posing the Square of Opposition *first and ask students to find the relationships between each categorical proposition. Or, choose one subject and predicate (like* dog *and* fluffy things, *for example) and present students with different categorical propositions to see which statements can be true or false at the same time (and why).*

is referring to different kinds of birds so the resulting propositions can both be true.

## Subalternation

If a universal proposition is true, then it follows that its corresponding particular proposition is also true. If *all birds are flying creatures*, then it follows that some particular application of that universal proposition is also true—i.e., that all birds, and every particular species of bird we can think of, are flying creatures. The same is true for E statements: If *no birds are flying creatures*, then it follows that some particular application of this universal proposition is also true—namely, that *some birds are not flying creatures*. This relationship is known in logic as **subalternation** because it goes from a universal subject (and all instances of that subject) to the particular subsumed under that universal to indicate that its corresponding particular proposition is also true. If you affirm that the universal proposition is true, then the particular proposition subsumed under that universal is also true.

At times, the relationship known as subalternation is divided into two different relationships, known as *subimplication* and *superimplication*. The relationship from the universal statement to the particular statement is known as **subimplication**, and the relationship from the particular statement to the universal statement is known as **superimplication**. In subimplication, if the universal is true, then the particular proposition falling under that universal claim must also be true since the Latin prefix *sub* means "under". If *all dogs are good*, then it stands that for each and every particular *dog* that exists, it must also be *good*, too.

**Superimplication** works in the opposite direction, going from a particular proposition (I, O, statements) to a universal proposition. The Latin prefix *super* implies that we are going from a particular proposition over and above to a universal proposition. If a particular proposition is false, then it holds that a universal proposition with the same subject and predicate is also false. If the proposition *Some dogs are good* is false, then the universal proposition *All dogs are good* must also be false, too, since a universal claim cannot be true if each and every particular instance of that claim is not also true.

In summary, the relationship of subimplication goes from A propositions down to I propositions, and from E statements to O statements. Likewise, the relationship of superimplication goes from I propositions up to A propositions.

## Vocabulary

**Subcontrariety**
The relationship between I and O statements, in that two particular propositions with the same subject and the same predicate can both be true, but they cannot both be false.

**Subalternation**
The relationship between A statements and I statements and between E statements and O statements, in that the truth of the universal proposition (A, E statements) implies the truth of the particular proposition (I, O statements) with the same subject and predicate, or that the falsity of the particular I or O statement implies the falsity of the universal A and I statement.

**Subimplication**
The relationship between A statements and I statements and between E statements and O statements, in that the truth of the universal proposition (A, E statements) implies the truth of the particular proposition (I, O statements)

**Superimplication**
The relationship between I statements and A statements, and between O statements and E statements, in that if a particular statement (I, O statements) is false, then by necessity, its corresponding universal proposition (A, E statements) must be false, too.

# Diagram / The Square of Opposition

Remember, the Square of Oppositions provides a visual means of demonstrating the relationships between proposition, namely, the relationships of *contradiction, contrariety, subcontrariety,* and *subalternation*.

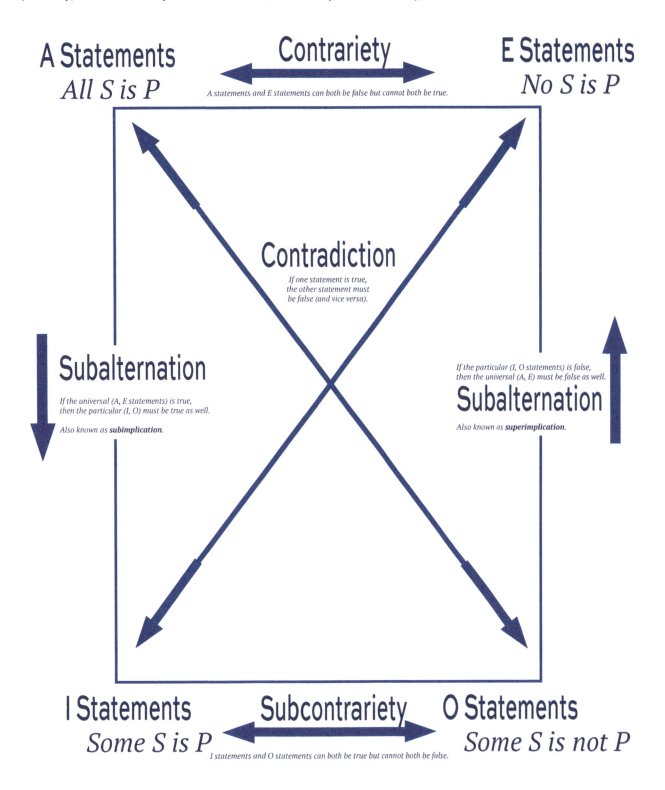

# Reading Comprehension Questions

What pair(s) of statements is/are contradictories (i.e., contradictory propositions)?

What is the rule of contradictories (i.e., contradictory propositions)?

What pair(s) of statements is/are contrarieties?

What is the rule of contrarieties?

# Reading Comprehension Questions

What pair(s) of statements is/are subcontrarieties?

What is the rule of subcontrarieties?

What pair(s) of statements is/are subalternate?

What is the rule of subalternation?

ACTIVITY

# The Square of Opposition / Part I

**Instructions**: Provide the statements of opposition for the following propositions. Put *Not Applicable* or *N/A* for not applicable if a particular statement does not have that type of relationship of opposition.

*Example*: Some propositions are true statements.

Contradiction: *No propositions are true statements* (an E statement)

Subalternation: *We are not told if the statement is true or false; if it were false, then the corresponding A statement must be false, too.*

Contrary: *Not Applicable, as I statements do not have contrary propositions.*

Subcontrary: *Some propositions are not true statements* (an O statement)

1. All triangles are three-sided shapes.

Contradiction:_____    Subalternation:_____

Contrary: _____    Subcontrary:_____

2. All friends are people who want your good.

Contradiction:_____    Subalternation:_____

Contrary: _____    Subcontrary:_____

3. Some bears are circus animals.

Contradiction:_____    Subalternation:_____

Contrary: _____    Subcontrary:_____

4. No syllogisms are things containing four terms.

Contradiction:_____    Subalternation:_____

Contrary: _____    Subcontrary:_____

ACTIVITY

# The Square of Opposition / Part I

**Instructions**: Provide the statements of opposition for the following propositions. Put "N/A" for not applicable if a particular statement does not have that type of relationship of opposition.

5. Some birds are flying creatures.

Contradiction:_____   Subalternation:_____

Contrary: _____   Subcontrary:_____

6. All animals are equal (from George Orwell's *Animal Farm*).

Contradiction:_____   Subalternation:_____

Contrary: _____   Subcontrary:_____

7. Some sharks are meat-eaters.

Contradiction:_____   Subalternation:_____

Contrary: _____   Subcontrary:_____

8. Some monkeys are curious creatures.

Contradiction:_____   Subalternation:_____

Contrary: _____   Subcontrary:_____

9. All *philosophes* are Enlightenment thinkers. [*Note: philosophe is a French term for an Enlightenment thinker.*]

Contradiction:_____   Subalternation:_____

Contrary: _____   Subcontrary:_____

10. No virtues are habits to be avoided.

Contradiction:_____   Subalternation:_____

Contrary: _____   Subcontrary:_____

# ACTIVITY

# The Square of Opposition / Part II

**Instructions**: Provide the statements of opposition for the following propositions. Put *Not Applicable* or *N/A* for not applicable if a particular statement does not have that type of relationship of opposition.

---

**Example:** *If an **A** statement is **true**, then its corresponding **I** statement is…*

| (True) | False | Undefined | because these statements are… |
|---|---|---|---|
| Contradictories | Contrariety | Subcontrariety | (Subalternate) |

**1.** *If an **I** statement is **true**, then its corresponding **A** statement is…*

| True | False | Undefined | because these statements are… |
|---|---|---|---|
| Contradictories | Contrariety | Subcontrariety | Subalternate |

**2.** *If an **I** statement is **false**, then its corresponding **O** statement is…*

| True | False | Undefined | because these statements are… |
|---|---|---|---|
| Contradictories | Contrariety | Subcontrariety | Subalternate |

**3.** *If an **O** statement is **true**, then its corresponding **I** statement is…*

| True | False | Undefined | because these statements are… |
|---|---|---|---|
| Contradictories | Contrariety | Subcontrariety | Subalternate |

**4.** *If an **O** statement is **true**, then its corresponding **A** statement is…*

| True | False | Undefined | because these statements are… |
|---|---|---|---|
| Contradictories | Contrariety | Subcontrariety | Subalternate |

**5.** *If an **O** statement is **true**, then its corresponding **E** statement is…*

| True | False | Undefined | because these statements are… |
|---|---|---|---|
| Contradictories | Contrariety | Subcontrariety | Subalternate |

ACTIVITY

# The Square of Opposition / Part II

**Instructions**: Provide the statements of opposition for the following propositions. Put *Not Applicable* or *N / A* for not applicable if a particular statement does not have that type of relationship of opposition.

6. *If an **O** statement is **false**, then its corresponding **I** statement is…*

| True | False | Undefined | because these statements are… |
|---|---|---|---|
| Contradictories | Contrariety | Subcontrariety | Subalternate |

7. *If an **A** statement is **false**, then its corresponding **E** statement is…*

| True | False | Undefined | because these statements are… |
|---|---|---|---|
| Contradictories | Contrariety | Subcontrariety | Subalternate |

8. *If an **E** statement is **false**, then its corresponding **A** statement is…*

| True | False | Undefined | because these statements are… |
|---|---|---|---|
| Contradictories | Contrariety | Subcontrariety | Subalternate |

9. *If an **I** statement is **true**, then its corresponding **E** statement is…*

| True | False | Undefined | because these statements are… |
|---|---|---|---|
| Contradictories | Contrariety | Subcontrariety | Subalternate |

10. *If an **E** statement is **true**, then its corresponding **A** statement is…*

| True | False | Undefined | because these statements are… |
|---|---|---|---|
| Contradictories | Contrariety | Subcontrariety | Subalternate |

11. *If an **E** statement is **true**, then its corresponding **I** statement is…*

| True | False | Undefined | because these statements are… |
|---|---|---|---|
| Contradictories | Contrariety | Subcontrariety | Subalternate |

# Diagram / The Square of Opposition

Remember, the Square of Oppositions provides a visual means of demonstrating the relationships between proposition, namely, the relationships of *contradiction, contrariety, subcontrariety,* and *subalternation*.

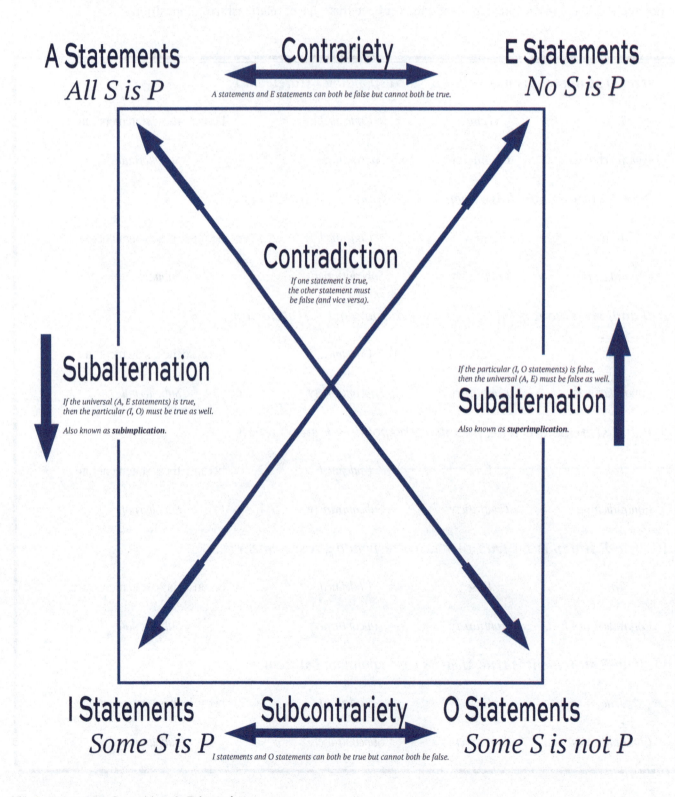

# The Enlightenment, Skepticism, & David Hume

**THE LAST PRIMARY SOURCE TEXT** that we will examine in this section is from **David Hume's** *Enquiry Concerning Human Understanding*. Thus far, we have focused on propositions and epistemology in Section II because logic aims at truth, only propositions can be true, and epistemology is the study of how we know what we know and whether what we know is actually true.

There have been two significant schools of thought concerning how we know what we know: **rationalism** and **empiricism**. Rationalism is the idea that what we know, we know through our unique ability to reason. To explore rationalism, we read a selection from René Descartes, a French philosopher who grounded his confidence in his ability to think. Then we turned to John Locke, a British empiricist who argued that the mind is more like a "blank slate" that lacks the kind of innate ideas that Descartes believed the human mind possessed. Locke argued that if we know anything at all, we know it through our senses, for empiricism says that what information we know about the world, we take in through our senses.

Let's assume, for the moment, we know for sure that empiricism is true. So much of what we know, we know because we saw it, heard about it, or in some other way experienced it. But there is one significant flaw in empiricism, for if we know things through our senses, and if our senses can mislead us, then we cannot wholly trust in or depend on the knowledge we think we have. Moreover, the world we see and experience is constantly changing—does that mean that the knowl-

|| **DAVID HUME / 1711 - 1776**

edge we gain from the world is in constant flux as well? Put another way, if our senses mislead us, if the world around us changes constantly, then we cannot have any real confidence in the knowledge we have gained through sense experience. Our senses may have wrongly interpreted such information, or the world has already changed so that knowledge has become practically worthless. What can we do?

This puzzle is the philosophical problem taken up by the Scottish **Enlightenment** philosopher David Hume, to whose life and works we will now turn—although, as we shall see, David Hume does not necessarily resolve this philosophical problem. Rather, he draws out all the logical implications of empiricism. If empiricism is true and we know things through our senses, then we learn values and moral absolutes through our senses, too. And if we learn morals and axioms through our senses, well, they are privy to the same problems of every other piece of information we take in through our senses, too.

David Hume (1711-1776) was born in Berwickshire, Scotland, near the city of Edinburgh. His father died when Hume was just two, leaving him and his siblings to be raised by their mother. His mother recognized a unique intellectual curiosity in David and allowed the boy to accompany his older brother to the University of Edinburgh, where David became well-versed in the Greco-Latin Classics as early as age 11. He spent time in fairly isolated study reading philosophy, preparing himself for a career as a self-described "Scholar and Philosopher".

In his early twenties, Hume journeyed abroad to France where he carried on his regimen of reading philosophy. During this time France was at the center of an exciting intellectual atmosphere known as the Enlightenment, a movement characterized by its confidence in the powers of human reason, its love for the classics of Greco-Roman antiquity, and its antipathy for organized religion. Hume already possessed the same love for the Latin classics, particularly Cicero, and had already rejected the beliefs held by the Presbyterian Church of Scotland in which he was raised. As a result, Hume rapidly absorbed the intellectual trends promoted by Enlightenment thinkers, commonly called **philosophes**. Hume began writing his first work *A Treatise of Human Nature* in 1734, a work that Hume's critics say promoted an unhealthy skepticism and irreverence, and Hume complained that most people simply ignored the work, which fell "deadborn from the press". The following text is an excerpt from Hume's *Enquiry Concerning Human Understanding*.

Published in 1748, Hume's *Enquiry* reworked many of the same themes and ideas from his earlier *A Treatise of Human Nature* (1739-40) which, despite the work that Hume put into it, barely raised enough "distinctions even to excite a murmur among the zealots", i.e., that work was not popular, and Hume felt like a failure. In both of these texts, Hume applied the rigors of the scientific method to the study of human nature with the hope that in the same manner in which Isaac Newton unlocked the secrets of the universe, Hume could reveal the mysteries of the human condition. This unlocking, Hume believed, could be accomplished if philosophers, building "on a foundation entirely new", confined themselves to a more scientific study of human nature and rejected the unfounded metaphysical assumptions made by Hume's predecessors (*A Treatise of Human Nature*, xvi.6).

But in the process, Hume jettisons other beliefs that cannot necessarily be supported by empirical evidence and scientific study. In this text, David Hume

# Vocabulary

**David Hume**
David Hume was a prominent, Enlightenment-era philosopher. Born in Scotland, Hume was a *skeptic*, meaning he denied the idea that human beings can have any certainty concerning the knowledge we think we know. His most significant works are the A *Treatise of Human Nature* and *An Enquiry Concerning Human Understanding.* He lived from 1711 to 1776.

**Rationalism**
Rationalism is the belief that all knowledge comes in and through the powers of man's reason.

**Empiricism**
From the Greek word for "experience," this is the belief that all knowledge comes through the senses.

**Enlightenment**
An age in European history from approximately 1650 to 1789 when European intellectuals placed incredible confidence in the powers of human reason to solve the problems of society.

**Philosophes**
The *philosophes* were a class of Enlightenment thinkers, who were mostly French but also included individuals from England, Scotland, and Prussia.

**Skepticism**
The denial, or at the very least, the doubt, that we human beings can have certainty of the knowledge we think we know.

follows the logical conclusions of empiricism: if we come to know things through our senses and our senses are unreliable, then we cannot have any real certainty of any knowledge whatsoever —at least nothing beyond sense experience. This philosophy is not empiricism but the idea of **skepticism**, the denial, or, at the very least, the doubting that we can know anything for certain to be true. This doubt is especially true for ideas related to morality, theology, and anything else pertaining to *metaphysics*, ideas and values that cannot be supported by empirical study. These ideas may be more complicated, but they still come to us from sense experience (remember Locke's nursemaid?) and remain as unreliable as any other forms of knowledge.

But as we shall examine later in this textbook, these kinds of arguments for traditional morality form part of the foundation for civilized society. If these beliefs form at least part of the foundation of society, and now we aren't sure if those beliefs are true anymore, well, what kind of society should we build? How should we live? What should we do with those ideas? Let's turn now to the *Enquiry*, for by the end of the work David Hume will have instructed his reader as to exactly what they should do with such arguments.

## Reading Comprehension Questions

1. Who was David Hume? Where is he from and where did he study? What influences contributed to his unique brand of philosophy?

2. What was the Enlightenment, and on what topics were the Enlightenment thinkers (called *philosophes*) focused?

3. How did Hume try to change philosophy?

4. What are the implications of empiricism? How did Hume deal with these implications in his writings?

# Enquiry Concerning Human Understanding / By David Hume

*In the ending to the* Enquiry, *Hume offers his recommendation for what should happen to books that are not based on experience and observation.*

131 It seems to me, that the only objects of the abstract science or of demonstration are **quantity and number**, and that all attempts to extend this more perfect species of knowledge beyond these bounds are mere **sophistry** and illusion. As the component parts of quantity and number are entirely similar, their relations become intricate and involved; and nothing can be more curious, as well as useful, than to trace, by a variety of mediums, their equality or inequality, through their different appearances. But as all other ideas are clearly distinct and different from each other, we can never advance farther, by our utmost scrutiny, than to observe this diversity, and, by an obvious reflection, pronounce one thing not to be another. Or if there be any difficulty in these decisions, it proceeds entirely from the unde-

## Vocabulary & Annotations

**...quantity and number**
In other words, the only sure sources of knowledge are things that can be observed.

**Sophistry**
The term *sophistry* refers to the attempt to make false arguments appear true and intended to deceive people.

**...imperfect definition**
"Imperfect" in the sense that it is incomplete and thus can be made to include another term.

**...syllogistical reasonings**
If a syllogism had clear terms, true propositions, and valid argumentation, then the conclusion of that syllogism had to be true. In contrast, Hume argues that syllogisms are more like imperfect definitions, wherein the syllogism expands to include the term in question.

**...incapable of demonstration**
According to Hume, a metaphysical claim cannot be replicated like an experiment.

**...a priori**
The phrase *a priori* refers to ideas or principles that one may reach apart from experience which, in Hume's estimation, is impossible.

**...to the flames**
The famous conclusion to Hume's *Enquiry* states that any work not supported by empirical observation should be cast into a fire.

**DAVID HUME / 1711 - 1776**
*Portrait by Allan Ramsay, 1766*

terminate meaning of words, which is corrected by juster definitions. That the square of the hypothenuse is equal to the squares of the other two sides, cannot be known, let the terms be ever so exactly defined, without a train of reasoning and enquiry.

But to convince us of this proposition, that where there is no property, there can be no injustice, it is only necessary to define the terms, and explain injustice to be a violation of property. This proposition is, indeed, nothing but a more **imperfect definition**. It is the same case with all those pretended **syllogistical reasonings**, which may be found in every other branch of learning, except the sciences of quantity and number; and these may safely, I think, be pronounced the only proper objects of knowledge and demonstration.

132 All other enquiries of men regard only matter of fact and existence; and these are evidently **incapable of demonstration**. Whatever is may not be. No negation of a fact can involve a contradiction. The non-existence of any being, without exception, is as clear and distinct an idea as its existence. The proposition, which affirms it not to be, however false, is no less conceivable and intelligible, than that which affirms it to be. The case is different with the sciences, properly so called. Every proposition, which is not true, is there confused and unintelligible. That the cube root of 64 is equal to the half of 10, is a false proposition, and can never be distinctly conceived. But that Caesar, or the angel Gabriel, or any being never existed, may be a false proposition, but still is perfectly conceivable, and implies no contradiction.

**133** The existence, therefore, of any being can only be proved by arguments from its cause or its effect; and these arguments are founded entirely on experience. If we reason **a priori**, anything may appear able to produce anything. The falling of a pebble may, for aught we know, extinguish the sun; or the wish of a man control the planets in their orbits. It is only experience, which teaches us the nature and bounds of cause and effect, and enables us to infer the existence of one object from that of another. Such is the foundation of moral reasoning, which forms the greater part of human knowledge, and is the source of all human action and behavior. Moral reasonings are either concerning particular or general facts.

All deliberations in life regard the former; as also all disquisitions in history, chronology, geography, and astronomy. The sciences, which treat of general facts, are politics, natural philosophy, physic, chemistry, &c. where the qualities, causes and effects of a whole species of objects are enquired into. Divinity or Theology, as it proves the existence of a Deity, and the immortality of souls, is composed partly of reasonings concerning particular, partly concerning general facts. It has a foundation in reason, so far as it is supported by experience. But its best and most solid foundation is faith and divine revelation.

Morals and criticism are not so properly objects of the understanding as of taste and sentiment. Beauty, whether moral or natural, is felt, more properly than perceived. Or if we reason concerning it, and endeavor to fix its standard, we regard a new fact, to wit, the general tastes of mankind, or some such fact, which may be the object of reasoning and enquiry. When we run over libraries, persuaded of these principles, what havoc must we make? If we take in our hand any volume; of divinity or school metaphysics, for instance; let us ask, Does it contain any abstract reasoning concerning quantity or number? No. Does it contain any experimental reasoning concerning matter of fact and existence? No. Commit it then **to the flames**: for it can contain nothing but sophistry and illusion.

## Reading Comprehension Questions

1. To Hume, what kind of knowledge can he have the most assurance of?

2. What is *a priori* knowledge, and why is it impossible?

3. Why are metaphysical arguments and historical events incapable of demonstration? (Hint: Be sure to define the word *demonstration* in your answer.)

4. Should we really cast books of metaphysics into the flames? Why or why not?

ACTIVITY

# The First Act of the Mind / Terms

Each row contains a term, the authors use of that term, or a definition of that term suitable for students. If the row contains a quotation, write down a clear, intelligible definition of that term in the box provided. If the term is already defined for you, please find the quotation from the text that supports the appropriate definition.

| Term | Quotes from the Text | Quote Rephrased as a Definition |
|---|---|---|
| Science | | By *science*, David Hume refers to *empirical science* and the Scientific Method, the process of forming a hypothesis, testing it via experimentation and data collection, analyzing that data, and then publishing the results of the experiment. The Scientific Method was still a relatively new phenomenon in Hume's day. |
| Imperfect Definition | But to convince us of this proposition, that where there is no property, there can be no injustice, it is only necessary to define the terms, and explain injustice to be a violation of property. This proposition is, indeed, nothing but a more imperfect definition. | |
| Sophistry | | Sophistry is a kind of logical sleight-of-hand, and it occurs when someone makes a bad, pernicious argument seem good; or makes a good, worthwhile conclusion seem bad. |

ACTIVITY

# The First Act of the Mind / Terms

Each row contains a term, the authors use of that term, or a definition of that term suitable for students. If the row contains a quotation, write down a clear, intelligible definition of that term in the box provided. If the term is already defined for you, please find the quotation from the text that supports the appropriate definition.

| Term | Quotes from the Text | Quote Rephrased as a Definition |
|---|---|---|
| Contradiction | | By the word *contradiction*, Hume refers to concepts that could both be and not be because they are ultimately contingent on something else. To say that a triangle has more than 3 sides implies such a contradiction, but to say Julius Caesar did or did not exist is not a contradiction because his existence is contingent upon something else. |
| Moral | *Moral reasonings are either concerning particular or general facts. All deliberations in life regard the former; as also all disquisitions in history, chronology, geography, and astronomy.* | |
| Sentiment | | *Sentiment* in the sense of mere opinion, not an absolute value that in some way, shape, or form exists independently of an individual who may hold to one such sentiment. |

CHAPTER 9 The Square of Opposition ◆ 265

ACTIVITY

# The Second Act of the Mind / **Propositions**

Each row contains an excerpt from the significant text included in this chapter. These selections include significant points and ideas the author uses to build his argument and reach a meaningful conclusion, one that was not apparent at the beginning of their work. In the space provided, write a summary of the quotation and try to express it in the form of a proposition.

| Quotations from Text | Quotations rephrased as Propositions |
|---|---|
| *It seems to me, that the only objects of the abstract science or of demonstration are quantity and number, and that all attempts to extend this more perfect species of knowledge beyond these bounds are mere sophistry and illusion.* | |
| *It is the same case with all those pretended syllogistical reasonings, which may be found in every other branch of learning, except the sciences of quantity and number; and these may safely, I think, be pronounced the only proper objects of knowledge and demonstration.* | |

ACTIVITY

# The Second Act of the Mind / Propositions

Each row contains an excerpt from the significant text included in this chapter. These selections include significant points and ideas the author uses to build his argument and reach a meaningful conclusion, one that was not apparent at the beginning of their work. In the space provided, write a summary of the quotation and try to express it in the form of a proposition.

| Quotations from Text | Quotations rephrased as Propositions |
|---|---|
| *The sciences, which treat of general facts, are politics, natural philosophy, physic, chemistry, &c. where the qualities, causes and effects of a whole species of objects are enquired into.* | |
| *If we take in our hand any volume; of divinity or school metaphysics, for instance; let us ask, Does it contain any abstract reasoning concerning quantity or number? No. Does it contain any experimental reasoning concerning matter of fact and existence? No. Commit it then to the flames: for it can contain nothing but sophistry and illusion.* | |

ACTIVITY

# The Third Act of the Mind / **Inferences**

In the space below, create an "argument map", a visual way of representing the premises, assumptions, and ultimately the conclusion that a writer is making in their work. You can also use this blank space provided to draw a "conversation map", a visual way of recording the discussion your class had over this text.

WRITING

# Writing Prompt

Remember, writing is thinking. To help us to write and think more clearly, we will spend considerable time this year writing essays based on the texts we read in class. These essays are descriptive in nature and answer one question that arises from the material we are reading in class. In such an essay, the writer wants to explain the meaningful ideas contained in this text by reading and rereading the text under analysis to better explain that author's argument and the consequences of his or her ideas.

**Question**: *What are the logical conclusions of empiricism, the implications that David Hume draws out for his readers?*

## Writing

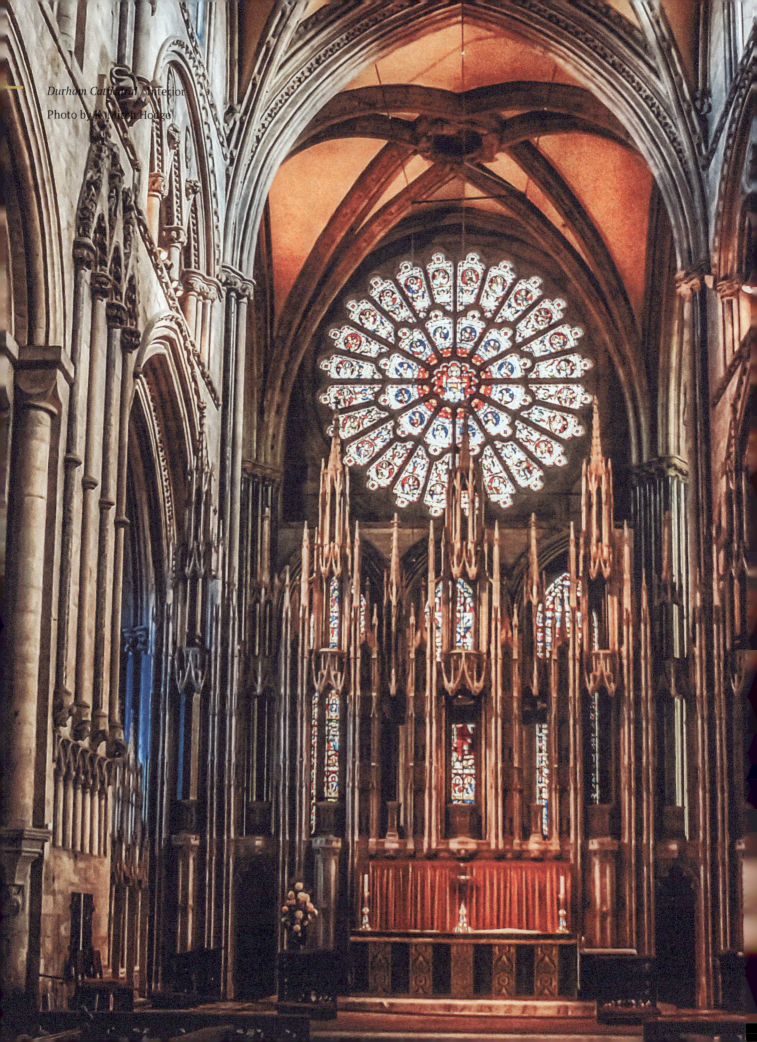
*Durham Cathedral* Interior
Photo by K. Mitch Hodge

APPENDIX

# Appendix

### ROADMAP

- A suggested rubric for formal writing assignments.
- A suggested rubric for formal, in-class presentations.
- A *Socratic Seminar* prep sheet to help students practice the skills of analytical reading. Teachers may give this prep sheet to students to complete as they are reading the primary source texts.
- A sample *Conversation Map*, which can be used to provide a visual diagram of seminar discussion.

ESSAY

# Essay Rubric

Logic is the art of right thinking. To help us to think more clearly, we will spend considerable time this quarter writing expository essays based on the texts we read in class. These expository essays are descriptive in nature and answer one question that arises from the material we are reading in class. Essentially, an expository essay is one that explains. In an expository essay, the writer seeks to explain by reading and rereading the text under analysis to better explain the author's argument and the consequences of their ideas. Each essay will be graded according to the following rubric (see below).

| Essay Component | Criteria |
| --- | --- |
| **Introduction** <br> 5 points per criterion <br> ___ / 25 points | ___ Hook <br><br> ___ Background Information of time period, author, philosophical problem, etc. <br><br> ___ Context, in terms of the author's background, the main idea of the text, the problem the author is trying to solve, etc. <br><br> ___ Underlined Thesis statement (a debatable claim that contains 1 to 2 reasons why that claim is correct) <br><br> ___ MLA Format (Heading, Double Spaced, etc.) |
| **Body Paragraph** <br> 5 points per criterion <br> ___ / 20 points | ___ Hook (short, pithy, includes language from thesis statement) <br><br> ___ Evidence (specific examples from reading, quotes from text, etc.) <br><br> ___ Explanation / Analysis / Synthesis (the significance of this information in light of the student's thesis) <br><br> ___ Transition |
| **Conclusion** <br> 5 points per criterion <br> ___ / 15 points | ___ Synthesis of main points <br><br> ___ Restatement of thesis <br><br> ___ Meaningful send-off to reader |

TOTAL: ___ / 60 POINTS

ESSAY

# Presentation Rubric

The third way of the trivium is *rhetoric*, the art of public speaking. In the ancient world, public speaking was equated with public service and leadership, for the speaker recognized the best course of action for his city and had to bring together the words, thoughts, and arguments to deliver a speech that fit whatever the occasion called for. Rhetoric encompassed all the skills needed to argue rightly on a subject and compose a speech that is logically sound, aesthetically pleasing, and powerfully delivered so that the audience is inspired to take up the course of action expounded upon by the orator. As a result, we will spend time this year writing and delivering speeches and developing our ability to speak persuasively.

| Presentation Component | Criteria |
|---|---|
| **Content of Speech** <br> 5 points per criterion <br> ___ / 20 points | ___ Student presents a clear, defensible, and persuasive claim. <br><br> ___ Thesis is clear and well-defined, uses interesting and engaging word choice, and is presented logically and precisely throughout the entire presentation. <br><br> ___ Student presents clear and accurate ideas in support of his/her thesis. <br><br> ___ The thesis topic arises out of the events, figures, and ideas of the Western tradition. |
| **Presentation** <br> 5 points per criterion <br> ___ / 20 points | ___ Student holds the attention of the audience with eye contact <br><br> ___ Student displays appropriate and professional movements (standing upright with a confident demeanor). <br><br> ___ Student speaks with an engaging tone of voice, interesting inflections for key points, and outstanding pacing. <br><br> ___ The presentation is enthusiastic, relevant, and engaging. |
| **Visual Aids and Preparation** <br> 5 points per criterion <br> ___ / 20 points | ___ Presentation is clear, attractive, and professional, free of errors. <br><br> ___ The presentation includes consistent, easy-to-read font choices. <br><br> ___ Text and images are centered, aligned, and consistent. <br><br> ___ Student chooses harmonious and appealing style, color, and template choices. |

TOTAL: ___ / 60 POINTS

ACTIVITY

# Socratic Seminar Prep Sheet

A Socratic seminar is a guided, yet free-flowing discussion about ideas that matter. They are lively conversations among teachers and students around the investigation of a great text, an inspiring work of art, or some other meaningful idea or concept worth discussing. To prepare for our Socratic seminar, let us examine some key pieces of information about this text by filling in the blank spaces of this *Socratic Seminar Prep Sheet*.

| | |
|---|---|
| Author | |
| Title | |
| Literary Genre | |
| Date of Composition | |
| **Key Ideas** *The ideas that we should understand well enough to analyze this particular text and evaluate the ideas within it.* | |
| **Key Vocabulary** *Words that are either so difficult, so crucial, or so abstract that they merit special consideration.* | |
| **The "Big Idea"** *The "Big Idea" may be the central claim (or claims) that the author is trying to advance in his or her work, or it may be an idea that speaks to transcendent values such as truth, beauty, justice, and virtue. Or, the text may interact with deeply-rooted issues in the human condition so that no matter how long ago the text was written, it can speak to and inspire us today.* *In short, the "Big Idea" is the most important idea or ideas circulating through this text.* | |

ACTIVITY

# Socratic Seminar / Conversation Map

A Socratic seminar is a guided, yet free-flowing discussion about ideas that matter. They are lively conversations among teachers and students around the investigation of a great text, an inspiring work of art, or some other meaningful idea or concept worth discussing. Use the space provided to take notes during the seminar.

> *In the space provided, consider drawing a conversation map, a visual representation of a seminar. To draw a conversation map, look around the room and take note of where each of your classmates is sitting; then write their initials on the space below in that order. As the seminar conversation moves forward, write down a brief comment about each contribution and a line connecting one speaker to another.*

# Works Cited

**Adler, Mortimer J. and Charles Van Doren.** *How to Read a Book: The Classic Guide to Intelligent Reading.* Simon & Schuster, 1972.

**Aquinas, Thomas.** *Summa Theologiae.* Translated by Fathers of the English Dominican Province, Benziger Bros, 1947, Christian Classics Ethereal Library, https://ccel.org/ccel/Aquinas/summa/summa.i.html.

**Archie, Lee.** "Venn Diagrams." Venn Diagrams for Categorical Syllogisms, https://philosophy.lander.edu/logic/syll_venn.html.

**Aristotle.** *The Complete Works of Aristotle.* Edited by Jonathan Barnes, I, Princeton Univ. Press, 1995.

**Aristotle.** *Categories.* Translated by E.H. Edgehill, https://classics.mit.edu/Aristotle/categories.html

**Aristotle.** *Metaphysics.* Translated by W. D. Ross, MIT Classics Archive, http://classics.mit.edu/Aristotle/metaphysics.html.

**Aristotle.** *Physics.* Translated by R. P. Hardie and R. K. Gaye, MIT Classics Archive, 2009, classics.mit.edu/Aristotle/physics.html.

**Aristotle.** *Poetics.* Translated by S. H. Butcher, classics.mit.edu/Aristotle/poetics.html.

**Aristotle.** *Rhetoric.* Translated by W. Rhys. Roberts, MIT Classics Archive, 1924. http://classics.mit.edu/Aristotle/rhetoric.1.i.html

**Aristotle.** *Topics.* Translated by W. A. Pickard-Cambridge, MIT Classics Archive, 2009, classics.mit.edu/Aristotle/topics.1.i.html.

**Arryn, Larry.** "Introduction to Aristotle's Ethics: How to Lead a Good Life." Hillsdale College, https://online.hillsdale.edu/landing/aristotles-ethics.

**Augustine.** *Confessions.* Translated by Henry Chadwick. Oxford University Press, 2008.

**Augustine.** *The Confessions.* Translated by E. B. Pusey, Project Gutenberg, https://www.gutenberg.org/files/3296/3296-h/3296-h.htm#link2H_4_0001.

**Bacon, Francis.** *Novum Organum,* edited by Jon Roland, Constitution Society, 2016. http://www.constitution.org/bacon/nov_org.htm

**Bastiat, Frédéric.** "That Which Is Seen and That Which Is Not Seen." 1848, Foundation for Economic Education, https://fee.org/resources/that-which-is-seen-and-that-which-is-not-seen.

**Bok, Hilary.** "Baron De Montesquieu, Charles-Louis De Secondat." Stanford Encyclopedia of Philosophy, *Stanford University*, 2 Apr. 2014, plato.stanford.edu/entries/montesquieu/.

**Booth, Wayne C., Gregory G. Colomb, and Joseph M. Williams.** *The Craft of Research.* University of Chicago Press, 2008.

# Works Cited

**Boyer, Carl B**. "Leonhard Euler". Encyclopedia Britannica, 14 Sep. 2021, https://www.britannica.com/biography/Leonhard-Euler. Accessed 1 November 2021.

**Brann, Eva.** "Plato's Theory of Ideas." *The Imaginative Conservative*, 2019. August 5. https://theimaginativeconservative.org/2019/08/plato-theory-ideas-eva-brann-90.html.

**Cohen, S. Marc, and C. D. C. Reeve**. "Aristotle's Metaphysics." Stanford Encyclopedia of Philosophy, Stanford University, 21 Nov. 2020, plato.stanford.edu/entries/aristotle-metaphysics/#SubjMattArisMeta.

**Cooper, John M.** editor. *Plato: Complete Works*. Cambridge: Hackett, 1997.

**Corbett, Edward P.J.** *Classical Rhetoric for the Modern Student.* Oxford University Press, 1971.

**Descartes, René.** *Discourse on Method.* Translated by John Veitch, 1637, Project Gutenberg, https://www.gutenberg.org/files/59/59-h/59-h.htm.

**Devey, Joseph**, editor. *Novum Organum*. Project Gutenberg, 2014, The Project Gutenberg EBook of *Novum Organum*, by Francis Bacon, https://www.gutenberg.org/files/45988/45988-h/45988-h.htm.

**Editors of Encyclopædia Britannica.** *"Phenomenon."* Encyclopædia Britannica. Encyclopædia Britannica, inc, n.d., britannica.com/topic/phenomenon-philosophy/

**Euclid.** *Elements.* Translated by John Casey. Project Gutenberg, 2021. https://gutenberg.org/files/21076/21076-h/21076-h.htm.

**Falcon, Andrea.** "Aristotle on Causality." Stanford Encyclopedia of Philosophy, Stanford University, 7 Mar. 2019, plato.stanford.edu/entries/aristotle-causality/#FouCau.

**Halsall, Paul**. "Medieval Sourcebook: Thomas Aquinas: Reasons in Proof of the Existence of God, 1270." Fordham University, http://legacy.fordham.edu/Halsall/source/aquinas3.asp. Accessed 1 Apr. 2016.

**Hatfield, Gary.** *"René Descartes."* Stanford Encyclopedia of Philosophy, Stanford University, 3 Dec. 2008, plato.stanford.edu/archives/sum2016/entries/descartes/.

**Hayek, Friedrich**. *The Road to Serfdom.* Edited by Bruce Caldwell. University of Chicago Press, 2007.

**Hobbes, Thomas**. *Leviathan, or the Matter, Forme, & Power of a Common-Wealth Ecclesiastical and Civill*. 1651, Project Gutenberg, https://www.gutenberg.org/files/3207/3207-h/3207-h.htm.

**Hume, David**. *An Enquiry Concerning Human Understanding.* Project Gutenberg, 2017, https://www.gutenberg.org/files/9662/9662-h/9662-h.htm.

**Hume, David**. *A Treatise of Human Nature.* Clarendon Press, 1739. Online Library of Liberty, https://oll.libertyfund.org/title/bigge-a-treatise-of-human-nature

**Humphreys, Justin.** *"Aristotle."* Internet Encyclopedia of Philosophy, www.iep.utm.edu/aristotl/#H7.

# Works Cited

**James, William.** *The Meaning of Truth.* 2016. http://fair-use.org/william-james/the-meaning-of-truth/preface

**Joyce, David E.** "Euclid's Elements, Book III." Clark University, 1996. Web. 13 Oct. 2016. aleph0.clarku.edu/~djoyce/java/elements/bookIII/bookIII.html>.

**Kennedy, George Alexander.** *Quintilian: A Roman Educator and His Quest for the Perfect Orator.* Sophron, 2017.

**Kraut, Richard.** "Plato." Edited by Edward Zalta. Stanford Encyclopedia of Philosophy, Fall, 2017. https://plato.stanford.edu/archives/fall2017/entries/plato/.

**Kreeft, Peter.** *Socratic Logic: A Logic Text Using Socratic Method, Platonic Questions, and Aristotelian Principles.* South Bend: St. Augustine Press, 2010.

**Larsen, Aaron, and Joelle Hodge.** *The Art of Argument: An Introduction to the Informal Fallacies.* Classical Academic Press, 2010.

**Locke, John.** *An Essay Concerning Human Understanding.* Project Gutenberg, 2017, *An Essay Concerning Human Understanding,* www.gutenberg.org/files/10615/10615-h/10615-h.htm.

"Ludwig Von Mises." Mises Institute, The Mises Institute, 28 July 2014, mises.org/profile/ludwig-von-mises.

**Machiavelli, Niccolò.** *The Prince.* Translated by W.K. Marriott. Edited by John Bickers, David Widger, et al. 1908. www.gutenberg.org/files/1232/1232-h/1232-h.htm#link2HCH0001

**Madison, James.** *The Federalist #10.* Ed. by Jon Roland. Constitution Society, 1 June. 2015. www.constitution.org/fed/federa10.htm>. Accessed 23 June 2015.

**Madison, James.** "The Federalist #51." Ed. by Jon Roland. Constitution Society, 1 June. 2015. www.constitution.org/fed/federa51.htm. Accessed 23 June 2015.

**McInerny, Ralph, and John O'Callaghan.** "Saint Thomas Aquinas." Stanford Encyclopedia of Philosophy, 1 May 2014, plato.stanford.edu/entries/aquinas/#Chr.

**Montesquieu, Charles.** *Complete Works, vol. 1 The Spirit of Laws.* T. Evans, 1748. Online Library of Liberty, oll.libertyfund.org/title/montesquieu-complete-works-vol-1-the-spirit-of-laws

**Mumma, John**, et al. "Diagrams." Stanford Encyclopedia of Philosophy, edited by Edward Zalta, 1 Jan. 2018, plato.stanford.edu/archives/win2018/entries/diagrams. Accessed 1 Apr. 2016.

**Plato.** *The Apology.* Edited by Daniel C Stevenson and Daniel Stevenson, Translated by Benjamin Jowett, MIT Classics Archive, http://classics.mit.edu/Plato/apology.html.

**Plato.** *Euthyphro.* Translated by Benjamin Jowett. MIT Classics Archive. n.d. classics.mit.edu/Plato/euthyfro.html.

# Works Cited

**Plato.** *Gorgias.* Translated by Benjamin Jowett. MIT Classics Archive. n.d. classics.mit.edu/Plato/gorgias.html.

**Plato.** *Phaedrus.* Translated by Benjamin Jowett. MIT Classics Archive. n.d. classics.mit.edu/Plato/phaedrus.html.

**Plato.** *The Republic.* Translated by Benjamin Jowett. MIT Classics Archive. n.d. classics.mit.edu/Plato/republic.3.ii.html.

**Quintilian.** *Institutes of Oratory, or, Education of an Orator.* Edited by Curtis Dozier and Lee Honeycutt, translated by J. S. Watson, 2015.

**Ricardo, David.** *On the Principles of Political Economy and Taxation.* Library of Economics and Liberty, 1999. www.econlib.org/library/Ricardo/ricP.html.

**Robinson, Howard.** "Substance." Stanford Encyclopedia of Philosophy, Stanford University, 16 Nov. 2018, plato.stanford.edu/entries/substance/#ArisAccoSubs.

**Rohlf, Michael.** "Immanuel Kant." Stanford Encyclopedia of Philosophy, Stanford University, 20 May 2010, plato.stanford.edu/archives/spr2016/entries/kant/.

**Roland, Jon.** *Rousseau: Social Contract.* Constitution Society, 1 June 2015. www.constitution.org/jjr/socon.htm. Accessed 24 June 2015

**Rousseau, Jean-Jacques.** *The Social Contract and Discourses.* J. M. Dent, 1761. oll.libertyfund.org/title/cole-the-social-contract-and-discourses

**Shields, Christopher.** "Aristotle." Stanford Encyclopedia of Philosophy. Stanford University, 25 Sept. 2008, plato.stanford.edu/entries/aristotle/

**Smith, Nicholas D.** "Plato." Edited by James Fieser and Bradley Dowden. *Internet Encyclopedia of Philosophy,* 2017. iep.utm.edu/plato/.

**Studtmann, Paul.** "Aristotle's Categories." Stanford Encyclopedia of Philosophy, Stanford University, 2 Feb. 2021, plato.stanford.edu/entries/aristotle-categories/#GenDis.

**Thatcher, Oliver, editor.** *The Early Medieval World.* Milwaukee: University Research Extension Co, 1907.

**Turabian, Kate L.** *A Manual for Writers of Research Papers, Theses, and Dissertations, Ninth Edition: Chicago Style for Students and Researchers.* University of Chicago Press, 2018.

**Zinsser, William.** *On Writing Well: The Classic Guide to Writing Nonfiction.* Harper Collins, 2006.

# Photography Credits

## Section I: Terms & Metaphysics

The portrait of the bust of Plato is available in the public domain and is accessible at <https://en.wikipedia.org/wiki/Plato#/media/File:Plato_Silanion_Musei_Capitolini_MC1377.jpg>.

The photo of the US Capitol, West Side, is available via a Creative Commons license, was taken by user Martin Falbisoner on September 5, 2013, and is accessible at <https://en.wikipedia.org/wiki/United_States_Capitol#/media/File:US_Capitol_west_side.JPG>.

The photo of the Roman Forum is available via a GFDL license and is accessible at <https://en.wikipedia.org/wiki/Roman_Forum#/media/File:Roman_forum_cropped.jpg>.

The photo of Chartes Cathedral is available via an Unsplash license, was taken by user K. Mitch Hodge, and is accessible at <https://unsplash.com/photos/5BksR6Ne-Vo>.

The photo of the bust of Socrates is available via a Creative Commons license and was made by user named Sting; the photo is accessible at <https://en.wikipedia.org/wiki/Socrates#/media/File:Socrate_du_Louvre.jpg>.

The fresco of Euclid from Raphael's *School of Athens* is available in the public domain and may be accessed at <https://en.wikipedia.org/wiki/Euclid#/media/File:Scuola_di_atene_23.jpg>.

The photo of Aristotle of a bust from the third century is available in the public domain and may be accessed at <https://en.wikipedia.org/wiki/Aristotle#/media/File:Aristotle_Altemps_Inv8575.jpg>.

The photo of the bust of Plato is available in the public domain and may be accessed at <https://en.wikipedia.org/wiki/Plato#/media/File:Plato_Silanion_Musei_Capitolini_MC1377.jpg>.

The illustration of Porphyry is available in the public domain and may be accessed at <https://upload.wikimedia.org/wikipedia/commons/a/a6/Porphyry.jpg>.

The diagram of the tree of Porphyr is available a Creative Commons license, was made by user VoiceoftheCommons on May 27, 2013, and is accessible at <https://en.wikipedia.org/wiki/Porphyrian_tree#/media/File:Porphyrian_Tree.png

The sketch of William of Ockham is available in the public domain and may be accessed at <https://en.wikipedia.org/wiki/William_of_Ockham#/media/File:William_of_Ockham_-_Logica_1341.jpg>.

The illustration of the liberal arts is available in the public domain and is accessible at <https://en.wikipedia.org/wiki/Liberal_arts_education#/media/File:Hortus_Deliciarum,_Die_Philosophie_mit_den_sieben_freien_K%C3%BCnsten.JPG>.

The drawing of Porphry is available in the public domain and is accessible at <https://en.wikipedia.org/wiki/Porphyry_(philosopher)#/media/File:Porphyry.jpg>.

The photo of the Greek and Latin text of Plato's Euthyphro is available in the public domain and is accessible at <https://en.wikipedia.org/wiki/Euthyphro#/media/File:Euthyphro_Stephanus_1578_p_2.jpg>.

The 6th-c. portrait of St. Augustine is available in the public domain and is accessible at <https://en.wikipedia.org/wiki/Augustine_of_Hippo#/media/File:Augustine_Lateran.jpg>.

The photo of the Chimera of Arezzo / Etruscan Bronze is available via a Creative Commons license, was taken by user Saliko on June 7, 2012, and is accessible at <https://

# Photography Credits

en.wikipedia.org/wiki/Chimera_(mythology)#/media/File:Chimera_d'arezzo,_fi,_04.JPG>.

The photograph of the mosaic of Plato's Academy is available in the public domain and is accessible at <https://en.wikipedia.org/wiki/Plato%27s_Academy_mosaic>.Section I / Terms & Metaphysics

The drawing of Canterbury Cathedral is available in the public domain and may be accessed at <https://commons.wikimedia.org/wiki/File:Wenceslas_Hollar_-_Canterbury_Cathedral-_south_side_(State_2).jpg>.

The photo of the bust of Plato is available in the public domain and may be accessed at <https://en.wikipedia.org/wiki/Plato#/media/File:Plato_Silanion_Musei_Capitolini_MC1377.jpg>.

The photo of the bust of Socrates is available via a Creative Commons license and was made by user named Sting; the photo is accessible at <https://en.wikipedia.org/wiki/Socrates#/media/File:Socrate_du_Louvre.jpg>.

The fresco of Euclid from Raphael's *School of Athens* is available in the public domain and may be accessed at <https://en.wikipedia.org/wiki/Euclid#/media/File:Scuola_di_atene_23.jpg>.

The photo of Aristotle of a bust from the third century is available in the public domain and may be accessed at <https://en.wikipedia.org/wiki/Aristotle#/media/File:Aristotle_Altemps_Inv8575.jpg>.

The illustration of Porphyry is available in the public domain and may be accessed at <https://upload.wikimedia.org/wikipedia/commons/a/a6/Porphyry.jpg>.

The sketch of William of Ockham is available in the public domain and may be accessed at <https://en.wikipedia.org/wiki/William_of_Ockham#/media/File:William_of_Ockham_-_Logica_1341.jpg>.

The illustration of St. Augustine is available in the public domain and may be accessed at <https://en.wikipedia.org/wiki/Augustine_of_Hippo#/media/File:Augustine_Lateran.jpg>.

The painting of Valle Romita Polyptych by Gentile da Fabriano (c. 1400) is available in the public domain and may be accessed at <https://en.wikipedia.org/wiki/Thomas_Aquinas#/media/File:Gentile_da_Fabriano_052.jpg>.

The drawing of Daedalus is available in the public domain and is accessible at <https://en.wikipedia.org/wiki/Daedalus#/media/File:Daedalus_escapes_(iuvat_evasisse).jpg>.

The picture of the Acropolis is available via an Unsplash license, was made by user Victor Malyushev, and is accessible at <https://unsplash.com/photos/WVrrQgjH6y4>.

The fresco of Aristotle from Raphael's "School of Athens" is available in the public domain and may be accessed at <https://en.wikipedia.org/wiki/The_School_of_Athens#/media/File:%22The_School_of_Athens%22_by_Raffaello_Sanzio_da_Urbino.jpg>.

## Section II: Propositions & Epistemology

The photograph of the lateral entrance of Westminster Abbey is available via an Unsplash license, was made by user Zaymuel, and is accessible at <https://unsplash.com/@zaymuel>.

The relief of Plato and Aristotle is available via a Creative Commons license, was made by user I, Sailko on July 12, 2007, and is accessible at <https://en.wikipedia.org/wiki/Aristotle#/media/File:Formella_21,_platone_e_aristotele_o_la_filosofia,_luca_della_robbia,_1437-1439.JPG>.

# Photography Credits

The photograph of the nave of Westminster Abbey is available via an Unsplash license, was made by user K. Mitch Hodge, and is accessible at <https://unsplash.com/@kmitchhodge>.

The illustration of the Library of Alexandria is available in the public domain and is accessible at <https://en.wikipedia.org/wiki/Library_of_Alexandria#/media/File:Ancientlibraryalex.jpg>.

The painting entitled "The Death of Socrates" by Jacques-Louis David is available in the public domain and is accessible at <https://en.wikipedia.org/wiki/The_Death_of_Socrates#/media/File:David_-_The_Death_of_Socrates.jpg>.

The painting entitled "Ecce Homo" by Antonio Ciseri is available in the public domain and is accessible at <https://en.wikipedia.org/wiki/Ecce_homo#/media/File:Ecce_homo_by_Antonio_Ciseri_(1).jpg>.

The painting entitled "The Christian Martyrs' Last Prayer" by Jean-Léon Gérôme is available in the public domain and is accessible at <https://en.wikipedia.org/wiki/Jean-Léon_Gérôme#/media/File:Jean-Léon_Gérôme_-_The_Christian_Martyrs'_Last_Prayer_-_Walters_37113.jpg>.

The fresco of St. Augustine is available in the public domain and is accessible at <https://en.wikipedia.org/wiki/Augustine_of_Hippo#/media/File:Augustine_Lateran.jpg >.

The map of the Fall of the Roman Empire is available via a Creative Commons license, was taken by user MapMaster on October 1, 2006 and https://en.wikipedia.org/wiki/Fall_of_the_Western_Roman_Empire#/media/File:Invasions_of_the_Roman_Empire_1.png>.

The portrait of Saint Augustine of Hippo and Saint Thomas of Aquino by Pieter Jozef Verhagen https://commons.wikimedia.org/wiki/File:Pieter_Jozef_Verhaghen_-_Saint_August_of_Hippo_and_Saint_Thomas_of_Aquino.jpg>.

The page from an illuminated manuscript of Lady Philosophy and Boethius is available in the public domain and is accessible at <https://upload.wikimedia.org/wikipedia/commons/1/1c/Boethius.consolation.philosophy.jpg>.

The image of a 14th century university lecture is available in the public domain and is accessible at < https://en.wikipedia.org/wiki/Scholasticism#/media/File:Laurentius_de_Voltolina_001.jpg>.

The portrait of William James is available in the public domain and is accessible at <https://en.wikipedia.org/wiki/William_James#/media/File:William_James_b1842c.jpg>.

The fresco of Aristotle is available in the public domain and is accessible at <https://en.wikipedia.org/wiki/Aristotle#/media/File:Francesco_Hayez_001.jpg>.

The drawing of Westminster Abbey is available in the public domain and may be accessed at <https://en.wikipedia.org/wiki/Westminster_Abbey#/media/File:Westminster_Abbey_c1711.jpg>.

The portrait of David Hume is available in the public domain and is accessible at < https://en.wikipedia.org/wiki/David_Hume#/media/File:Allan_Ramsay_-_David_Hume,_1711_-_1776._Historian_and_philosopher_-_Google_Art_Project.jpg>.

# Glossary of Terms

## A

**A Statement**: A universal affirmative proposition that affirms something is true (and is always true) about the entirety of the subject. A Statements take the form, "All [S] is [P]."

**Accident**: A characteristic that can be present or be missing from a subject without detracting from or adding to the essence of that particular subject.

**Acropolis**: The Acropolis was the main citadel at Athens, located on top of a massive, rocky outcropping in the center of the city.

**Adam Smith**: A Scottish moral philosopher who lived from 1723-1790; he is credited with inventing economics as the modern scientific discipline we know today; author of The Wealth of Nations (1776) and The Theory of Moral Sentiments (1759).

**Affirmative**: When the proposition affirms something about the subject.

**Alexandria, Egypt**: Founded by Alexander the Great, this was a cosmopolitan port city located in the Nile delta; the city was one of the largest in the ancient world and, despite being in Egypt, was a center for Greek culture.

**Allegory**: An allegory is an extended metaphor where different people, places, and things have a deeper meaning that is often moral, philosophical, or theological.

**Analogical Terms**: A term that has multiple but related shades of meaning and thus can describe many different things; such terms include adjectives like "good," "bad," "love," etc.

**Analogy**: A comparison between two things to illustrate a point.

**Antecedent**: In a hypothetical statement, this term refers to the proposition that comes first after "if". The word "antecedent" comes from the Latin "to go before," with the prefix "ante" meaning "before" or "in front of."

**Apprehension**: This is the first act of the mind that focuses on the clear understanding of terms. Also known as simple apprehension.

**Aquinas, Thomas**: A philosopher and theologian from Italy, author of the *Summa Theologiae*, and amongst the most noteworthy members of the Scholastics; amongst his most notable accomplishments are integrating the ideas of Aristotle with elements of Christian faith and doctrine. Aquinas lived from 1225 to 1274 AD.

**Argument**: In logic, an argument is composed of two or more propositions called "premises" that, if those premises contain clear terms and true propositions, lead to a conclusion.

**Argument to the Greater**: An argument from the lesser to the greater, so that if some smaller and less significant thing is true, then a greater and more significant instance of this thing should be true as well. At times, this argument is referred to as argumentum a fortiori.

**Argument to the Lesser**: An argument from the greater to the lesser, so that if some greater and more significant example is true, then a lesser significant instance of this thing should be true as well. At times, this argument is referred to as *argumentum a maiori ad minus*.

**Aristotle**: A Greek philosopher whose writings on *Politics, Poetics, Physics, Metaphysics, and Rhetoric* form the basis for the Western canon. He lived from 384 to 322 BC.

**Aristotle's Rules**: These are the ways by which we can determine the validity of an argument. Some logic

# Glossary of Terms

books cite six rules and others seven; our book cites seven rules.

**Augustine**: A philosopher and theologian from North Africa, author of *The Confessions* and *City of God*; amongst his most notable accomplishments are integrating ideas of Platonism with elements of Christian faith and doctrine. He lived from 354 to 430 AD.

**Austrian School**: Austrian Economics is a school of economic thought dating back to the late 19th century, deriving its name from the home country of the economists who are credited with founding this unique theoretical approach to economics. Austrian economics focuses on the choices individuals make to achieve ends they find desirable.

### B

**Bacon, Francis**: English philosopher and government official who is credited with inventing the Scientific Method. He lived from 1561 to 1626.

**Barbara**: The name for a syllogism comprised of three A statements and in the first figure.

**Bastiat, Frédéric**: A French economist, most famous for his writings on classical economics and for developing the idea of the opportunity cost in economic thinking.

**Bramantip**: The name for a syllogism comprised of an A statement for its major premise, an A statement for its minor premise, and an I statement in the conclusion; this syllogism is in the fourth figure.

### C

**Categories**: Aristotle's *Categories* are ten ways in which language may reflect being and include the ideas of substance, quantity, qualities, relation, place, time, posture, possession, action, and passion.

**Categorical Form**: The particular arrangement of terms in a proposition. A syllogism in categorical form contains three sentences arranged in categorical form, with the major premise appearing first, the minor premise second, and the conclusion third.

**Categorical Logic**: The kind of logic that focuses on the relationship between categories of things.

**Categorical Propositions**: The particular arrangement of terms in a proposition containing a subject, predicate, copula, and quantifier.

**Cathedral**: A church constructed during the medieval period made of marble or limestone. They were hundreds of feet in height and were constructed to resemble beams of light.

**Causation**: The idea that one thing, event, person, idea, etc. causes another thing, event, person, idea, etc. to come into being.

**Cesare** The name for a syllogism comprised of an E statement for its major premise, an A statement for its minor premise, and an E statement in the conclusion; this syllogism is in the second figure.

**Christianity**: A religion that grew out of 1st century Judaism, centered on the life, teaching, death, and resurrection of Jesus Christ, whom Christians believe to be the Messiah and the Son of God.

**Circle**: A 360° shape wherein each point on its circumference is equidistant from the center.

**Classical Economists**: Influenced by the work of Adam Smith, this is a school of economic thought that favors free trade and minimal government interference.

# Glossary of Terms

**Compound Syllogism**: A compound syllogism is a syllogism whose first premise is technically two different propositions; the second premise then affirms or denies something about the first premise, leading to the conclusion.

**Comprehension**: The inward, subjective understanding of a term and the various attributes of that term.

**Concept**: The image in our mind of a thing, which transcends space and time.

**Conclusion**: The point that an argument is making.

*Confessions*: The spiritual autobiography of the philosopher Augustine.

**Conjunctive Syllogism**: A conjunctive syllogism is one that begins with a conjunctive statement, one using the correlating conjunctions "both" and "and". A conjunctive statement that has been negated states that the two propositions cannot both be true at the same time.

**Connotation**: The thought or feeling invoked by the use of a word alongside its dictionary definition.

**Consequent**: In a hypothetical statement, this term refers to the proposition that comes after "then" and follows after the antecedent. The word *consequent* comes from the Latin "to follow after", with the prefix "con" meaning "with".

**Contingent**: A proposition or state of affairs that could have existed otherwise.

**Contradictions**: The relationship between A and O statements, and between E and I statements. These pairs of statements cannot both be true at the same time; an A statement is proven false by an O statement (and vice-versa), and an E statement is proven false by an I statement (and vice-versa).

**Contrariety**: The relationship between A and E statements, in that two universal propositions with the same subject and the same predicate can both be false, but they cannot both be true.

**Conversion**: The process of interchanging the subject and predicate in a sentence to create an equivalent statement; conversion only works on E statements and I statements.

**Copula**: The linking verb that joins together the subject and the predicate in a categorical proposition; most often, it is a form of the verb to be.

**Corollary**: A proposition that is derived from a proposition that has already been proved.

**Correlation**: The idea that two events often happen in near proximity to each other, but one does not directly cause the other.

**Correspondence Theory of Truth**: A proposition is true in as much as that statement corresponds to reality (or the best evidence we have available).

**Cronos & Uranus**: Cronos & Uranus were deities that existed before the Olympians; Cronos rebelled against Uranus and took his kingdom, and Zeus rebelled against Cronos and took his kingdom.

D

**Daedalus**: Daedalus was a famous inventor and architect in Greek mythology, credited with building the Labyrinth for King Minos of Crete.

**Darapti**: The name for a syllogism comprised of an A statement for its major premise, an A statement for its minor premise, and an I statement in the conclusion; this syllogism is in the third figure.

# Glossary of Terms

**Data**: Derived from the Latin *datum* meaning "the thing given," these are the noteworthy events, characteristics, and facts that can be collected in aggregate and analyzed from a mathematical perspective.

**Deductive Reasoning**: Reasoning that goes from premises to particulars that utilizes clear terms, true propositions, and valid reasoning in the construction of formal arguments.

**Denotation**: The dictionary definition of a word.

**Dependent Variable**: The output that changes in regard to changes in the independent variable.

**Descartes, René:** A French philosopher and mathematician who wanted to ground logic in the same sort of rigorous chain of reasoning found in geometry. He is most famous for his practice of methodological skepticism and the phrase, "I think; therefore, I am." He lived from 1596 to 1650.

**Descriptive Statistics**: The systematic collection and analysis of a data set to find patterns in that data set including measurements such as mean, median, mode, and standard deviation.

**Direct Inference**: The act of drawing a conclusion from only one premise. The term *direct inference* is also called *immediate inference*.

**Disjunctive Syllogism**: A compound syllogism built upon the correlating conjunctions "either" and "or"; the wording of a disjunctive syllogism implies that at least one of the propositions, maybe both, is true. If a logician denies either one of the two propositions, then its corresponding proposition must be true.

**Distributed**: A term is distributed if it refers to all of the things that are in its category.

**Distribution**: The idea of *distribution* and the *distribution of terms* refers to how much of one term is identified with, or found in, the corresponding term it is joined to in a proposition. In negative propositions, distribution refers to the extent to which a term is excluded from its corresponding term.

**Distribution of Powers**: As originally formulated by Montesquieu, this idea referred to separating the powers of making laws, enforcing laws, and interpreting laws to different branches of government.

E

**E Statement**: A universal negative proposition that denies something is true (and it is always not true) about the entirety of the subject. E Statements take the form, "No [S] is [P]."

**Economics**: Economics is the study of the use of scarce resources which have alternative uses.

**Economy**: The sum total of all the commercial activity in a given nation related to the production, sale, and distribution of goods and services.

**Efficient Cause**: The agent that brings a thing into being or produces changes in a thing.

**Empiricism**: From the Greek word for "experience," this is the belief that all knowledge comes through the senses.

**English Civil War**: Lasting from 1642 to 1651, the English Civil War was fought between the forces of King Charles I and the New Model Army of the English Parliament. The English Civil War ended in the victory of Parliament over King Charles I.

**Enlightenment**: An age in European history from approximately 1650 to 1789 when European intellectu-

# Glossary of Terms

als placed incredible confidence in the powers of human reason to solve the problems of society.

**Enthymeme**: A syllogism with one premise omitted, implied, or "kept in mind"; these are especially important in rhetoric.

**Epistemology**: The study of how we know what we know.

**Equivocal Terms**: Terms that can have more than one meaning or are ambiguous.

**Euclid**: A mathematician from Alexandria, Egypt, and the author of *The Elements*, perhaps the most influential math textbook in history.

**Euler's Circle / A Statement**: Two circles labeled for the subject and predicate terms respectively, with the circle for the subject term located entirely within the circle for the predicate term.

**Euler's Circle / E Statement**: Two circles labeled for the subject and predicate terms respectively, with the circle for the subject term entirely separated from the circle for the predicate term.

**Euler's Circle / I Statement**: Two partially-overlapping circles; the subject term is located in the area overlapping with the predicate term to show that part of the subject is identified with part of the predicate.

**Euler's Circle / O Statement**: Two partially-overlapping circles; the subject term is located in the area that is separated from the predicate term to show that part of the subject is identified with part of the predicate.

**Euler's Circles**: A visual means of representing the terms in a categorical proposition. By layering Euler's Circles for different propositions on top of each other, we can determine whether or not a syllogism is valid or invalid.

**Euthyphro's Dilemma**: Euthyphro's Dilemma refers to the difficulty of defining and understanding the meaning of abstract terms like goodness and piety. If something is pious because the gods love it, the piety of that thing may be arbitrary and unfair; if it is pious and then the gods love it, then the love of the gods seems irrelevant and unnecessary.

**Extension**: All the real things to which a term refers (i.e., the population of a species) and is generally quantitative.

**Extreme Realism**: Ideas really exist outside of minds and in another world as real entities; this view derives from the writings of the philosopher Plato.

F

**Faith and Reason**: A formula derived from Thomas Aquinas that helps define the relationship between faith, the truths we find revealed to man in religious writings like the Bible, and reason, the truths that we primarily find through our intellect and our senses.

**Fallacy of an Affirmative Conclusion from a Negative Premise**: This fallacy occurs when a syllogism has at least one negative premise and an affirmative conclusion.

**Fallacy of a Negative Conclusion from Affirmative Premises**: This fallacy occurs when a syllogism has a negative conclusion but has two affirmative premises.

**Fallacy of Exclusive Premises**: This fallacy occurs when a syllogism uses two negative premises.

**Fallacy of Four Terms**: This fallacy occurs when a syllogism has more than the three required terms.

**Fallacy of Illicit Major**: This fallacy occurs when the major term is distributed in the conclusion but is not distributed in the major premise.

# Glossary of Terms

**Fallacy of Illicit Minor**: This fallacy occurs when the minor term is distributed in the conclusion but is not distributed in the minor premise.

**Fallacy of Illicit Process**: This fallacy occurs when either the major or minor term is distributed in the conclusion but is not distributed in the premise in which that term first appears.

**Fallacy of the Undistributed Middle**: This fallacy occurs when the middle term is not distributed at least once in the syllogism.

**de Fermat, Pierre**: A French mathematician and thinker who contributed to the field of statistics and probability (lived 1607-1665).

**Figure**: This idea refers to the location of the middle term in a syllogism.

**Final Cause**: The purpose or goal for which a thing is made.

**First (1st) Figure**: The middle term is the subject of the major premise and the predicate of the minor premise.

**First Order Enthymeme**: An enthymeme where the implied proposition is the major premise.

**Formal Cause**: The essence of a thing.

**Formal Fallacy**: A formal fallacy is an error in the structure of an argument so that its premises do not necessarily lead to its conclusion.

**Forms**: Plato's term for ideas such as truth, beauty, and goodness that, for Socrates and Plato, exist in an independent spiritual realm known as the "World of Forms". The term is derived from the Greek word for "seeing", so the term is ironic since the Forms can only be seen with the mind.

**Fourth (4th) Figure**: The middle term is in the predicate of the major premise and the subject of the minor premise.

**Free Market**: The market is composed of people exchanging goods and services, and because individuals are capable of making meaningful, rational choices, the market should be free from as much interference from third parties as possible.

## G

**Genus**: The general category in which a thing exists.

**Geometry**: One of the four roads of the quadrivium, geometry is the study of space relative to the size and distance of shapes.

**Glorious Revolution**: In 1688, the English Parliament successfully (and without bloodshed) replaced the unpopular King James II with the Dutch Prince William of Orange. William and his English wife Mary supported the goals of Parliament including increased support for Protestant Christianity, a national bank, and protections for freedom of expression and other liberties.

**Grammar**: The subject of grammar focuses on the rules of language and communication to read and understand texts and write in clear, intelligible prose; at times, grammar, as a road of the trivium, may also refer to the basic, fundamental building blocks of a subject.

## H

**Hephaestus**: The god of blacksmiths, metallurgy, and fire in Greek mythology.

**Hera**: The queen of the gods, as well as the goddess of marriage. In Greek mythology, Hera is the mother of Hephaestus but threw him off of Mount Olympus upon recognizing he was crippled.

# Glossary of Terms

**Historical Analogy**: An event that has happened in the past that has enough similarity to a possible future event that we can predict whether or not that future event will be successful.

**Hobbes, Thomas**: An English philosopher best known today for his seminal work on political theory, *Leviathan*. He lived from 1588 to 1679.

**Hume, David**: A philosopher, skeptic, and a member of the Scottish Enlightenment; his two most famous works are *A Treatise of Human Nature* and *The Enquiry Concerning Human Understanding* (lived, 1711 - 1776).

**Hypothetical Syllogism**: A hypothetical syllogism is a syllogism made up of two premises, the first premise being an if/then statement composed of two propositions; the second premise then affirms or denies one of the propositions in the first premise.

I

**I Statement**: A particular affirmative proposition that affirms something is sometimes true, or is true part of the time, about a certain undefined part of the subject. I Statements take the form, "Some [S] is [P]."

**Independent Variable**: The input that the researcher has under his or her control and whose changes are not under the control of another input.

**Indicator Variables**: A way of numerically representing yes or no questions with a *1* for *yes* or a *0* for *no*.

**Inductive Reasoning**: A form of reasoning that goes from observations to broad, universal principles; these arguments depend more on content and evidence than on form or structure.

**Inference**: The third act of the mind, a process that takes information we already know and uses that information to reach a new conclusion.

**Inferential Statistics**: The systematic collection and analysis of a data set to make inferences or predictions.

**Invalid**: An argument is invalid if the conclusion does not follow logically from the premises; if the argument breaks any of the rules governing the formal construction of syllogisms.

**Invisible Hand**: Adam Smith's metaphor for the uncoordinated yet orderly workings of the free market.

J

**Jesus of Nazareth**: A 1st-century itinerant preacher and teacher from the Roman province of Judea whose teachings, miraculous acts of healing, and accounts of his resurrection from the dead led to the founding of Christianity, whose adherents believe Jesus to be the Son of God.

**Judgment**: The second act of the mind, which is the mental act of connecting one term with another to form a proposition.

K

**Keynes, John Maynard**: A British economist who argued that government intervention could play a positive role in the economy by boosting aggregate demand via deficit spending; his most famous work is *The General Theory of Employment, Interest and Money* (1936). Keynes lived from 1883 to 1946.

**Keynesian Economics**: Derived from the writings of John Maynard Keynes, this is the macroeconomic theory that describes how increased government spending could stimulate economic activity and thus mitigate the effects of economic downturns.

# Glossary of Terms

## L

**The Liberal Arts**: The liberal arts are the subject areas that free the mind from ignorance; they are composed of the trivium and the quadrivium and thus include grammar, logic, and rhetoric (known as the *trivium*) and music, arithmetic, geometry, and astronomy (known as the *quadrivium*).

**Logic**: The art of right thinking and the rules for organizing a wide array of thoughts, facts, and propositions into a coherent and organized system.

**Logos**: A Greek word that means "reason," "reckoning," or "account." John uses the word to describe Jesus himself, and Aristotle uses the word to refer to a rational appeal in an argument.

**Louis XIV**: Nicknamed *The Sun King*, this French monarch centralized huge amounts of power and built the massive palace known as Versailles to keep his nobles under his control. Louis XIV reigned as king of France from 1654 to 1715.

**Locke, John**: The *father of Liberalism*, this political theorist said that all human beings have natural rights, chief amongst them being life, liberty, and property; He lived from 1632 to 1704.

## M

**Major Term**: The term used as the predicate in the conclusion of a syllogism.

**Middle Ages**: The approximately one-thousand-year period between the fall of the Roman Empire in 476 AD to the fall of Constantinople in 1453, whose worldview was shaped mainly by the influence of Christianity and the Catholic Church.

**Middle Term**: The term appears in both premises and joins the major term and the minor term, but this term does not appear in the conclusion.

**Minor Term**: The term used as the subject in the conclusion of a syllogism.

**Major Premise**: The premise in which the major term (the predicate of the conclusion) originally appeared.

**Market**: A constantly changing pattern of production and exchange, in which buyers and sellers engage in trades of goods and services at an agreed-upon price.

**Material Cause**: The composition of a thing and the things from which it is made.

**Mercantilism**: An economic philosophy popular in the 17th and 18th centuries arguing for more government oversight and interference in the economy. This view is based on the assumption that because the world's wealth is finite, European states should endeavor to have more gold and silver relative to other countries.

**Metaphorical Terms**: One term that can be (and is commonly used) to make a comparison between two unlike objects to illustrate an important idea.

**Metaphysics**: The branch of philosophy that focuses on the fundamental nature of causes, as well as certain issues concerning the nature of being and reality. The word comes from the title of a book that literally came after Aristotle's Physics—hence, Metaphysics.

**Methodological Skepticism**: In his philosophical works, Descartes famously described subjecting each and every belief he had to rigorous testing to make sure each belief was, in fact, true.

**Mill, John Stuart**: A British philosopher and writer most famous for developing the school of ethics known as *utilitarianism*.

# Glossary of Terms

**Minor Premise**: The premise in which the minor term (the subject of the conclusion) originally appeared.

**Modified Realism**: A universal exists in the world in the particulars, and in our mind as universal concepts abstracted from other real things; also called *moderate realism*.

**Modus Ponens**: The mode of affirming the antecedent or, in Latin "the mode that by affirming affirms." If the antecedent is true, then the consequent must also be true.

**Modus Tollens**: The mode of denying the consequent or, in Latin, "the mode that by denying denies". If we deny the consequent, then we can say with certainty that its corresponding antecedent is not true, either.

**Montesquieu**: Unique amongst the French *philosophes*, Montesquieu was both a member of the French aristocracy and a strong proponent of the Enlightenment. Amongst his famous works is *The Spirit of the Laws*.

**Mood**: The quality and quantity of the three propositions that comprise a syllogism.

## N

**Necessity**: A necessary truth is one that cannot exist otherwise.

**Negative**: When the proposition denies something about the subject.

**Nominalism**: Universals exist only as names that we use for convenience, but don't express anything truly outside of the idea brought to our minds by that name; this position is identified with the English philosopher William of Ockham.

***Novum Organum***: Francis Bacon's work on the potential of inductive reasoning, the *new instrument* in contrast to the deductive reasoning of Aristotle. The title is Latin for *New Instrument*.

## O

**O Statement**: A particular negative proposition that denies something is true, or is not true part of the time, about a certain undefined part of the subject. O Statements take the form, "Some [S] is not [P]".

**Obversion**: The process of negating the predicate of a proposition and changing the quality of that statement to create an equivalent statement. These work for all statement types.

**Oikonomikos**: A Classical Greek term meaning house management, as the study of economics is, in part, the study of how to take care of one's household.

**Opportunity Cost**: The next best opportunity that was foregone when an individual chose to act to satisfy a specific end. In other words, it is the number two ranking on their value scale.

***Organon***: The title of Aristotle's work on logic and reasoning; the word comes from the Greek word for "tool" or "instrument" in the same way that logic is very much a tool for constructing and evaluating arguments.

## P

**Panathenaea**: A festival held in ancient Athens celebrated every four years that included religious ceremonies and athletic events, alongside other events.

**Parable**: A very short story or example that illustrates an important moral lesson.

**Partial Conversion**: Because the subject and predicate terms in an A statement are not evenly distributed, A statements convert to I statements.

# Glossary of Terms

**Particular**: The individual thing that exists in the observable world; also, the notion that the subject of a proposition only discusses or touches upon one particular, undefined group within that subject.

**Pascal, Blaise**: A French mathematician and philosopher, one particularly famous for contributing both to the field of statistics and calculus (lived 1623-1662).

**Peripatetics**: From Greek for "to walk about", these were the students of Aristotle. The nickname was given because Aristotle habitually walked around while he lectured.

**Phenomenon**: Things which we can observe to exist in the real world and whose characteristics we can record and measure, and make inquiries about their nature and their causes.

*Philosophes*: A French term for a class of Enlightenment-era thinkers and writers.

**Philosophy**: Literally, the "love of wisdom", philosophy is the academic subject that examines significant, overarching questions of the human condition concerning ethics, values, epistemology, and ontology.

**Piety**: As an abstract value, piety refers to one's respectful and reverential dealings with one's elders, including one's parents and the gods.

**Plato**: An Athenian philosopher whose writings serve as the basis for much of Western philosophy; he wrote dialogues that explored the fundamental nature of reality and morality.

**Platonism**: A philosophical school of thought that, following the influence of Socrates and Plato, holds as its central idea the existence of ideas such as truth, beauty, and goodness in the World of Forms.

**Political Theory**: The philosophical study of government in terms of the best form of government, its powers, and its responsibilities, as well as issues of justice, liberty, and stability.

**Porphyry**: Roman philosopher and author of commentaries on the works of Aristotle. He lived from AD 234 to 305.

**Predicables**: Aristotle lists five different types of predicables, the different ways in which we can affirm or deny something is or is not true about our subject.

**Predicate**: This part of the sense includes the verb and everything following the verb; this part of the sentence either affirms or denies the subject of the sentence.

**Premise**: The reasons given in an argument that lead to its conclusion.

**Primary Substance**: Something that exists, such as the individual man or horse.

**Probability**: The likelihood that one particular, desirable outcome should occur.

**Property**: An essential quality that derives from the species of a thing, from the essence of that thing what that thing is in itself.

**Proposition**: A sentence that joins together a term with another term in order to communicate some idea about the world, an idea that could either be true or false.

**Proteus**: Proteus is a Poseidon-like sea god capable of changing his shape and predicting the future, but he only tells people who ask him about future events if they can capture and hold onto him.

# Glossary of Terms

### Q

**Quadrivium**: Literally, the place where *four roads meet*; metaphorically, those *four roads* are the arts of music, arithmetic, geometry, and astronomy.

**Quality**: The notion that a predicate may affirm or deny something about the subject.

**Quantifiers**: These are words such as "all", "some", or "no" that indicate the quantity and the quality of a given proposition.

**Quantity**: The notion that a subject is either universal or particular.

### R

**Rationalism**: From the Latin word for "reason" or "account", this term refers to the belief that all knowledge comes in and through the powers of man's reason.

**Reason**: The unique ability to solve problems, make inferences, and think about subjects that go above and beyond human experience.

*Reductio ad absurdum*: A *reductio ad absurdum* argument is a form of modus tollens that begins by assuming the consequent is true, then draws out a series of ridiculous conclusions that follow, all of which show that the consequent can, in fact, not be true.

**Regression Analysis**: Regression analysis is one form of statistical modeling used to predict the relationship between the dependent y-variable and any number of independent variables used in the regression. This kind of analysis predicts future changes in the dependent y-variable based on increases or decreases in the independent variables used in the model.

**Relationships of Equivalence**: These are ways to alter a proposition to create ones that have the same meaning.

**Resources**: Items like time, money, and labor that can be used to create finished goods; resources are limited and must be allocated carefully.

**Rhetoric**: The art of public speaking and the skills and strategies needed to compose and deliver a stirring speech.

### S

**Second (2$^{nd}$) Figure**: The middle term is in the predicate of both the major premise and the minor premise.

**Schema**: A means of identifying a syllogism by its mood and its figure.

**Scholastics**: A movement amongst well-educated professors, bishops, and priests that arose in European universities during the Middle Ages.

*Scientia*: From the Latin word for "knowledge," which forms the basis for our English word "science"; Francis Bacon famously said that "Knowledge is power."

**Second Order Enthymeme**: An enthymeme where the implied proposition is the minor premise.

**Secondary Substance**: The things predicated of a primary substance, including a thing's species, genus, and other predicables.

**Simple Apprehension**: This is the first act of the mind that focuses on the clear understanding of terms.

**Skepticism**: A lack of confidence, at times even the outright denial, that human beings can have certain knowledge of anything at all.

# Glossary of Terms

**Slope-Intercept / Linear Equations**: The equation $y = mx + b$, with $y$ being the dependent variable, $m$ being the slope of the line, $x$ being an independent variable, and $b$ being the $y$-intercept when $x$ equals zero.

**Socrates**: A Greek philosopher and "gadfly of Athens" whose incessant questioning and probing into the nature of the good life led to his execution in 399 BC.

**Sound**: If an argument employs valid reasoning and all of the propositions are true, then that argument is sound.

**Species**: What a thing is in itself, the essence, the fundamental nature of its being; for example, we can take Aristotle's definition of man as a rational animal as the species or the essence of man.

**Specific Difference**: A quality that separates one thing from its genus and thus serves as the defining characteristic that makes a species what it is.

**Square of Opposition**: As formulated by Aristotle, this is a visual way of showing the relationships between categorical propositions, providing that they all have the same subject and predicate terms.

**The State**: The political institutions in a given country that have a monopoly on the use of force.

**State of Nature**: A thought experiment wherein an author such as Hobbes, Locke, or Rousseau, imagined what human beings were like before the beginning of civil society and civil government. In conducting this thought experiment, they hoped to understand what man was really like.

**Statistics**: The systematic, mathematical collection and analysis of "actual events" in large quantities for the purposes of finding useful, practical insights.

**Subalternate Moods**: These are mnemonic devices that were not included in the original list of mnemonic devices, but they are valid under the rule of subalterns.

**Subalternation**: The relationship between A statements and I statements and between E statements and O statements, in that the truth of the universal proposition (A, E statements) implies the truth of the particular proposition (I, O statements) with the same subject and predicate, or that the falsity of the particular I or O statement implies the falsity of the universal A and I statement.

**Subcontrariety**: The relationship between I and O statements, in that two particular propositions with the same subject and the same predicate can both be true, but they cannot both be false.

**Subimplication**: The relationship between A statements and I statements and between E statements and O statements, in that the truth of the universal proposition (A, E statements) implies the truth of the particular proposition (I, O statements).

**Subject**: The main actor in the sentence; the principal person, place, or thing that the sentence is about.

*Summa Theologiae*: The great work of Thomas Aquinas wherein he attempts to reconcile the philosophy of Aristotle with the worldview of Christianity. Aquinas' great work was unfinished at the time of his death.

**Superimplication**: The relationship between I statements and A statements, and between O statements and E statements, in that if a particular statement (I, O statements) is false, then by necessity, its corresponding universal proposition (A, E statements) must be false, too.

**Supply and Demand**: The relationship between the amount of goods a producer may produce (the supply)

# Glossary of Terms

and the amount of goods consumers wish to purchase (the demand).

**Syllogism**: A formal, structured argument composed of two premises leading to a conclusion; the written expression of the mental act of inference.

**Syllogism Mnemonic**: A means of quickly and efficiently determining the validity of a syllogism by analyzing its mood and its figure; in logic, these devices apply a name to a syllogism, whose vowels indicate what categorical propositions are used in that syllogism.

### T

*Tabula Rasa*: Latin for *blank slate*, John Locke used this metaphor to describe the human mind at birth: a blank slate, upon which information and knowledge is inscribed through experience.

**Term**: A term is the most basic, most fundamental unit of meaning; terms are held or apprehended in the mind when we think of a particular idea or concept.

**The Pragmatist Theory of Truth**: A proposition is true in as much as that statement works--in short, truth is what works.

**The Problem of Induction**: The human mind tends to see two events happening in quick succession and assume (wrongly) that the first event caused the second event.

**The Problem of the Points**: A thought experiment that contributed to the beginnings of statistical analysis and probability, based on how to divide up the money at stake in a game of chance if that game was interrupted.

**Theorem**: A theorem is a statement that is not self-evident (that is, it is not obviously true) but has been proven to be true on the basis of other axioms or other theorems.

**Third Order Enthymeme**: An enthymeme where the implied proposition is the conclusion.

**Third (3rd) Figure**: The middle term is the subject of both the major and the minor premise.

**Three Acts of the Mind**: The three ways that human beings can think about thinking, which include the acts of simple apprehension, judgment, and inference.

**Treatise**: Lecture-like texts that focus on one particular subject, investigate one particular phenomenon, or solve one particular problem.

**Triangle**: A three-sided shape whose interior angles sum to 180°.

**Trivium**: The place "where three roads meet," this was an ancient and medieval way of organizing education, whose *three roads* included the study of grammar, logic, and rhetoric.

### U

**Undistributed**: A term is undistributed if it refers to only some of the things that are in its category.

**Universal**: One idea or concept that can be predicated, or said about, many other ideas or concepts. For example, the idea of animal may be predicated of many different things such as the individual man, the idea of man, or the idea of other kinds of animals. Also, the notion that the propositions discuss or encompass the entire category of a subject.

**Univocal Terms**: A term that has only one meaning.

**Utilitarianism**: The ethical framework that resolves difficult moral dilemmas by focusing on the consequences of actions and judging those consequences by

# Glossary of Terms

their utility, or the marginal usefulness and happiness an action produces for society.

## V

**Valid:** An argument in which the conclusion follows logically from the premises; the argument follows all the rules governing the construction of syllogisms.

**Venn Diagram:** A visual way of testing syllogisms for validity that uses three overlapping circles to show the relationship between terms.

**Venn Diagram / A Statement**: The Venn diagram for an A statement is comprised of two overlapping circles; the region not in common between the subject and the predicate is shaded. The shading indicates that of all the possible instances of that subject, none of them are identified with the predicate.

**Venn Diagram / E Statement**: The Venn diagram for an E statement is comprised of two overlapping circles; the region in common between the subject and the predicate is shaded. This shading indicates that of all the possible instances of that subject, none of them are not also identified with the predicate.

**Venn Diagram / I Statement**: The Venn diagram for an I statement is comprised of two overlapping circles, with an X placed in the region in common between the subject and the predicate. The X indicates that the proposition refers to the part of the subject that is identified with the predicate.

**Venn Diagram / O Statement**: The Venn diagram for an O statement is comprised of two overlapping circles, with an X placed in the region that is not in common between the subject and the predicate. The X indicates that the proposition refers to the part of the subject that is not identified with the predicate.

GLOSSARY OF TERMS

# NEVER ✦ CEASE
# LEARNING

© 2023 THALES PRESS

All rights reserved. Originally published in Raleigh, North Carolina for use in Thales Academy, a network of low-cost, high-quality private schools in North Carolina, South Carolina, Tennessee, and Virginia.

Made in the USA
Columbia, SC
13 April 2025